A HISTORY OF THE PACIFIC ISLANDS

PALGRAVE ESSENTIAL HISTORIES
General Editor: Jeremy Black

This series of compact, readable and informative histories is designed to appeal to anyone wishing to gain a broad understanding of a country's history – whether they are a student, a traveller, a professional or a general reader.

Published

A History of the British Isles   *Jeremy Black*
A History of Ireland   *Mike Cronin*
A History of the Pacific Islands   *Steven Roger Fischer*
A History of the United States   *Philip Jenkins*
A History of India   *Peter Robb*
A History of China   *J.A.G. Roberts*

A History of the Pacific Islands

Steven Roger Fischer

palgrave

First published 2002 by
PALGRAVE
Houndmills, Basingstoke, Hampshire RG21 6XS and
175 Fifth Avenue, New York, N. Y. 10010
Companies and representatives throughout the world

PALGRAVE is the new global academic imprint of
St. Martin's Press LLC Scholarly and Reference Division and
Palgrave Publishers Ltd (formerly Macmillan Press Ltd).

ISBN 0–333–94975–7 hardcover
ISBN 0–333–94976–5 paperback

This book is printed on paper suitable for recycling and made from fully managed and sustained forest sources.

A catalogue record for this book is available from the British Library.

A catalogue record for this book is available from the Library of Congress.

10   9   8   7   6   5   4   3   2   1
11   10   09   08   07   06   05   04   03   02

Printed in China

To H. G. A. HUGHES

Contents

List of Maps

Preface

As I begin these lines, a single Monterey pine planted in 1875 is being felled on One Tree Hill here in Auckland, New Zealand, where I live. For most New Zealanders, the solitary sentinel, with historic predecessors, had come to symbolize this country's proud unity. Others saw in it European domination. Dangerously weakened by repeated assaults, the pine falls this afternoon by City Council decree. No one knows what will replace it.

In many ways it is symbolic of today's Pacific Islands. (Hereinafter 'Pacific Islands' will be used in the singular without the article *the* in order to call attention to its special identity.) The last half of the twentieth century witnessed the dissolution of time-honoured allegiances in the region, the transformation of colonial patronages into new trading partnerships, and the creation of interregional organizations. It was also a time of independence from colonial masters in many islands and, more recently, of violent demonstrations addressing greater autonomy, indigenous rights and ethnic segregation in Irian Jaya, Bougainville, Guadalcanal, New Caledonia, Fiji, New Zealand, Hawai'i and Tahiti. A region experiencing accelerated change, Pacific Islands has been fraught of late with political tension and social friction, with mass migration and renewed foreign intrusion. A saddening malaise now vexes many of the island nations which stretch from Micronesia's tropical atolls to New Zealand's alpine fjords. Some are even calling Captain Cook's erstwhile paradise the 'coconut ghetto'.

It is not only the human story that causes concern. Global warming imperils Pacific existences. This is heralding short-term destruction of coral ecosystems and their fish stocks, razing regional economies. It further threatens long-term submersion of low-lying atolls, razing entire nations.

Yet a 'New Pacific' is emerging in this era of foment, home to an innovative hybrid people wishing to incorporate the best of both worlds, the Pacific and the West.

Directed at a popular audience who possess no specialist training in Pacific Studies, this book is a contemporary measure of Pacific Islands' greater story. Through retrospective analysis it addresses current issues confronting small islands in a globalized marketplace and environment. In accordance with the format of the Palgrave Essential Histories series, it adopts a Western-derived chronological structure. (A chronological framework is easiest for students to understand and recall.) The book's length and format similarly conform to those of the series; prescribed brevity will explain why certain favourite topics will be missed by some specialists. This work eschews the modern penchant for theoretical 'bell-tingling'. As the eminent Pacific historian Kerry Howe has reminded us, a 'primeval' function of history is to tell stories. This volume is first and foremost a story.

Please note the following conventions in writing Pacific languages:

Vowels   Each vowel is pronounced as in Spanish or Italian. Thus:

> **a** is *ah*
> **e** is *eh*
> **i** is *ee*
> **o** is *oh* (American) / *aw* (British)
> **u** is *oo*

What appear to be diphthongs are actually separately pronounced syllables:

> **ae** is *ah-eh* (Tahitian *tae* 'arrive' is *tah-eh*, not English 'tie')
> **ai** is *ah-ee* (Easter Island *tai* 'ocean' is *tah-ee*, pronounced quickly)
> **ao** is *ah-oh* or *ah-aw*
> **au** is *ah-oo*
> **ei** is *eh-ee* (close to the vowel in English 'day')
> **oe** is *oh-eh* or *aw-eh*
> **ou** is *oh-oo* or *aw-oo*

Consonants All Pacific consonants closely resemble their English equivalents, with the exception of the *g* which is always hard. In Samoan and Fijian (and some minor orthographies) the *g* is pronounced as the *ng* in English 'sing': Pago-Pago, capital of American Samoa, is therefore pronounced *Pango-Pango*. Fijian further pronounces the *b* as /mb/; the *d* as /nd/ (Nadi, the site of Fiji's International Airport, is thus /Nandi/); *c* as /θ/ (the 'th' in 'thin'); and the *q* as /ŋg/ (the 'ng' in 'singer', but with a pronounced *g*).

The celebrated Pacific glottal stop, as in Hawaiian *ali'i* ('chief, noble'), a consonant as frequent in Pacific languages as *k* and *t*, is in fact the same sound heard in American *uh-uh* and Cockney *li'o* ('little').

Pacific names of Austronesian origin usually comprise two words, sometimes even more. These are frequently written together: such as Honolulu (of *hono* 'bay' and *lulu* 'shelter') and Rapanui (Easter Island's Polynesian name, of *rapa* 'extremity' and *nui* 'great').

Acknowledgements

All recent histories of Pacific Islands are heirs of Douglas L. Oliver's epochal *The Pacific Islands* (1951). Oliver was the first rigorously trained scholar to offer a comprehensive survey of a region so vast as to nearly defy comprehension. A small handful of brave successors have published new surveys within the past decade. *A History of the Pacific Islands* owes a great debt to both Oliver and this new generation of scholars, being a synthesis of their labours and my own studies. I am particularly beholden to those who have challenged the foreign hegemony, integrated the indigenous franchise and achieved a new hybrid scholarship which counters the unhappy revisionism of certain vested countries' historiography. It is my hope that the 'New Pacific' will continue to maximize all ethnic inheritances in order to fashion a Pacific story which can stand on its own merits as an indigenous product of, and more accurate medium for, all Pacific Islanders, irrespective of heritage.

The past 36 years in Pacific Studies and linguistics have often brought me together with outstanding personalities in the fields of Pacific history, anthropology, archæology, sociology, linguistics and other related disciplines. Over a decade as editor of the journal *Rongorongo Studies: A Forum for Polynesian Philology* has connected me to most of the leading names in the Pacific today, whose perspicacity and liberality have been inspirational. The roll call of 'unforgettables' is too long to intone here, but I wish to mention a few Pacific luminaries, colleagues and mentors who have influenced my studies, each in their own special way: Wallace Ambrose, Sir David Attenborough, Paul Bahn, Thomas Bargatzky, †Terrence Barrow, †Thomas S. Barthel, Nona Beamer, Peter Bellwood, Byron Bender, †Bruce Biggs, Mark Blackburn, Olaf Blixen, Frank Brosnahan, Nikolai A. Butinov, Horst Cain, †Ramón Campbell, John Charlot, Ross Clark, Kenneth Cook, Ron Crocombe,

Peter Russell Crowe, †Bengt Danielsson, Irina Fedorova, Ben Finney, John R. Flenley, Francina Forment, Paul Geraghty, George W. Gill, Roger Green, Niko Haoa, Sonia Haoa, Ray Harlow, Toru Hayashi, Futa Helu, Thor Heyerdahl, Robin Hooper, Even Hovdhaugen, H. G. A. Hughes, †Kauraka Kauraka, Robert Koenig, Viktor Krupa, Joan Seaver Kurze, Robert Langdon, Hugh Laracy, Georgia Lee, Charles M. Love, John Lynch, Grant McCall, Donald S. Marshall, Francisco S. Mellén Blanco, Sidsel Millerstrøm, Claire Moyse-Faurie, Douglas Oliver, Margaret Orbell, Kiko Paté, Andrew Pawley, Nancy Pollock, J. Douglas Porteous, John E. Randall, Malcolm Ross, Albert J. Schütz, Gunter Senft, Arne Skjølsvold, †Carlyle Smith, Wolfgang Sperlich, Dorota Starzecka, Christopher Stevenson, Robert C. Suggs, Jennifer Terrell and Darrell T. Tryon.

To Jeremy Black at the University of Exeter, who invited me to write this volume for the Palgrave Essential Histories series, my heartfelt gratitude. And to Terka Acton and Felicity Noble, my profound appreciation for their excellent editorial support at Palgrave in Basingstoke, Hampshire.

This book is dedicated to H. G. A. Hughes of Wales.

Introduction

The Pacific Ocean is the largest geographical feature on Earth, covering a third of the planet's surface. It hosts more than 20 000 islands, 80 per cent of the world's total. With each square kilometre of land – about 1 300 000 in all – come 130 of ocean. This is the 'water continent' that encompasses **Pacific Islands** (Map 1), a specialist term – based on geographical, biological, historical and ethnic criteria – for a specific Pacific region which excludes the Asian and American islands and archipelagos that are part of the greater Pacific Rim. New Guinea alone claims 70 per cent of Pacific Islands' land, New Zealand a further 20 per cent. The remaining 10 per cent is made up of small, usually palm-fringed atolls and high islands lying hundreds, sometimes even thousands (as with Rapanui or Easter Island) of kilometres apart.

Already over 40 000 years ago, it appears, humans were settling offshore islands of the Southwest Pacific – long before rising seas separated New Guinea from Australia. Pacific Islands also experienced Earth's last human settlements (New Zealand's Chatham Islands were first colonized only around 600 years ago). Over tens of thousands of years, in other words, the history of Pacific Islands has been one of never-ending migration: eastwards and northwards, with 'back-migrations' southwards and westwards. This human ebb and flow created new cultures as communities adapted to differing island environments and new social challenges.

Pacific Islanders were the last people on Earth to encounter Europeans, in some places nearly 500, in others only 50 years ago. The collision of the two worlds changed both the Pacific and Europe, as this history will show.

Melanesia, **Micronesia** and **Polynesia** are Pacific Islands' three distinct culture areas. The name Polynesia – from Greek *poly* ('many') and *nēsos* ('island') – was coined by French historian and geographer Charles de Brosses in 1756 who applied it to all of Pacific Islands. French explorer Jules Sebastien César Dumont d'Urville gave the term its current restricted usage in 1831 when he also suggested the labels Melanesia (from Greek *melas* 'black') and Micronesia (*mikros* 'small') for the rest of Pacific Islands. These Greek-derived names have recently been challenged by those who reject Western nomenclature in the Pacific. Yet the names remain peerless as useful regional and cultural distinctions, especially to describe the last 500 years of Pacific Islands.

Melanesia (Map 2) comprises the subequatorial islands of the Southwest Pacific: New Guinea (Irian Jaya and Papua New Guinea, with its many offshore island groups), the Bismarck Archipelago (including the Admiralties), the Solomon Islands, the Santa Cruz Islands, the Banks Islands, Vanuatu (formerly the New Hebrides) and New Caledonia (with the Loyalty Islands). Fiji – a Tongan corruption of the indigenous name Viti – stands at the crossroads between Melanesia and Polynesia.

Lying east of the Philippines and mostly north of the equator, **Micronesia** (Map 3) includes the scattered high islands and coral atolls of Belau (formerly Palau), the Marianas (including Guam), the Federated States of Micronesia (formerly the Carolines), the Marshalls, Nauru and Kiribati (formerly the Gilberts).

The eastern half of the South Pacific is claimed by **Polynesia**: Tonga, Samoa, Tokelau, Tuvalu, Niue, the Cook Islands, Hawai'i (in the North Pacific), the Society Islands, the Marquesas, the Tuamotus, the Australs, the Gambiers, Rapanui and many others. Situated far south of the Tropic of Capricorn – normally Pacific Islands' southern 'border' – and below Melanesia, New Zealand represents Polynesia's greatest landmass. Several Polynesian 'Outliers' also occupy Melanesian and Micronesian waters.

Precontact – that is, pre-European – Polynesia enjoyed historical and cultural 'homogeneity', as it comprised a rather recent uni-ethnic settlement. In comparison, Melanesia and

Micronesia are historically and culturally far more complex and diverse. A similar complexity and diversity, however, has characterized Polynesia of the last 200 years, because of European intrusion and its effects.

The present volume is a general history of Pacific Islands, informed by the most recent developments in Pacific archæology, biology, linguistics, sociology and ethnography, among other disciplines. It reflects the changing patterns of cross-cultural dynamics, gender relations and Islanders' enfranchisement. It acknowledges the heterogeneity of island populations and the struggle towards uniformity and consolidation: the dynamics of the 'New Pacific' identity. Some scholars believe that, because of the region's vastness, cultural diversity and convoluted record of cross-cultural contacts, a comprehensive historical survey of Pacific Islands should not even be attempted. I oppose this view, on the grounds that a comprehensive history of Pacific Islands in one volume is not only possible, but greatly useful. The increasing number of undergraduate courses – from Britain to New Zealand – dedicated to Pacific Islands and its history require comprehensive, compact and easily accessible information. It is the purpose of this book to provide this.

Let me briefly explain this work's theoretical orientation. Half a century ago, Douglas Oliver's Pacific Islanders were viewed chiefly as naive victims of foreign exploitation (the so-called 'Fatal Impact' approach, addressing effects). A recent polemic response then re-analyzed the role of Pacific Islanders as historical agents and equal partners in cross-cultural events ('Islander Agency', addressing causes). Many Pacific scholars have since combined the two approaches – addressing both effects and causes – in order to present Pacific Islands history not as one or the other separate pole of a historical dialectic (that is, the historical continuum of unifying opposites), but as waxing and waning tides of endless human confrontation.

According to this most recent historiographical approach – the one this book also adopts – early on in the contact period (that is, the age of encounter with European outsiders)

Islander agency was strong. Later, this Islander agency diminished, with only sporadic revivals. Even later and more frequently,
foreign exploitation and domination prevailed, with the former
exploiters, as New Islanders, finally being exploited themselves
by distant cosmopolitan powers. No Pacific Islanders have
been eternally passive victims. No Pacific Islanders have been
eternally active agents, either. As everyone else, Pacific
Islanders have always been doers and receivers. The historical
truth of any society or region appears to lie in the interplay of
forces and in the switching of foci. The last 500 years of Pacific
Islands history reveal the increasing accommodation of all
peoples of the region to the demands of cosmopolitan powers.
This is the dynamic which determines the course of Pacific
Islands today.

This book includes the dimension of disciplinary emphasis,
too. Pacific Islands historiography has long suffered from the
contradictory methodologies of historians and anthropologists –
of those seeking history and of those describing cultures. Yet
the tension this has created has also, in recent years, inspired
a new approach to Pacific historiography, one that analyses
the interplay between event (history) and structure (culture).
Pacific historians are now profiting from the judging of past
events according to the ethics of the current vantage point, but
effecting this in knowledge of the responsibility of each historian
to retrospective dispassion and objectivity. The event is thus
seen in the structure, and the structure in the event.

The theoretical basis of this book lies, then, in taking an
ethnographic approach towards historiography which is also
firmly rooted in those principles mentioned above. Concretely,
it affords an understanding of how Pacific Islands' sociocultural
systems were constituted and functioned before Western invasion, and of how they have changed because of that invasion. It
further provides a historical (explanatory) framework for
comprehending sociocultural change in the Pacific, and the
historical contexts of the regional ethnographies. And it
demonstrates one cogent method of reconstructing the past in
a rational, positivistic way while also integrating, here and

there, the subjective, non-linear 'historiography' of indigenous Islanders.

The history of the Pacific is understood to be the story of all Islanders, old and new. The belief underlies this book's theme: that the recent Pacific was wholly transformed by Western arrivals, but that the transformation was co-directed by the same Islanders who were the product of tens of thousands of years of continuous Pacific history.

Steven Roger Fischer

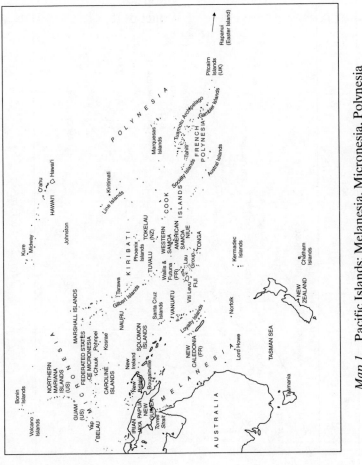

Map 1 Pacific Islands: Melanesia, Micronesia, Polynesia

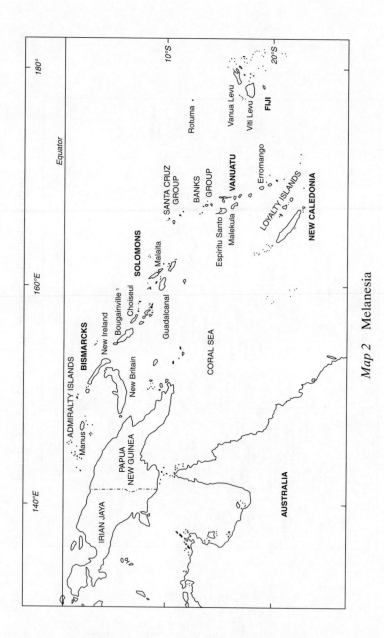

Map 2   Melanesia

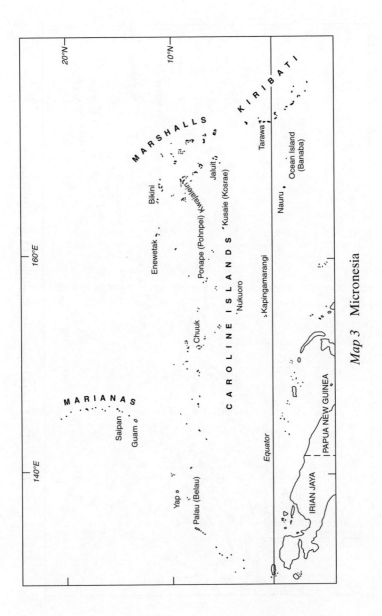

Map 3 Micronesia

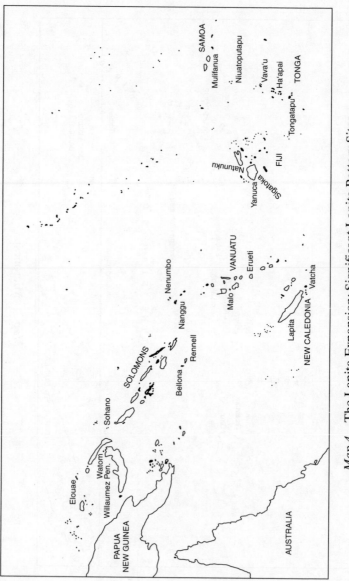

Map 4   The Lapita Expansion: Significant Lapita Pottery Sites

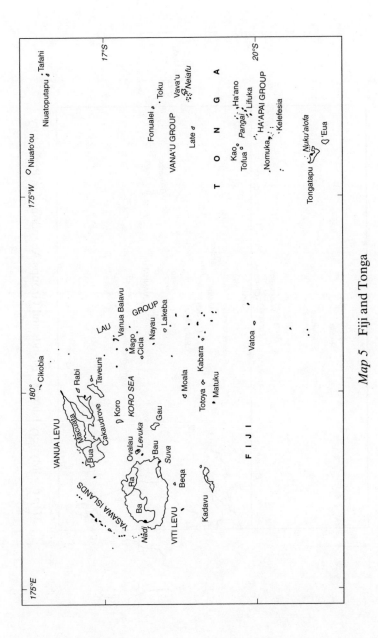

Map 5 Fiji and Tonga

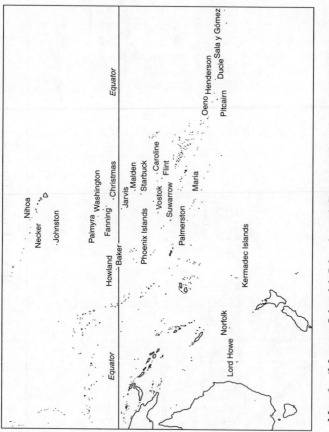

Map 6 'Mystery Islands': Islands and Groups Abandoned in Prehistory

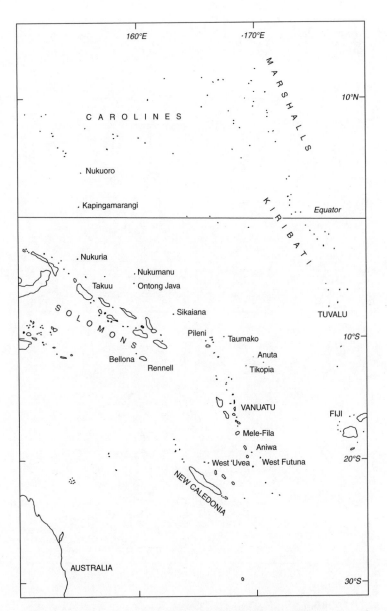

Map 7　The Outliers: Polynesian Communities in Melanesia and
Micronesia

1

The First Islanders

FROM SUNDA TO SAHUL

Sea levels were as much as 120 metres lower than today's during the last Ice Age – the Pleistocene epoch – which lasted from 1.8 million to 12000 years ago. Southeast Asia then included the maritime subcontinent of Sunda, that ancient and immense 'Boot of Asia' which separated the South China Sea from the Indian Ocean. East and southeast of the Sunda subcontinent lay enormous Sahul: ancient Australia, Tasmania and New Guinea, which were then still connected as one massive continent.

Sahul's separation from Sunda throughout the Pleistocene epoch demarcated not only land, but also mammals. Sahul's primitive marsupials (pouch-bearers like kangaroos and oppossums) and monotremes (primitive mammals like the duck-billed platypus and several species of anteater) remained distinct from the more evolved placental mammals of the 'Old World': that is, of Asia, Europe and Africa. This is an important consideration with regard to the presence of humans in the Pacific. For humans are also placental mammals. From this one can deduce that any early humans in Sahul had to come, then, from the Old World. However, many Aboriginal Australians and Papuans (the indigenous people of New Guinea and parts of the Solomon Islands) believe humans are autochthons, descendants of the spiritual ancestors of Dreamtime.

There might be something tangible to the indigenous belief, though the true story would differ significantly from the Aboriginal Australian and Papuan account. Sunda, or sub-continental Southeast Asia, was already home to the hominid species *Homo erectus* by the beginning of the Pleistocene epoch some 1.8 million years ago. We now know that some-time between 900 000 and 800 000 years ago a small flotilla of *Homo erectus* migrants, probably carrying an entire com-munity which had devised watercraft of bamboo-log rafts expressly for the purpose, deliberately crossed Wallace's Line. This was the strait of 17 (now 24) kilometres in width separat-ing Sunda from the Indonesian island of Lombok. It has always been one of the world's major biological boundaries, separating the fauna of Asia from that of Australia and Oceania. That this *Homo erectus* community would have effected the sea migration deliberately is deduced from the fact that they drifted even further than Lombok: they went on to settle Flores Island east of Lombok, rapidly causing the extinction there of pygmy stegodons (bony-plated quadrupeds) nearly one million years ago. On Flores Island they also left behind stone tools and dietary remains, which archæologists discovered in 1997.

It is a contentious issue whether *Homo erectus* ever ventured further than Sunda's offshore islands. Only related or descend-ant hominid species appear to have progressed all the way to the continent of Sahul. The exact origin of the first hominids in Sahul is still unclear. Australian archæologists announced in 2001 that an archaic human skeleton had been discovered at Lake Mungo in eastern Australia, subsequently dated, using three different techniques, as being 60 000 years old. As the skeleton indicated a DNA sequencing different from that of Australia's Aborigines, it was suggested that it might represent a hominid species which had not survived evolution. Perhaps it had been a precursor of *Homo sapiens sapiens* or modern humans in the region, as some now hypothesize. Archaic human societies were likely to be far more genetically complex than that Trinity of early human species – *Homo erectus*,

Homo neanderthalensis and *Homo sapiens* – still popularly peddled today. But the results of the Lake Mungo discovery require external confirmation through other, comparative analyses. It is too soon to definitively evaluate the discovery. Still, one should appreciate that the trend of the past half century has been one of ever-earlier dates for a hominid presence in Sahul.

All *living* humans in the region are, as most scholars agree, descendants of *Homo sapiens sapiens* who more recently came 'out of Africa', as particularly modern genetic studies witness. From 100 000 to 50 000 years ago, modern humans were ranging out to populate nearly all the Old World (and perhaps the Americas, too, as some scholars are now claiming). Migrating southwards from Asia down into the Sunda 'Boot', they would have crossed the sea also in small flotillas of bamboo-log rafts or perhaps dug-out canoes. They made their first traverses north via Celebes and the Moluccas to occupy northern Sahul. Others would have ranged further south, along the detached Lesser Sunda islands of Lombok, Flores, Timor and others to occupy the coastal regions of northwestern Sahul. Coming from both directions, Sahul could be reached only after several successive sea-crossings, some as far as 100 kilometres in distance: that is, beyond visible land.

It appears these migrants of around 50 000 years ago would be the Aboriginal Australians' and Papuans' ultimate ancestors, those true spirits and lawgivers of Dreamtime.

New Guinea, today less than 200 kilometres north of Australia's Cape York Peninsula, was evidently an early centre of *Homo sapiens sapiens* intrusion when New Guinea still comprised Sahul's elongated northern appendage. Its great diversity of cultures and large population testify to perhaps as long as 50 000 years of uninterrupted human development on the island, Earth's second largest. Various Highland and Lowland societies speak of their descent from ocean gods or from ancestors who rose up from an underworld; various coastal tribes tell of legendary voyages of settlement. Using Western scientific methods, practitioners of modern archæology and genetic profiling can confirm prehistoric migration paths, particularly through Sahul's northern reaches, which were plied tens of thousands of years ago.

The region's tangible archæological record is impressive, and continually deepening. We now know, for example, that one northern site on New Guinea's Huon Peninsula served Archaic Papuans as prolonged shelter as early as 40 000 years ago. The Matenkupkum cave site on New Ireland in the Bismarck Archipelago, northeast of Papua New Guinea, apparently accommodated a small community around 33 000 years ago. Five thousand years later other Archaic Papuans were calling a site on Buka Island in the northern Solomon Islands, south of the Bismarcks, their home. By about 25 000 years ago, Near Oceania – that is, New Guinea, the Bismarcks (comprising the Admiralties, New Britain and New Ireland) and the Solomons – would certainly have held hundreds of discrete Archaic Papuan communities.

These Archaic Papuans, who are sometimes called Australoids, were preoccupied with various methods of food acquisition. In the New Guinea Highlands, at ancient sites such as Kosipe, local Papuan communities primarily comprised hunter-gatherers. Occupants of lowland settlements engaged in both hunting-gathering and marine-life activities. But marine pursuits, including shellfish and urchin gathering, dominated the lives of coastal Papuans in the shoreline settlements of New Britain, New Ireland and Bougainville in the Solomons. Changing domiciles often in search of new habitats, Archaic Papuans were a migrant people who seem to have seldom shied from close sea-crossings.

With such movements and differentiated settlement patterns, networks of exchange increased and diversified. Some archæologists hold that obsidian (volcanic glass) from New Britain's Talasea site made its way to a number of further sites within the Bismarck Archipelago as early as 20 000 years ago; the trade continued for thousands of years. Having adapted to a variety of local coastal and inland environments, the First Islanders were already benefiting from established societies which evidently practised sophisticated techniques of exchange involving repeated sea-crossings.

New Guinea's earliest stone tools – hoe-like waisted blades and flaked ax-adzes – suggest that forest-edge clearance was taking place. It has been hypothesized that this Palæolithic (Old Stone Age) population was already practising a rudimentary form of horticulture, that is, of cultivating simple crop gardens. If true, then New Guinea's Archaic Papuans would have been among the world's first crop gardeners (in contrast to the hunting-gathering practised everywhere else on Earth during the Palæolithic era). However, the required evidence to confirm the hypothesis, such as drainage ditches and measurable pollen changes, has not been forthcoming. It is believed that New Guinea's earliest assemblage of flaked-stone tools – a mainstay of comparative archæology – reveals features characteristic of those of both Palæolithic Australia (Sahul) and Southeast Asia.

However, external connections of lineage and trade began gradually to decline around 12000 years ago. Sea levels started rising as kilometre-thick sheets of ice which, until then, had covered large parts of Earth melted in warmer mean temperatures that have continued up to the present day. Entire land masses 'detached', one from the other, as waters rose. In geological perspective, this happened overnight. In human cultural terms, it was an extremely protracted process. Maximum sea levels were not reached until around 8000 years ago, when the neck of land near Cape York, Australia, connecting Sahul to its northern appendage (New Guinea) finally disappeared under what became Torres Strait.

New Guinea had become a separate island, part of Near Oceania. (Near Oceania itself demarcates the distribution of major fauna and flora from those of northern, southern and particularly eastern islands, all known as Remote Oceania.) Well before 12000 years ago, Archaic Papuan hunter-gatherers had occupied Highland, Lowland and coastal regions of New Guinea, the Bismarcks and the Solomons (it is assumed). As most ancient coastal sites were gradually inundated over the

4000 years of rising sea levels, those sites which had once represented the most densely populated Archaic Papuan settlements now lay underwater. (This explains why discovered Archaic Papuan sites comprise exclusively the erstwhile higher habitats and cave or rock shelters which, back then, had been only sparsely populated; most ancient sites, pending improved technology, are still too deeply submerged to investigate.) New Papuan societies and languages began differentiating under drastically changed geographical and environmental conditions.

ANCIENT NEAR OCEANIA

The outgrowth of these changed conditions, 'Pacific Islands' as a human habitat began in New Guinea and the Bismarck and Solomon Archipelagos. Near Oceania's profound human history – far longer than Remote Oceania's – reveals a vast social diversity and immense cultural variation. Isolated from its Sahul parent continent since the filling of Torres Strait around 8000 years ago, New Guinea houses the world's richest treasury of languages within one confined geographical area: over a thousand Papuan and Austronesian tongues. Though one would expect genetic connections with the languages of Australia, whose Aborigines once shared Sahul with their northern neighbours the Archaic Papuans, none with reliable systematic correspondences has ever been found (perhaps because of the profound time depth which thwarts the limited capabilities of historical linguistics).

The fact that other Near Oceanian islands reveal a similar extreme of linguistic diversity indicates that these islands, too, were initially settled by the two genetically and linguistically distinct peoples. The continued development and interaction of these diverse cultures produced one of Earth's most ancient and elaborate cultural complexes.

It is assumed, for want of hard archæological evidence, that Archaic Papuans had already settled the southernmost islands

of the Solomon Archipelago by the height of the last glaci-
ation, around 18 000 years ago. There is no indication that
Papuans proceeded further than this – that is, into Remote
Oceania – until shortly before the arrival of Austronesians
many thousands of years later. Scholars now believe that it was
probably not the greater sea distances (that is, beyond visible
landfall) between islands and archipelagos which prevented
Papuans from extensively settling Remote Oceania. The
reluctance to do this was probably attributable instead to
the paucity of naturally occurring fauna and flora in Remote
Oceania to provide long-term sustenance after arrival. Such
natural resources prevailed only in Near Oceania. Throughout
Near Oceania – from the northwest Admiralties to the southeast
Solomons – Papuans had adapted to various environments.
They established sophisticated networks of exchange and
rapidly grew in numbers, with accelerating complexity and
further differentiation.

Nothing has disrupted the Papuan continuum up to the
present day.

Early Papuan sea-crossings were hardly the famed open-
ocean voyages of those celebrated Micronesian and Polynesian
seafarers who came much later. Early voyages probably
occurred in bamboo-log rafts or dug-out canoes, with minimum
navigational control. Voyages nearly always took place between
nearby shorelines, 'hopping' from one visible island to the
next. Papuan mariners clearly relied on the time-honoured
principle of the shortest crossing. The crucial factor in such
early crossings was time: the danger of a raft or canoe becoming
waterlogged – and as a result its occupants drowning – was
always present. As large numbers of people were needed with
a first settlement in order to avoid human extinction within
two or three generations of arrival on a previously uninhabited
island, early sea-crossings could not have been accidental.
They were clearly intentional. But why did Archaic Papuans,
time after time, drift away on tiny rafts or canoes to distant,
hazy islands on the horizon? It was evidently their way of
experiencing the world. Archaic Papuans, too, had no other

motive in mind but to search out new habitats, exploit the exploitable and thrive where possible. It was the very purpose of life, and offered continued survival.

The First Islanders were hunter-gatherers and fishers, then, who possessed intricate strategies which transcended mere subsistence. Before the end of the last Ice Age, Archaic Papuans were even introducing mammals to New Ireland in the offshore Bismarcks. The best defined archæological sequence of early human presence in the region comes from New Guinea's Highlands. By around 15 000 years ago, the Kaironk Valley had become home to hunter-gatherers. However, actual Highland regions were occupied only once Ice Age glaciers had receded globally (no glaciers were ever in New Guinea itself). Before then, coastal regions, warmed by ocean currents, had been preferred habitats. The rock shelters at Kafiavana and Kiowa in the Eastern Highlands Province of Papua New Guinea accommodated hunter-gatherers over 10 000 years ago. One may assume that rising mean temperatures world-wide finally allowed the general settlement of the Highlands at about this period, as evidenced by pollen changes over the following millennia, indicating forest clearance.

At this time in Near Oceania, Archaic Papuans lived in villages of some 30 individuals who often relocated to other sites. Networks of exchange remained internal within a given archipelago. Ocean gaps did not link but divided the First Islanders, who in this way continued to differentiate culturally. Rising sea levels and mean temperatures enabled crop cultivation in the Western Highlands of Papua New Guinea. There is convincing evidence for the earliest ditch and drainage systems, such as those at the swamp margins of Kuk in the Mount Hagen region. Taro was apparently cultivated in Kuk's hollows and gutters from 9000 to 5500 years ago.

Taro had originally come from Southeast Asia. The name taro includes a number of plant species belonging to the Arum family, *Araceae*. There is evidence that taro was already being used by the northern Solomon Islanders of Buka as early as

28 000 years ago. Purposely cultivated in New Guinea for more than 6000 years, taro is used for its large, starchy rhizomes (root-like stems emitting roots and usually producing leaves). Cultivated taro, *Colocasia esculenta*, was to become a staple food crop throughout Pacific Islands. It is still popular today.

Bismarck sites of similar antiquity reveal plantings of *Canarium indicum*, an almond and tree crop probably brought from New Guinea in the late Pleistocene. It appears Archaic Papuans at this time also intentionally introduced such wild fauna as large rats and bandicoots (insect-eating Sahul marsupials) to Manus Island in the Admiralties, and rats and possums to New Ireland in the Bismarcks. (Later migrants introduced the small wallaby as well.) No obsidian or animals were taken by Papuans to the Solomons, however, suggesting infrequent contact with the southernmost archipelago of Near Oceania.

In the Eastern Highlands, agriculture developed at a slower pace. Here, hunting-gathering still prevailed and the root *Pueraria lobata* – not taro – was cultivated.

One assumes that other crops which later formed the basis of Pacific Islands horticulture and agriculture, such as certain species of bananas and sugarcane, were also cultivated at a relatively early date in New Guinea.

That New Guinea Highlanders practised frequent exchange with coastal regions is evidenced by the discovery in Highland sites of marine shell ornaments dating from around 9000 years ago. One assumes that the shells came from the many Papuan coastal settlements today under the sea. But around 4500 years ago, polished stone tools and pottery-making also appear to have reached New Guinea's Highlands from the coast. At this time, Highland Papuan communities were rapidly becoming mixed hunting-gathering and horticultural societies. Highland swamp management comprised complex systems of channelling water – such as at Manton in the Western Highlands, whose archaic stone ax-adzes and wooden spades are almost indistinguishable from today's. (These demonstrate a continuity of local culture over a span of approximately 4500 years.)

Highlanders perhaps began clearing swathes of forest for food production at this time, too. Fruit and nut species were being cultivated in the Sepik-Ranu region. In the islands of Near Oceania, a low-level vegetation impact distinguishes the pollen record from around 4500 years ago. One might surmise that a rapid population increase caused an increased demand for food which was only satisfied by an intensification of production, leading to intentional forest clearance. (However, there might be other, non-agricultural explanations for forest loss at this time.) Domestic animals (pigs, dogs, fowl) appear for the first time in the cultural assemblage, sustained by Highlanders who obviously had sufficiently diversified their agriculture to feed these animals. Some scholars believe that this Papuan development prepared the way for a subsequent settlement of Remote Oceania by Papuans. However, the cumulative weight of evidence suggests that many, if not all, of the abovementioned developments were the result of contact with culturally more sophisticated intruders arriving from Island Southeast Asia:

The Austronesians.

THE AUSTRONESIANS AND LAPITA

The first Islanders had been Archaic Papuans or Australoids, the first *Homo sapiens sapiens* to settle, perhaps as early as 60 000 years ago, all the ancient lands from continental Southeast Asia (Malaysia, Kampuchea, Vietnam) in the west to the Solomon Islands in the east. With the arrival around 4500 years ago of Austronesian-speaking Island Southeast Asians, a people of Southern Mongoloid stock – ultimately hailing from Southern China – made Pacific Islands their tenure.

They are still there today.

Constant change – that is, internal development, migration, adaptation to environmental and climatic variations, and external contact – was affecting the human history of early Pacific Islands as much as it was all other regions on Earth around 4500 years ago. The constant change continued. No archæological discoveries show Papuan settlement beyond the Solomon Islands before the arrival of Austronesians. Yet today's Melanesians in this region comprise a Papuan-Austronesian (Australoid-Southern Mongoloid) hybrid people. The Papuan-Austronesian features now so evident in Vanuatu, New Caledonia and Fiji would have emerged within the last 2000 years. Before then, Remote Oceania was exclusively Austronesian. Micronesians and Polynesians owe most of their genetic and cultural make-up to Austronesian (Southern Mongoloid) ancestors. As Papuans were the first Islanders of Near Oceania, Austronesians were the first Islanders of Remote Oceania.

Around 4500 years ago Austronesians brought with them to the northern coastline of New Guinea their food plants, domesticated animals, polished stone tools and agricultural and sea-voyaging skills. Most of this cultural baggage was of immediate Island Southeast Asian, some of ultimately coastal Chinese origin. By then, the indigenous Papuans had already elaborated a rudimentary horticulture, based in part on such Southeast Asian plant species as taro and ti. However, they had never attained to the agricultural and fishing skills suddenly witnessed in the archæological record of Near Oceania once Austronesians had arrived. More significantly, Austronesians were expert seafarers, capable both of deep-sea fishing (as opposed to shoreline fishing and angling) and of extensive voyaging for trade and exploration. They were Earth's premier mariners.

The Austronesians' saga is fascinating. Some 8000 years ago, once rising seas had attained maximum levels and global mean temperatures had effected a major climate change, a distinct cultural complex (only now being identified by scholars) singled out a diverse, but interrelated Southern Mongoloid population which was settled along China's southern coast. Around 6000 years ago members of this complex left the Asian mainland – probably sailing, not drifting, approximately 130 kilometres of open ocean – to settle Taiwan where, over centuries, their language(s) developed into Proto-Austronesian. Having increased their numbers significantly on Taiwan, descendant Austronesian speakers sailed south to colonize the nearby Philippines, then west and southwest to establish settlements in eastern Vietnam and Kampuchea, on the Malay Peninsula and on the islands of Borneo, Sumatra and Java. Other Austronesians sailed directly south of the Philippines to colonize Sulawesi, Timor, southern Halmahera and Irian Jaya (Western New Guinea). Speakers of a proto-language which, in time, would become the Oceanic languages were probably settling regions of Papua New Guinea's northern coast beginning around 4500 years ago. They finally settled on the islands of New Britain and New Ireland in the Bismarcks around 4000 years ago. Here, Austronesians colonized coastal regions, generally keeping apart from the indigenous Papuans.

Austronesians' peregrinations are perhaps best followed through historical linguistics. Formerly known as Malayo-Polynesian, the Austronesian language family contains the world's greatest number of member tongues: around 1200, or 30 per cent of all the world's languages (if one accepts there are currently around 4000). Spoken today by approximately 270 million people, the Austronesian family includes nearly all the languages of the Philippines, Indonesia, Malaysia, Madagascar (east of Africa), Melanesia, Micronesia and Polynesia. It is the first language family in history to be spoken in over two-thirds of the globe. In Near Oceania, Austronesian languages still coexist alongside numerous Papuan languages, generally in coastal regions.

Most Austronesian settlements in the Bismarcks and Solomons had not been previously inhabited by Papuans. Austronesians were the ones who first brought New Britain's Talasea obsidian to the Solomon Islands. They also brought the first pottery to Island Melanesia. (New Guinea had had pottery, but of a different type.) Indeed, it was their characteristic pottery – possibly elaborated in the Bismarcks, along with a new and distinctive culture – which provided a name for these first Austronesians in Pacific Islands:

The Lapita people.

The name comes from the site on New Caledonia's west coast where this representative pottery came to light in significant quantities in the 1950s. 'Lapita ware' is an earthenware formed of slabs of clay usually tempered with sand and fired in the open (not in kilns). The ware encompasses open bowls, shouldered pots, globular cooking pots and flat-bottomed dishes. Lapita ware is commonly undecorated, though some pieces carry a red 'slip' – that is, clay mixed with water to a creamy consistency and used for decoration or patching. Others bear a highly distinctive and intricate assortment of patterns either incised or stamped into their surface. For stamping, a small-toothed instrument was used, one very similar to the later Polynesian tattooing chisel.

In time Lapita came to identify the Austronesians' entire cultural complex in Pacific Islands. It is believed that Lapita ware may have been fired in the Bismarcks as early as 4000 years ago. Already by this time, stable settlements of more than a hectare (2.47 acres) were providing long-term residence to sizeable populations of Austronesians engaged in long-distance trade. Early Lapita ware – those pieces older than 2800 years – bearing similar patterns appear from the Bismarck Archipelago throughout Island Melanesia, with the exception of the contiguous Solomons, to as far as Samoa more than 4000 kilometres away (Map 4). Fragments of a Lapita pot have also been discovered in New Guinea, at Aitape. It is clear that it was this Lapita people who initiated expansion into Remote Oceania. That is to say, the colonization of Remote Oceania was an Austronesian initiative.

The Lapita complex embraced an entire cultural assemblage of ornaments, tools (stone axes and adzes, shell adzes, shell scrapers, fishhooks, files of sea-urchin and coral spines), permanent villages of stilt houses, animal domestication, an array of agricultural techniques, sophisticated seafaring skills and vessels, and other things. The Lapita people characteristically cooked, for example, with hot stones in earth ovens – still a commonplace in Pacific Islands today.

It was also around 4000 years ago that specifically Melanesian languages and cultures, as distinct from indigenous Papuan languages and cultures, first emerged. They arose out of Austronesian traditions which admitted a restricted Papuan contribution. (Micronesian and Polynesian languages and cultures were to emerge around a thousand years later, at the northern and eastern peripheries of the Lapita culture, on islands uninhabited until then.) A revealing characteristic of Lapita sites is that these occur almost exclusively on coastlines. This is true also of the settlements on previously unoccupied islands. Some Lapita settlements were built on piles over the water of fringing coral reefs, a practice still common among many Southeast Asian communities. Though the Lapita people perpetuated the cultivation of common Island Southeast Asian crops such as taro, yam and banana, and the husbandry of pigs, dogs and fowl, their preferred resource was the sea.

INTO REMOTE OCEANIA

If it ever existed, Lapita 'unity' in the Bismarcks – genetically, culturally, linguistically – would certainly have been of extremely brief duration. Lapita expanded far, and it expanded rapidly. First branches of Lapita tentatively advanced throughout Island Melanesia around 3300 years ago then continued on to settle Fiji about a century later. (Tonga and Samoa would soon follow.) In such different locales the imported culture mutated rapidly under altered environmental and social conditions. For this reason one cannot speak of 'Lapita society'. There were many Lapita societies. Those in Near Oceania included Papuan communities which did not always enjoy Lapita's full complement of plants and animals, for example, while those in Remote Oceania beyond the Solomons appeared to experience only Lapita – that is, essentially Oceanic Austronesian – refinements.

Papuans had practised a maritime tradition of bamboo-log rafts and dug-out canoes which, until then, had allowed adequate sight-crossings. Lapita people, whose Austronesian antecedents had been sailing vast expanses of ocean since the settling of Taiwan around 2000 years earlier, either brought with them or invented in the Bismarcks the outrigger canoe, double-boom triangular sails and complex open-ocean navigational techniques which no longer required sight of land. In particular, Lapitans invented the double-hulled canoe, one of the greatest technological innovations in the history of seafaring. The double-hulled canoe allowed greater loads to be carried, meaning that Lapitans could take on board not merely provisions for one voyage but an entire culture, ensuring sustenance on distant islands lacking basic resources. In this way, settler populations could thrive, with the existences of settlers' children and grandchildren secured. This, more than anything else, allowed the Lapita people to colonize Remote Oceania.

Ultimately of Island Southeast Asian origin, Lapita was, then, an Austronesian culture. However, it integrated indigenous elements from the various Papuan communities it encountered as well as Austronesian solutions to specifically Bismarck problems. Lapita culture was therefore no Austronesian 'importation', but the indigenous creation of the new arrivals in Pacific Islands. Around 4000 years ago, Lapita first emerged with a small group of Proto-Oceanic speakers who first fired a distinctive type of pottery. Within around 500 years, however, members of this community – or influenced neighbours of shared pedigree – began moving out of New Britain and New Ireland, ranging eastern coastlines and sailing narrow ocean gaps. Their culture first spread through the Solomon Islands (it is assumed). Around 1300 BC, Lapita people left the Solomons and dared to sail into Remote Oceania in large double-hulled canoes: east to the Santa Cruz Islands, and south to Vanuatu and New Caledonia.

New Caledonia's mainland is the Grande Terre; a small offshore island, the Île des Pins, punctuates its southeastern tip. Around 80 kilometres east of the Grande Terre lie the Loyalty Islands, from northwest to southeast: West 'Uvea, Lifu and Mare. Though not found in the Loyalties, hundreds of earthen mounds, each about 2.5 metres tall and 8000 years old or more, dot both the Grande Terre and the Île des Pins. Some writers have alleged these are human artefacts, which is not impossible. But recent studies have suggested they are the remains of the nesting mounds of an extinct megapode: ground-living birds of ancient Sahul and adjacent islands. It appears the Austronesian-speaking Lapita people, the first humans to arrive on New Caledonia around 3300 years ago, were responsible, either directly or indirectly, for the megapode's extinction at around this time or slightly later. Archaic New Caledonians produced two types of pottery: Lapita ware, and one decorated by impression (using dies of carved wooden paddles) which was sometimes supplemented by incise work and clay reliefs. The later complexity of New Caledonian culture suggests there might have been two or three different settlements of the island.

New Caledonia's first settlement was paralleled by a series of Lapita migrations in multiple directions. A Western Oceanic subgroup of Austronesian speakers spread from Papua New Guinea's coast to Santa Isabel in the Solomon Islands, then later westwards and southwards into the Papuan Gulf. From Vanuatu, southeast of the Solomons, one community sailed southeast to Fiji, arriving around 3200 years ago. After an initial period of consolidation, the Fijian Lapitans sailed, around 2900 years ago, to the southeast to colonize Tonga. (Within two centuries, during which time Lapita potters had developed a distinctive Polynesian Plainware type of pottery on Tonga, the settlers' heavy reliance on natural resources had caused several species' extinction there.) Descendants, who were then developing an ancestral Polynesian society, set sail for the northeast and colonized Samoa. And it was there, at distant Samoa in the Central Pacific, that the Lapita seafarers apparently came to a halt after many generations of almost continuous colonization.

The settlement of Fiji had been a watershed in Austronesian exploration. (Austronesians of southeastern Borneo and Sumatra would not set sail for Madagascar east of Africa until approximately AD 700, or 1900 years later.) As measured from the southernmost tip of the Vanuatu chain, Fiji lies around 850 kilometres away, east-northeast. A voyage there meant an unheard-of distance in open sea. It could well have demanded up to several weeks' sailing, depending on winds. Once arrived at Fiji, the Lapita voyagers would have had to accept this isolation as a kind of sentence: limited exchange with the western homeland and its resources would have been the acknowledged price of permanent settlement there.

The settlers established 'gateway communities' on Fiji through which subsequent settlers and goods were funnelled throughout a protracted period of colonization there. Communities were then connected to less complex secondary sites serving as dispersal areas for tertiary hinterlands.

The great distance between Vanuatu and Fiji produced, in time, two distinct Lapita cultures: one in western, the other in eastern Pacific Islands. As generations passed, several 'provinces' of Lapita emerged: Far Western (New Guinea, Admiralty Islands, Bismarck Islands), Western (Solomon Islands, Bellona, Rennell, Santa Cruz, Tikopia), Southern (Vanuatu, New Caledonia, Loyalty Islands) and Eastern (Fiji, Tonga, Futuna, East 'Uvea, Samoa). Exchange still continued between west and east. Indeed, it was during the Lapita era that New Britain's Talasea obsidian finally realized its widest geographical distribution: from Borneo to Fiji, a distance of some 7000 kilometres. But the exchange occurred with nowhere near the frequency of that within neighbouring provinces. This is clearly demonstrated by those Lapita ware patterns that are almost indistinguishable from New Britain to New Caledonia: these are seldom, if ever, found in Eastern Province. Linguistically, the several languages of Remote Oceanic (Far Eastern Solomons, Micronesian, North Central

Vanuatu, Southern Vanuatu, New Caledonia) were also not at all involved in the many innovations which were now taking place in the emerging Central Pacific languages (Rotuman-West Fijian and Tokalau Fijian).

Judging by the immediate prerequisites of colonizing distant islands, one would conclude that settler societies of Remote Oceania had to be strongly hierarchical in their structure; only a strong hierarchy of command ensured survival in settlement events, maintaining social order while safeguarding food production. Initial settlement of a previously unoccupied island in Lapita times would have been small: one or two canoes of approximately 70 settlers, consisting almost entirely of an equal gender ratio of young adults. Whereas Near Oceania would have allowed local recruitment to stimulate population growth, Remote Oceania saw their populations increasing only naturally.

Lapita settlers' crops comprised both Southeast Asian and Near Oceanian cultivars, a package of foodstuffs which, once combined with the Austronesians' pigs, dogs and fowl, created a sophisticated agricultural collection. Many scholars believe it was this collection, borne on long-distance double-hulled canoes, which enabled Near Islanders to become Remote Islanders in the first place, providing necessary sustenance for prolonged settlement of islands lacking these staples. The Lapita colonization of both Near and Remote Oceania caused the extinction of many species of fauna and flora. In addition, forest clearance on a scale far exceeding that of earlier Papuans had caused irreversible environmental degradation. Once land became unusable, conservation practices such as terracing had to be introduced to safeguard crop production, particularly on the high islands of Remote Oceania. These and other measures ravaged island ecologies.

Today's Melanesians – that is, the indigenous people of Near Oceania and neighbouring archipelagos (now including Fiji) – still reveal contrasting degrees of Papuan-Austronesian mixture, the greatest being in western Near Oceania. Subsequent migrations of Near Oceanians into Remote Oceania over the last 2000 years have considerably raised the east's Papuan contribution. Before these migrations, Austronesian ethnicity and culture characterized all of Remote Oceania. Settling Fijians, for example, would have been 'Archaic Polynesian' in appearance: more the tall, thin, straight-haired and long-headed Rapanui Polynesians than modern Melanesians. This is because, many centuries ago, Island Melanesians with a stronger Papuan strain had overtaken Fiji and covered Lapitan roots. Most scholars believe the same thing occurred on Vanuatu and New Caledonia.

Lapita encompasses one of the most important homogeneous voyaging and colonizing events in Earth's human history. The nearly 3000-year-old Lapita ware found from the Bismarcks to Samoa attests to the early Lapita people's extraordinary seafaring skills. Such skills of course heralded the possibility of more distant colonies: the settlement of Micronesia and Polynesia (see Chapter 2). No direct genetic link exists between Micronesians and Polynesians. That is, Micronesia was not settled from Polynesia, nor Polynesia from Micronesia. All Micronesians, though extremely diverse, also originated in an Austronesian (Island Southeast Asian) population; southern Micronesians display varying degrees of Melanesian admixture. However, even before the Lapita people started ranging southeastwards, related Austronesian speakers were migrating from islands southeast of the Philippines to colonize Palau (now Belau) in western Micronesia. It is revealing that these first Island Southeast Asian settlers of Micronesia were evidently employing a sailing technology remarkably similar to that of the related Lapita people.

ARCHAIC PACIFIC ISLANDS

Despite the fact that prehistoric Austronesians had come to populate most of Pacific Islands, statistically fewer than half of all Pacific Islanders speak Austronesian tongues today. This is largely because of New Guinea, whose 6.5 million people chiefly speak Papuan languages. In comparison, populations of Remote Oceania have generally remained small, until the very recent European and American colonization of New Zealand and Hawai'i. Individual communities of archaic Pacific Islanders – little, isolated and with infrequent contact outside their respective region – differentiated rapidly into autonomous descent groups with characteristic traits. External influences and genetic replenishing occurred only with infrequent trading visits of distant neighbours who nearly always belonged to the same archipelago.

Along with Lapita ware these Pacific traders of 3000 years ago trucked in pottery-making materials, oven stones, chert, adzes...and the ever-prized obsidian. During the 'Lapita Millennium' – the era of principal Lapita activity that lasted from c. 1500 to 500 BC – obsidian remained one of the Pacific's most valuable trade items, used chiefly for fashioning cutting tools. The Talasea site on New Britain continued to be an important source for Pacific Islands obsidian, its stock traded in Vanuatu, New Caledonia, the Santa Cruz Islands and even in remote Fiji. Both Lapita ware and Talasea obsidian, above all, prove that interregional trading was indeed taking place, though far less frequently than inner-archipelagic trading.

The colonization of Archaic Pacific Islands did not occur as sporadic settlement events by disconnected 'exiles': it comprised regular human investments by connected entrepreneurs. Participants on both ends remained actively involved in maintaining exchange. Why did the Lapita Austronesians populate Remote Oceania? Austronesians had already been populating islands for well over two millennia. Colonizing remote islands was apparently their way of experiencing the world. They simply continued doing in the Pacific what they had been doing before they got there, until nearly every inhabitable Pacific island was reached and settled.

'Lapita-like' pottery was still being produced around AD 200. But already 700 years before this, Lapita ware was everywhere gradually being replaced by a different kind of pottery or by a similar plain style known as 'Lapitoid'. Lapita soon lost most of its distinctive features. The unifying identity of its dynamic creators had weakened. Communities had started developing in different directions, creating their own island societies which required new forms of expression.

New Guinea displayed its own uniquenesses. Papuan society there had elaborated singular items relating to agriculture. Characteristic are the stone mortars and pestles already in use before 1000 BC which are limited to the Western Highlands, the island's northeast, the Bismarcks and the Solomons. Often assuming decorative forms such as stylized birds, the stone pestles were perhaps used to grind kernels and seeds. Such artefacts are indicative of the Papuans' continued development while the Lapita people were differentiating within Remote Oceania.

By around 2700 years ago, the expanding Pacific Islanders – and their hybrid progeny – of both Near and Remote Oceania were harvesting taro, yam, sugarcane, breadfruit, ti, coconuts and many other crops. To all Islanders ti, for example, was a very special plant with supernational affinities, used for healing, garments, wrapping food, as well as for invoking or warding off magic and sorcery. Holy to Papuans and Austronesians alike, ti was indigenous to Island Southeast Asia. It was included in a variety of rituals performed to herald war or peace; it also marked boundaries, holy precincts and altars. When other foodstuffs failed, ti would become an important part of the diet. The specifically Papuan contribution to Pacific Islands alimentation comprised kava, breadfruit, certain species of banana, sugarcane and a variety of nuts. For protein, all Islanders kept pigs, dogs and fowl. Maritime resources – fish, eels, shellfish, seaweed, sea urchins and other things – assumed a principal dietary role for all coastal dwellers; such items could also be traded for the crops of inlanders. Deep-sea fishing supplied surpluses for coastal communities, allowing the leisure time which inland communities often lacked. It is assumed that a local specialization (such as a food crop) or resource (such as a special type of stone) would encourage more frequent exchange with immediately neighbouring communities, promoting exogamy – marriage outside one's tribe. Valuable commodities, like obsidian, would make long-distance voyages profitable, in terms of wealth and prestige for oneself and one's community.

In New Guinea, the Bismarcks and the Solomons, the 'first Islanders' or Papuans were still living alongside the 'newcomers' or Austronesians much in the same way as they had done for well over a thousand years, with only infrequent union. In Remote Oceania, however, from Vanuatu to Samoa, Austronesians were on their own, creating wholly new identities: Micronesians and Polynesians.

2

Melanesians, Micronesians, Polynesians

The prehistory of Melanesia, Micronesia and Polynesia is largely unknown. Pacific Islanders in precontact times – that is, before the European trespass – possessed no writing. Oral traditions mixed legend, myth and tribal agenda to create a 'group promotion' which is the antithesis of the modern West's linear, cause-and-effect historiography. Still, travellers' accounts, ships' logs and other reports from earlier centuries have revealed much about traditional Pacific Islands societies, and various fledgling fields of research at the same time provided a better understanding of such societies as first encountered by outsiders. These, together with such modern disciplines and techniques as archæology, historical linguistics, palynology, physical anthropology, DNA analyses, computer navigating and the like, have enabled a partial 'reconstruction' of Pacific Islands' human past. Though the reconstruction will never substitute for the accuracy of written history as one knows it from Europe, Egypt, the Middle East and Asia, a new understanding has nevertheless in these ways been achieved.

In the period following the Lapita expansion – that is, between approximately 3000 and 1500 years ago – New Guinea, the Solomons, Vanuatu, New Caledonia, Fiji and Tonga all experienced changes in their material cultures, as witnessed particularly by their pottery. These changes took place 'in step' throughout most of the area. Some islands failed to participate in some changes, but then participated in others. By *c.* AD 500, enormous cultural diversity characterized Pacific Islands.

The European labels 'Melanesia', 'Micronesia' and 'Polynesia' are useful distinctions which hold instructive, if limited, value in describing what was gradually emerging out of this prehistoric process. Their differences are ethnic, linguistic and cultural, encompassing Pacific Islands' three most salient human features, which also happen to be geographical in the main. Melanesia now claims more than 1000 Papuan and Austronesian languages within widely diverse cultural groups sharing only broad features in common. Micronesia has a large number of Austronesian subgroups in three major cultural divisions. And Polynesia, geographically the largest of the three regions, is culturally and linguistically the most homogeneous.

MELANESIA

Generally ignored in the 1800s and 'rediscovered' by scholars in the 1900s, Melanesia is now the focus of intense scientific research. Most of it involves New Guinea, Pacific Islands' largest landmass. Central to all investigation is the diversity brought about by the interactive development of two distinct peoples: the region's first inhabitants, the Papuans who occupy the Highlands of New Guinea and isolated communities in the Solomons; and the later Austronesians, who entered the region in small groups over a protracted period beginning around 4500 years ago.

Melanesia is characterized foremost by its enormous ethnic, social and cultural diversity. While some generalizations obtain, not one is valid for the entire region. Unusual for Pacific Islanders, Melanesians are not sailors. They do not frequently travel and are traditionally aggressive towards strangers. Networking has always been achieved through a series of near-neighbour partnerships. Goods which travel far pass through many hands. Horticulture has sustained most Melanesian communities, emphasizing one staple crop – such as taro – which was then supplemented by an assortment of minor crops. Slash-and-burn agriculture is still common today, enriching the earth with nutrimental charcoal.

Unlike the open island world of the rest of Pacific Islands, Melanesia comprised a closed chain. New Guinea allowed the rapid passage of parasites, pests, dangerous animals and diseases; countless communities situated relatively close to one another hastened proliferation. Malaria has forever ravaged Melanesian populations. Ancient and modern Melanesians have always worked hard, suffered much and died young. Particularly in the lowlands and coastal areas, life is hot, humid and disease-ridden. In fear of strangers and their sorcery, Melanesians have kept to themselves as much as possible. In this way, thousands of communities with distinct cultures have developed.

Melanesia possesses autochthonous Papuans, Austronesians and varying Papuan-Austronesian mixtures. A Papuan-Austronesian culture developed in Near Oceania only after Lapita. It engendered Island Melanesians who practised seafaring skills quite different from those of evolving Micronesians and Polynesians. In a series of migrations – even multiple settlements to the same chains – these Island Melanesians overran the Austronesian-occupied islands of New Caledonia, the Loyalties, Vanuatu, the Santa Cruz Islands, Fiji and others. There they mixed with resident Austronesians and elaborated distinct 'Melanesian' societies. Because Austronesian tongues were always retained, no matter how intense the western influx, this suggests that the invaders themselves were Austronesian speakers.

Ancient Melanesia began producing its own distinctive type of pottery, different from Lapita ware. On Buka at the northern tip of the Solomons potters used coils of clay (rather than Lapita's slabs) to form pots into which incisions were made as decorations, sometimes also applying relief images. First appearing *c.* 500 BC, such pots were popular for more than a thousand years. However, already by *c.* 700 BC, on Vanuatu's central islands, a related type of pottery had appeared: Mangaasi ware. The people producing this had apparently migrated to a Lapita community which no longer had pottery of its own. Only after *c.* AD 1200 did Vanuatu's production of Mangaasi pottery cease, the culture perhaps forced away by a new wave of Melanesian intruders, as some scholars allege.

The allegation might be corroborated by a rare marriage of oral tradition and Western archæology. Vanuatu's southern island of Efate recalls the legend of the arrival of a group of chiefs who founded a new society. Prominent in this legend is the name Roimata, who is believed to have once ruled northern Efate and, upon his death, to have been buried on Eretoka together with sacrifical attendants for the afterlife. In 1967, on Eretoka, archæologists unearthed a several centuries-old burial complex consisting of a main pit with a man's skeleton and four 'attendants'; 35 further burials surrounded the main pit. A rich assortment of funerary goods filled the site. Though proof that this was Roimata is lacking, a sacrificial mass burial of a powerful leader did occur, perhaps at the time the legend claims, perhaps several centuries later.

Though archæologists believe Vanuatu had been invaded from the north, oral tradition has Roimata and his people coming from the south. South of Vanuatu lie New Caledonia and the Loyalty Islands, logical 'stepping stones' for any would-be invader. It is possible that several Melanesian advances, over hundreds of years, took place. The small island of Rotuma, 500 kilometres northwest of Fiji, was settled by an early group of westerners who were no longer (or not yet) Melanesians but not yet Polynesians, perched on the divide between both regions. The Rotumans' position suggests an erstwhile commonality that was once far more prevalent in Pacific Islands – the 'Melanesia' that was in fact Oceania, the Pacific of prehistory.

MICRONESIA

North and northeast of Melanesia lies Micronesia, several chains of *c.* 3000 islands dotting 7.4 million square kilometres of ocean: over 3100 square kilometres of water for each square kilometre of land. Most Micronesian islands are low coral atolls, the majority of these uninhabited as well as uninhabitable. The region has been one of the most difficult places on Earth to settle: droughts and typhoons are common, plantings are restricted and hard to cultivate, and extreme isolation threatens survival.

There are three main cultural divisions: Western (Chamorros of the Mariana Islands; Yapese; Palauans); Central (Caroline Islanders' scattered atolls, including Pohnpeians and Kosraeans in the far east; Polynesian Outliers' Nukuoro and Kapingama-rangi in the southeast); and Eastern (Marshallese; Nauruans; Gilbertese of the Kiribati chain). In addition, the Tuvalu chain situated between Fiji and Kiribati is perhaps today Polynesian, but its geographic proximity to Micronesia as well as certain cultural features suggest a more intimate relationship with Micronesia in prehistory.

Though Micronesians may closely resemble Polynesians in culture, society and ethnicity, they have little to do with Polynesians. Micronesians were never a part of Lapita culture. Micronesians have always had a subsistence economy lacking the resources of Melanesia's and Polynesia's larger islands. This material privation has forced Micronesians to create different coping strategies to survive and thrive in an austere environment. Though their culture is much less diversified than the Melanesians', it is considerably more diversified than the Polynesians'.

The region's prehistory has enjoyed less scholarly attention than that of either Melanesia or Polynesia. Only now are investigators beginning to research in earnest what was investigated already in Polynesia a century ago. One specific problem is the archæology of atolls. Compared to that of high islands, the archæology of atolls is far more difficult and less productive. The problem is only now being addressed adequately, using an array of modern disciplines and techniques.

In consequence, prehistoric generalities are emerging for the region. For example, it is now appreciated that different waves of settlers at different periods entered Micronesia from the southwest (Philippines and Indonesia) and southeast (Solomons and northern Vanuatu). Already around 4500 years ago, centuries before Lapita emerged in the Bismarcks, humans were apparently occupying Palau in western Micronesia. These settlers would probably have been Austronesians. They came from Island Southeast Asia by way of Halmahera, easily 'island hopping' to the northeast. Around 3300 years ago a second incursion, following the same route, appears to have progressed far into the Marianas. The western highlands of Saipan and Guam in the Marianas show a distinctive pottery from this period known as 'Marianas Red', a plain red-slipped ware whose less common decorated type resembles ancient Philippine pottery; this would also have arrived through Halmahera and intervening islands. The languages of the Marianas and Palau are Western Austronesian, most closely resembling those of Island Southeast Asia.

Though the languages of Yap (in the Caroline Islands) and Nauru have no ascribeable origins, they are also Austronesian tongues. This suggests that all Micronesia's western high islands were settled from Island Southeast Asia, as the presence of rice and the loom in western Micronesia further suggests. The Marianas, Palau, Yap and Nauru were probably settled very early by several Austronesian voyagers of similar island origins.

Surprisingly, Bikini Atoll in the Marshalls shows evidence of human activity dating from around 1500 BC. Bikini might also have figured, then, in a very early expansion which occurred from the western islands of Micronesia. However, not all specialists accept this early date.

Palau and Yap developed independently as of around 500 BC. Palau exhibits certain cultural influences from Indonesia and the Philippines: it built great hill fortifications with terracing, for defence and taro cultivation; stone house platforms and pavements were preferred. In later centuries Yapese sought in Palau a special stone used to produce Yap's large stone disks, regarded as a valuable commodity. However, little is known about early western Micronesian exchange networks. Differing cultural evolutions suggest only infrequent mutual contact.

Central and eastern Micronesia is generally believed to have been colonized later, from eastern Melanesia. The nuclear proto-community of central and eastern Micronesia is believed to have originated in northern Vanuatu: historical linguistics clearly shows that the languages of these islands are closely related to those of the southeast Solomons and northern Vanuatu.

Kiribati was settled around 2200 years ago. From there, subsequent voyagers then settled the rest of eastern and central Micronesia. Expansion occurred gradually, from south to north – first into the Marshalls, which were settled around 2000 years ago – and then from east to west. The Carolines' high islands of Chuuk (Truk), Kosrae and Pohnpei were perhaps settled between 2000 and 1500 years ago. It is possible that the pottery of Pohnpei is a descendant of the last stage of Lapita ware. For this reason, and for the unequivocal linguistic data, it appears reasonable to see eastern Micronesian settlers hailing from a Lapita people or their Austronesian descendants.

Last to be reached were the central Micronesian islands of Nukuoro and Kapingamarangi, southeast of the Carolines. These two Outliers – that is, Polynesian-inhabited islands situated outside the 'Polynesian Triangle' – were settled only around 900 years ago.

Around AD 900, the long cultural continuity of the Marianas ended with the beginning of the Latte Phase. Micronesians there were supporting raised house floors using *latte*: pillars of coral limestone or volcanic tuff up to five metres in height and topped by bowl-like bases for floor beams. The largest *latte* structures may have supported communal men's houses. Some scholars have suggested that the Latte Phase signals foreign intrusion. However, it probably marks an indigenous transition of an ancient architectural feature from wood to stone. Among the artefacts found in *latte* sites are pounders similar to those for pounding taro throughout Pacific Islands, as well as maritime implements which suggest a heavy reliance on sea resources. The seventeenth-century Spanish intrusion finalled caused the abandonment of *latte* sites, when population patterns were fundamentally changed.

The high islands of the Carolines display Micronesia's greatest cultural complexity. On Pohnpei and Kosrae large stratified populations raised enormous structures in stone. Micronesia's most visited site today is eastern Pohnpei's Nan Madol settlement, ceremonial centre and burial enclosures. Built of basalt 'beams' in tiered ramparts and distributed on some 100 artificial islets within a shallow lagoon, this was the 'Venice of the Pacific'. According to oral tradition, Nan Madol was the seat of power of the Lords of Teleur, controlled by the Saudeleur Dynasty. Construction of such stone cities began in the ninth century AD, perhaps to signal social status; over the centuries, they became more elaborate. Similar structures on Kosrae are smaller and less imposing than Nan Madol. The culmination of a long tradition, Nan Madol was probably abandoned before the Europeans arrived in the sixteenth century.

Micronesian prehistory asks more than it answers. Specialists can at last identify Island Southeast Asian influences. Central and eastern Micronesians are now known to once have shared Austronesian proto-languages with eastern Melanesians. And many Polynesian features are now recognized in eastern Micronesia. A heterogeneous people with a complex prehistory, Micronesians still await their definitive biography.

POLYNESIA

Western Polynesia was first settled by Lapita people *c.* 3200 years ago. There in the Fiji-Tonga-Samoa Crescent over the following 500 years an Archaic Polynesian society emerged, distinct from any other on Earth. Only Polynesian languages were ever spoken in precontact Polynesia. Descendants only of the Lapita people, prehistoric Polynesians most closely resembled Island Southeast Asian ancestors and carried the least Papuan admixture of all prehistoric Pacific Islanders.

Fiji was the cradle of the Eastern Lapita Culture which gave rise to Archaic Polynesia (Map 5). Lapita culture continued to diversify throughout the Fiji-Tonga-Samoa Crescent. Eastern Lapita displays ever-greater simplification in its pottery, until Lapita ware finally vanished from the area *c.* 500 BC. Thereafter, Samoa started using simple bowls which scholars now call Polynesian Plainware. After Tonga and Samoa discontinued making pottery around two thousand years ago, for reasons which are still unclear, Fiji went on developing different types. As of 700 BC Fiji was already producing paddle-impressed pottery, like New Caledonia's. Beginning around AD 1100 a pottery like Vanuatu's Mangaasi ware was being produced in Fiji, at the same time that its main islands of Vanua Levu, Viti Levu and Taveuni were constructing earthen fortifications, suggesting social unrest.

Though linguists can point to Fiji's eastern islands as the probable point of origin for the Polynesians, a new and distinct Polynesian culture was emerging only out of the greater 'voyaging sphere' – an area of oceanic exchange and interaction – which was the Fiji-Tonga-Samoa Crescent. At the same time, the people of this region were losing contact with their Western Lapita 'homeland'. For perhaps a thousand years they developed, under mutual stimulation and competition, an Archaic Polynesian Culture which was unique, inspired and enriched by local environmental resources. Voyaging still continued, but only within the Crescent and with such distant neighbours as Tokelau, Niue, Rotuma, East Futuna, East 'Uvea and other islands which were beginning to develop distinct societies of their own.

The Tuvalu chain, situated between Fiji and Kiribati, was colonized around two thousand years ago. Its southern atolls were eventually claimed by Samoa, the northern by Tonga. Warrior groups arrived in recent centuries from Kiribati, the neighbouring archipelago in Micronesia; the inhabitants of the Tuvaluan island of Nui still speak Gilbertese, though their culture is entirely Tuvaluan. For these reasons Tuvalu occupies another 'threshold' position in Pacific Islands: neither one region nor the other, it is an Oceanic hybrid.

Archaic Polynesian society was characterized foremost by remarkable ethnic, linguistic and cultural homogeneity. From the Fiji-Tonga-Samoa Crescent sporadic voyages were undertaken. For example, it appears the first external archipelago to be discovered by Archaic Polynesian voyagers was the Cook Islands, around 700 BC; but no permanent settlement was apparently established there at the time. Because long-distance seafaring was regularly practised by Archaic Polynesians, they were well prepared for a second major expansion into Remote Oceania. However, this apparently occurred only after a long hiatus.

Perhaps prompted by favourable climatic conditions and the particular social situation, Samoans at last crossed 3000 kilometres of open ocean to colonize the Marquesas Islands in Eastern Polynesia around AD 300. A voyage that is normally against winds and currents, this crossing perhaps occurred during a rare reversal of prevalent oceanic conditions. After settling in the Marquesas, the Samoan emigrants probably returned often to Samoa. However, it would have been far more difficult to return to the Marquesas, as they would have needed a similar oceanic anomaly.

Prehistoric Pacific Islanders made use of various canoes, depending on region and era – from small fishing canoes to enormous voyaging canoes. In more recent times, Micronesians preferred outrigger canoes with raised platforms and transportable sails that changed stem to stern for quick course changes. In Fiji and Western Polynesia, large canoes had twin hulls commonly of unequal size. The great ocean-going voyaging canoes of the Eastern Polynesians had hulls of equal size, commonly with two lateen (triangular) sails and raised platform with storage and shelter constructions. Those celebrated eighteenth-century oils and watercolours by European visitors to the region in all likelihood memorialize a form of craft which was used during the millennium of Eastern Polynesian colonization: that is, from *c.* AD 300 to 1400.

The carrying capacity of double-hulled canoes was immense. Thousands of nautical miles could be crossed in one month, and such a distance was necessary in order to colonize many of the islands and island groups of Eastern Polynesia. Sailing with Captain Cook in the late eighteenth century, natural scientist Joseph Banks reported of Tahitian canoes that they 'carry a tolerable stock [of water] in hollow Bamboes'. Some stores, especially fermented foodstuffs like breadfruit, could last up to three months. Settling canoes were indeed expected to carry provisions for this length of time, as well as the staple food plants (taro, yams, sugarcane, bananas, breadfruit, ti and others) for several months ashore while awaiting first harvest.

Polynesians alone of all Pacific Islanders devised intricate ways of preserving foodstores. This allowed storage of large surpluses which guarded against times of famine. It also worked as a stimulus to cultural attainment: food storage freed Polynesians from constant food production, inviting greater challenges such as island exploration. Eastern Polynesians, in particular, had to innovate new strategies to cope with the more limited resources and extreme conditions they encountered: they 'desacralized' the ti plant, for example, by nullifying the ancient taboo which had always forbidden the eating of the holy plant's rhizomes, its root-like stems.

Their canoes also held domesticated animals (pigs, dogs, fowl), images of deified ancestors, entire toolkits and many other items. Each bore up to 30 or more settlers, many of whom were *tohunga* (canoe builders, tool-makers, irrigation experts, house builders, priests, orators and so on), and a large complement of women of child-bearing age. Each Polynesian settling canoe held a complete Polynesian society.

Despite the many competing theories about remote island settlement – 'accidental' drift, fanning out (with great losses) and several others – most scholars now agree that initial discovery was accomplished by scouts on two-way exploratory journeys. These would have set out with a given amount of food, sailing close to the wind; if no land had been found by the time half the food was consumed, then the scouts easily returned to their home island, sailing downwind. If land was found, then the scouts returned to report its location and suitability for settlement. Settlers then repeated the voyage after having completed careful preparations involving a complex arrangement of safeguards initiated by the entire community. Once settlement occurred, communication was maintained with the founding community. The new island was no isolate, but an addition to the network.

Islands were thus deliberately navigated to, using an array of navigational skills. Shore alignments provided an initial trajectory. Rising stars offered bearings, compensating for currents and wind drift. Differences in inter-island and open-ocean swells were noted, as well as subtle changes in water temperature which marked changing currents. Cloud movements were followed; cloud accumulations and underside reflections were heeded. The paths of certain birds – both those which feed at open sea at day and return, and those which range between archipelagos – were observed. Collections of driftwood and seaweed told of landfalls. At night, volcanic eruptions and natural fires informed observant navigators. On dark, wet nights, the fortuitous backwards-and-forwards flashing 'blue streak' pointed straight to land: a two-metre deep phosphorescent glow trailing up to 140 kilometres offshore which was probably caused by leaching from high-island valley rains, it led navigators to within 15 kilometres of land. Once near, expert navigators were then able to smell vegetation and perilous reefs.

There were many reasons for the continued colonization of Eastern Polynesia, in geographical terms the greatest migration of one people in the history of the planet. Historians frequently quote such clichés as drought, conflict, over-population, resource depletion, status competition and the like. However, these seem insufficient to explain the colonization of so vast a region over so many centuries. It appears instead that exploring and colonizing had simply become a vital part of Pacific Islanders' cultural heritage, as science and technology was to do in the West. However, one must own that Eastern Polynesians excelled all previous navigational achievements in Earth's human history, and this by several degrees of magnitude.

Once arrived at the Marquesas *c.* AD 300, the founding population of Samoans prospered. They found that breadfruit thrived in particular; it also stored well, up to decades in fact, in enormous pits. About AD 500 their descendants left to colonize the Eastern Tuamotus, the Gambiers (Mangareva), Pitcairn, Henderson and – *c.* 700 – Rapanui (Easter Island). Over these two centuries the first Marquesan departees had become a distinct Southeastern Polynesian people. However, the founding population back in the Marquesas was at this time emerging as Central Eastern Polynesians who began further voyages: northwest to Hawai'i and southwest to the Society Islands.

Whereas the Hawaiian archipelago remained an isolate – indeed, it is Earth's most isolated group of islands – Tahiti in the Societies became a major dispersal area. Probably in the tenth century Tahitians colonized the Northwestern Tuamotus, Australs and Cook Islands. New Zealand, Polynesia's largest landmass, was settled, perhaps in the late thirteenth century, from the Cooks. At around the same time, distant Norfolk Island (today under Australian authority) and the Kermadec Islands (New Zealand) were also colonized; these were probably then used as staging posts during the era of interactive voyaging. Shortly after 1400, South Island Māori of New Zealand then colonized Rēkohu (Chatham Islands) *c.* 1300 kilometres due east of Christchurch.

The Marquesans themselves had not done with colonizing, however. In the twelfth century they had apparently sailed south again to conquer and subjugate the Eastern Tuamotus and Mangareva, substantially altering the Southeastern Polynesian

culture and language there. Marquesan-dominated Mangarevans, around the year 1300, then voyaged *c*. 1300 kilometres
southwest to colonize Rapa, the southern isolate of the
Austral chain.

By the fifteenth century, then, Polynesians had settled the
eastern, northern and southern Pacific in the greatest maritime
expansion known to history. By this time, Polynesians alone
occupied a 'triangle' whose extremities were Hawai'i, New
Zealand and Rapanui. Only Asia's Mongol Empire had encompassed a greater range.

After settlement, each Polynesian island experienced unique
development. The first consequence was invariably adverse.
Every island had been a fragile, finely balanced ecosystem.
With the first Polynesian footfall, this balance was lost forever.
The result was the destruction of fauna, flora ... and the tres-
passers themselves.

Rapanui, for example, situated at the geographical terminus
of the millennia-old Austronesian expansion, had initially been
a subtropical 'paradise'. With flowing water, an abundance
of tall palms unique to the island (*Jubæa rapanuiensis*) and
bountiful marine and avian resources, the founding population on the western coast thrived on these and their successful
plantings of taro, yam, sugarcane, banana, ti and other cultivars.
They rapidly grew in numbers and, within 200 years of settlement, began settling the island's northeastern coast.

Around AD 1000 the Rapanui commenced the building of
larger stone *ahu* (ceremonial platforms), erecting on them
stone ancestral figures called *moai*. Around 300 *ahu* lined
primarily the shoreline, each facing inland towards its respective
settlement; only half of these had statues. Almost a thousand
moai were eventually quarried, carved, transported and
erected. Probably in the tenth or eleventh century, Rapanui
explorers apparently sailed to South America and returned
with two cultivars foreign to Pacific Islands: the sweet potato
and bottle gourd. Both thrived on Rapanui and swiftly entered
the interaction network, eventually making their way to Hawai'i
in the far northwest and New Zealand in the far west.

Up until 1500 peace and prosperity favoured the Rapanui; it was then that the island's southern coast and inland areas were settled extensively. Two major confederations of clans then emerged: the Tuʻu in the west and the ʻOtu ʻIti in the east. At the same time, Rapanui society became highly stratified, with several classes (nobility, high priests, experts, commoners and slaves). Nobility and high priests lived near the *ahu*; the rest of a community – around 70 villages in all populated the island – dwellt in low thatched huts like upturned boats which were scattered some distance apart. All clans shared the Rano Raraku quarry in the east for volcanic tuff for *moai*; later they also shared the Puna Pau quarry in the west for red scoria for *moai* topknots. Clans were wealthy enough, with sufficient surpluses, to afford constructing ever larger *ahu* with more and taller *moai*. Indeed, they created on the Pacific's most isolated inhabited island its greatest ceremonial architecture.

After this, climatic change and resource depletion meant less wood, hence fewer boats for open-ocean fishing and voyaging. Access to the ancient Southeastern Polynesian network became restricted. Once the trees were gone, all running water dried up. Conflict over land and water erupted, and warrior clans assumed power. By European contact in 1722, the 7000 to 10 000 Rapanui were living in a state of almost permanent warfare on a barren, near-waterless isolate, scarcely able to subsist.

New Zealand tells a different story, though similarities do obtain. Of the many contradicting Polynesian myths and legends about the discovery of this land, one in particular relates how Kupe, a chief of Hawaiki, mythical 'homeland' of many Polynesians (though not the Rapanui), was out at sea fishing one day and pursued an octopus which kept stealing his bait – until Kupe finally caught sight of New Zealand. Whoever did arrive there first did not do so until *c.* 1280, making New Zealand one of the last places in Pacific Islands to be permanently colonized. The first settlers found a land of extremes. At over 250 000 square kilometres New Zealand is larger than the rest of Polynesia combined; in all Pacific Islands, only New Guinea is larger. It is not tropical but subtropical, which forced an adaptation of traditional Polynesian customs and diet. Many species of large and small flightless birds were hunted down, most to extinction. This included the *moa* – up to 250 kilograms in weight and 3.7 metres in height – which ranged the forests of the North Island and the eastern South Island. The first settlers, their children and grandchildren apparently embarked on a hunting 'blitzkrieg', annihilating the islands' 11 species of *moa* in less than a century. Another settling group had simultaneously arrived at the South Island and just as rapidly eradicated the *moa* stocks there, apparently their main diet. The last firm evidence of living *moa* dates from *c.* 1360.

Because of the climate difference, some imported cultivars – such as coconut, banana and breadfruit – did not survive in New Zealand. Pigs and fowl were no longer bred, simply because there was an initial abundance of *moa*, seabirds and fishes. Hunting, fishing and gathering supplied nearly all needs, particularly in the south. Multiple arrivals to New Zealand, prompted by continued contact with the home island(s), settled other, usually eastern, coastal areas.

New Zealand's settling populations grew swiftly and became indigenous Māori. More people lived on the warmer North Island; both populations preferred sheltered eastern coasts. Maritime resources were keenly pursued: whales, seals, dolphins, as well as countless seabirds and shellfish. Crops were cultivated foremost on the North Island; the South Island was simply too cold, except for northern areas. Though the Polynesian staples of taro, yams, sugarcane, ti and other tropical plants were cultivated, it was the import from South America, which had probably been introduced into the Eastern Polynesian voyaging sphere in the tenth or eleventh century, that became, as on Rapanui, New Zealand's most important crop: the *kūmara* or sweet potato. It thrived in the land's harsh climate. (Also because of local climatic and soil conditions, breadfruit had become the Marquesans' preferred food crop and taro the Hawaiians'.) The roots of the native fern and of the cabbage tree were eaten as well on New Zealand. Since barkcloth, such as that furnished by the paper mulberry throughout Polynesia, was unavailable south of the northern half of the North Island, the Māori used fibre from the native flax to make clothing in these southerly latitudes (a custom copied by the northern Māori after the 1840s when paper mulberry became extinct because of damage by introduced cattle and because of human neglect). A special resource for prestige and trade was the greenstone of certain South Island locations; this nephrite jade was carved to create elegant and highly treasured ornaments and ceremonial clubs. Māori tribes grew large and began to develop a highly competitive society which, because of almost continuous warfare, failed to centralize, so there was never a paramount chief of New Zealand. Situated far from the main Eastern Polynesian voyaging spheres, New Zealand never competed in such elaborate undertakings as the construction of holy precincts in massive stone or the erection of monolithic ancestral statuary.

Unlike the pioneering Rapanui who in the end were perishing in privation and conflict on their small isolate, the Māori latecomers on the other side of the Pacific had settled islands so large that neither environmental depredation nor internal warfare could ever seriously threaten their survival. Free to exploit both their ecosystem and themselves without limits, the Māori thrived prodigiously. Indeed, by the time of European contact – only three and a half centuries after the first Polynesians had arrived at New Zealand – they had become one of Remote Oceania's most populous nations, numbering perhaps as many as 250 000.

Over the centuries fundamental differences emerged between Western Polynesians and Eastern Polynesians. Westerners fished primarily with nets, Easterners with hook and line. Westerners emphasized taro production, Easterners breadfruit (where possible) and sweet potato. Western art had no anthropomorphs, Easterners venerated ancestral figures. Westerners performed elaborate kava-drinking ceremonies, Easterners drank kava without ceremony. Westerners addressed chiefs in honorific language, Easterners lacked honorific language. Westerners told 'evolutionary' creation myths, Easterners intoned 'procreative' chants. Westerners buried their dead, Easterners placed them in caves or trees. Many such differences separated the two: their canoe designs and sailing techniques differed greatly, for example. In other words, they were rapidly becoming two separate Polynesian societies. Though each maintained an internal network of exchange for over a millennium, the infrequency of extra-regional contact had produced a major cultural division.

The Polynesian networks of exchange and social communication were most active after c. AD 1000. Major events also caused cultural diffusion: as when Marquesans likely overran and subjugated the Eastern Tuamotuans and Mangarevans around 1200, or when Society Islanders 'engaged' the Hawaiians – either by invasion or networking – around a century later.

Local empires emerged. The island of Tongatapu in Tonga, for example, preserves a regal legacy in the trilithon Ha'amonga 'a Maui, one of Polynesia's premier archæological sites. Over five metres in height, it comprises two upright coral monoliths crowned by an enormous coral lintel, apparently all that is left of an ancient gateway from an erstwhile chiefly centre at Heketa in Tongatapu's northeast. Tradition holds that the trilithon was built around 1200 by the eleventh Tu'i Tonga, Tu'itatui, to memorialize the special bond of brotherhood between his two sons.

But the era of Polynesian expansion and interaction did not last. Some 27 islands were abandoned altogether, probably because their small size and isolation made permanent settlement too difficult. (See 'Mystery Islands' below.) Voyaging became less frequent among all Polynesians around AD 1500, or perhaps even earlier: the internal networking between Northwest Marquesans and Southeast Marquesans, for example, appears already to have broken down c. AD 1300. No longer did a voyaging sphere unite the Southeastern Group (Eastern Tuamotus, Mangareva, Pitcairn, Henderson, Rapanui), Australs or Cooks. Those Tuamotuan pearl shells so prized in the Marquesas were simply no longer obtainable. And no one in Mangareva traded in Marquesan adzes any longer.

REGIONAL CHARACTERISTICS

Though many similarities obtained in Pacific Islands throughout most of prehistory, by AD 1500 Melanesia, Micronesia and Polynesia had developed distinct characteristics of their own, finally fully justifying these three labels. Many of the characteristics still survive today, particularly among those isolated Melanesian and Micronesian communities which have been little affected by several centuries of Western intrusion.

In its settlement patterns, Melanesia generally displayed nuclear villages of concentrated populations. Micronesia preferred extended settlements. Polynesia also preferred extended settlements, but some islands had concentrated populations.

In their social organization, both Melanesia and Micronesia experienced matrilineal and patrilineal societies. In contrast, Polynesia was both ambilineal (mothers' and fathers' lines together) and patrilineal. Melanesian society was classless, Micronesia had either two or three classes, while Polynesia usually displayed three classes or more. Both Melanesia and Micronesia had men's clubhouses; Polynesia had none. Melanesia acknowledged egalitarian descent, but Micronesia and Polynesia showed ramage (ranked family branching). Melanesia had the 'Big Man' concept (see below), Micronesia and Polynesia an aristocracy. Melanesia did have hereditary chiefs in some places, but these were not commonly hierarchical chiefs. Micronesia and Polynesia had weak hierarchies on atolls and strong hierarchies on larger high islands. Melanesia displayed 'consensus' rule, Micronesia decision by council, and Polynesia autocratic chiefly rule. Melanesia generally contained small social units with a village focus. Micronesia experienced military alliances between lineages. Polynesia had larger political units which transcended kinship groups.

Concerning land rights, Melanesia's kinship groups occupied a given territory. Micronesian atolls comprised distinct lineages claiming specific areas. Ancient Polynesia at first had lineages holding tenure, but territory in later centuries became defined in political terms beyond the lineage. All three regions had community leaders – almost always male – who controlled or managed land in a variety of ways.

The legal system of Pacific Islands as a whole was arbitrary, with both supernatural and secular sanctions. In Melanesia, a common form of punishment was sorcery. Whereas Melanesia displayed more legalistic practice, Micronesian and Polynesian law was applied principally according to rank.

In its economy, Melanesia had only limited marine exploitation; 'slash and burn' horticulture by both males and females, with separate duties; little food preservation; some irrigation; and non-specialist craftsmen. Micronesia experienced intensive marine exploitation; 'slash and burn' horticulture commonly, but not exclusively, by females; food preservation; and specialist craftsmen. Polynesia had intensive marine exploitation; all horticulture by males; complex food preservation; sophisticated irrigation and terracing; and many types of specialists for crafts and rituals.

With respect to a value system, Melanesians were highly competitive, particularly in their 'Big Man' system (a relatively localized and possibly quite recent phenomenon), yet communal at special times while suspicious and aggressive towards all outsiders. Micronesians were also highly competitive, but generally hospitable towards guests and strangers. Polynesians normally determined whether to be competitive or communal according to class, family or island, always mindful of the political or social circumstances; otherwise, Polynesians were generally hospitable to guests and strangers alike.

In their 'religion', which actually encompassed a variety of phenomena, all three regions acknowledged a local version of the *tapu/mana* complex (see below). Melanesians had creator-regulator 'gods' as well as ghosts and spirits who invariably worked harm. Micronesians valued an assortment of ancestors, spirits and 'gods'. Early Polynesians and Western Polynesians acknowledged ancestral spirits, ghosts and household 'gods'; later Eastern Polynesians retained many of these and also attached importance to anthropomorphic 'sky-gods', departmental 'creator gods' of sea, warfare, horticulture and so on.

No Pacific Islanders practised any form of worship. Melanesian and Micronesian devotion was placatory, to be manipulated by ritual; Polynesians had supplication and bargaining rituals. Melanesians often practised magic and sorcery; Micronesians also used magic; and Polynesians believed in trances, spirit possession and sacrifice (including human). Melanesians recognized sorcerers, but no specialist priesthood; Micronesians had shamans, diviners, mediums and sorcerers; and Polynesians acknowledged all of these as well as a hierarchy of priesthood on larger high islands, believing only chiefs experienced an afterlife of some kind.

Pacific Islands' rituals included the Melanesians' 'betel nut' chewing, and the kava drinking of the Micronesians (ceremonial) and Polynesians (ceremonial/unceremonial). All three regions shared feasting and competitive giving with elaborate display. Varying degrees of cannibalism were common throughout most of prehistoric and early historic Polynesia (see below), while head-hunting, in restricted contexts, was endemic to Melanesia.

In their networking, most Melanesians traded with immediate neighbours, rarely travelling beyond the next village; Melanesian society, especially in New Guinea and the Bismarcks, was of highly restricted mobility. In stark contrast, Micronesia's atoll dwellers travelled frequently; long sea-voyages were common, for social calls, trade, crisis relief and other things. Polynesians elaborated extensive 'voyaging spheres' which enabled inter-insular and inter-archipelagic communication for social, political and economic purposes.

'MYSTERY ISLANDS' AND OUTLIERS

Fluctuating populations of satellite settlers regularly 'commuted' to where resources were: fishes, whales, dolphins, birds, turtles, wood, basalt for adzes and other foodstuffs and objects. Islands were not always permanent bases: a 'homeland' might consist of an entire group of neighbouring islands, with migrations between constituent member islands taking place according to season, situation or ritual. This was particularly the case with low-lying atolls such as the Tuamotus, which still maintain many seasonal and satellite islands.

However, some islands of Polynesia were permanently settled for hundreds of years, then abandoned. This situation highlights the problems inherent in settling smaller islands: water and food shortage, internal conflict, natural disasters, illness, homesickness (psychological isolation) and others. The depletion of local bird populations can be a major factor, particularly on atolls which discourage gardening and animal husbandry. Henderson Islanders, for example, wiped out their breeding colonies of storm petrels and caused two separate species of large pigeon to become extinct. So, by 500 years ago, there were also no more Henderson Islanders.

The so-called 'Mystery Islands' are those Polynesian isolates which were found abandoned by the time of European contact, for any of the above reasons (Map 6). There is little real mystery to these approximately 27 known islands (and probably a greater number of unknown ones). Archæological evidence suggests that these settlements survived only as long as their prehistoric voyaging spheres lasted. Once active exchange and disaster relief ceased, isolated populations either sailed away or perished. Among the more prominent of these are Pitcairn of *Bounty* fame, neighbouring Henderson, Hawai'i's Necker and Nihoa, the Cooks' Palmerston and Suwarrow, the Kermadec Islands north of New Zealand, and Australia's Norfolk Island. Most of these appear to have been abandoned *c.* AD 1500, or slightly earlier. The climate change that occurred during the Little Ice Age might have also caused the abandonment of many of these islands.

Outliers are something altogether different (Map 7). These are the Polynesian-inhabited islands situated outside the 'Polynesian Triangle'. Some – like Tikopia, Anuta, Taumako and other southern islands – were settled around 3000 years ago when Archaic Polynesian society was first emerging. It is possible that a number of these were settled even before

Western Polynesia, describing the route of initial Lapita expansion. Others, like Nukuoro and Kapingamarangi in the Southern Carolines of Micronesia, were settled by Polynesians as recently as 900 years ago. The Outliers are, then, not the result of a single Polynesian thrust outward, but of many different voyages of discovery and settlement. Their subsequent histories were equally diverse and complex, with influences from many sources.

Most of the Outliers were settled during the first millennium AD when Polynesians from the Fiji-Tonga-Samoa Crescent set out to colonize isolated, small islands west and northwest of Fiji. This was a 'back-migration' only in so far as it reversed the general eastern thrust of Austronesian expansion. In navigational terms it is significant that all the Polynesian Outliers lie along the windward reaches of Melanesia and Micronesia (except Rennell and Bellona, southwest of the Solomons, which lie to leeward).

The Polynesian inhabitants of Rennell and Bellona preserve a tradition of an indigenous darker-skinned population whom they encountered when they migrated from legendary 'Ubea': perhaps East 'Uvea (Wallis) northeast of Fiji. They tell of coexistence, then conflict and massacre. It appears that, until then, Rennell and Bellona had been occupied exclusively by settlers from the Solomons called the 'Hiti', who were conquered, then annihilated, by the Polynesian immigrants. It is a tale common to prehistoric Pacific Islands.

Most Outliers evidently derive from a later stage of Samoan society. Some of these islands were then resettled by conquering populations within the last 700 years or so. Others had apparently been abandoned, then resettled hundreds of years later. Outlier populations have borrowed a number of features from Melanesian and Micronesian neighbours; in most cases, multiple contacts have occurred. In addition to the Outliers, several Melanesian locales show a significant Polynesian contribution, though the prehistoric source is unknown – such as the Loyalty Islands by New Caledonia, and even Port Moresby, capital of Papua New Guinea.

Though the inhabitants of the Outliers speak Western Polynesian languages and display Western Polynesian social and cultural traits, all differ from Western Polynesian islands and among themselves. Despite these differences, the Outliers exhibit a 'peripheral coherence': all are close enough to their Melanesian and Micronesian neighbours (who form tighter internal groupings) not to be wholly abandoned in the areal network, but lie far enough distant to maintain ethnic individuality without assimilation. The occupants of the Outliers are thus Melanesians and Micronesians who speak and behave as 'Polynesians'. All Outliers have had extensive communication with their Melanesian and Micronesian neighbours; only intermittently did Polynesians contribute. Of course, the longer the prehistory – such as with Anuta, Taumako and Tikopia – the more complex the situation, with many external influences. It cannot be ignored that the languages of the Outliers most closely resemble Samoan, East Futunan and Tuvaluan. (Some scholars have suggested that all of 'Polynesian' Tuvalu is in fact an Outlier Chain within Micronesia.) However, this tells only of the finale of a very long and complicated saga which, in the end, saw Western Polynesia imposing its languages on the area. A founding population may have experienced later Samoan, then Tongan domination, for example, concealing original ethnicity.

The lesson of the 'Mystery Islands', the Outliers and such further cases as Nauru, Banaba and Rotuma is that the greater the islanders' isolation, the harder it is to maintain ethnic integration, indeed even to survive. Small isolates tend to differ, dwindle and die. Outliers and larger isolates which maintain a threshold network with ethnically different neighbours profit from external sustenance and relief. The extreme case of Tikopia, isolated from Polynesia for over 3000 years, reveals an Outlier which has had varying influences from larger islands lying far away: the Solomons, the Banks Islands, Vanuatu and Western Polynesia. Here, one must really question what is meant by the label 'Polynesia', as the Tikopians are clearly Oceanians who throughout prehistory absorbed a heterogeneous heritage.

Our Western terminology breaks down here. An upshot of the recent focus of attention on the Outliers is just this: it has called into doubt the validity of the labels 'Melanesia', 'Micronesia' and 'Polynesia' as *prehistoric* categories. The names may be eminently useful in describing Pacific Islands since European contact. However, they appear to fail in adequately comprehending the complex situation before then. The Outliers witness what most of Pacific Islands might once have resembled, and this is evidently something quite different from what the three labels denote.

OCEANIC SYSTEMS

All prehistoric Pacific Islanders were self-sufficient in food. However, some local communities specialized, trading their specializations for lacking foodstuffs and other things. Merchants facilitated such trade: the Siassi people of Papua New Guinea's northwest coast, for example, were seafaring middlemen, exchanging pigs, dogs, pottery and other commodities between the mainland and New Britain in the Bismarcks. Melanesian leaders derived status from the possession of prestige objects usually acquired elsewhere through exchange. The exchange could be simple barter – bamboo tubes of oil for packs of salt, for example – or extended ceremonial networking: shell necklaces for armshells or bracelets.

Over the centuries Melanesian communities were linked in both commodity networks and ceremonial exchange networks, the two systems ultimately legitimizing those in authority and therefore rigidly maintained. The form of exchange most common throughout Pacific Islands has always been inland-and-coastal barter. In Melanesia's Solomon Islands, for example, as everywhere on larger islands, the inlanders exchanged garden crops for the coastal dwellers' fish, shellfish, eels, seaweed and other marine resources. In a very large area like

New Guinea, goods would pass through many hands before reaching their destination, organized through 'trade-friends' or a network of relationships between discrete pairs of individuals, each profiting from a share in the transaction. In this way, coastal dwellers of New Guinea enjoyed their treasured salt and oil from the Highlands while the Highlanders of Mount Hagen received highly valued shells which played such a large part in local ceremonies, bringing descent groups prestige and greater status.

One of the Highlands' main expressions of wealth is pigs. In the *tee* exchange system of the Tombema-Enga clan of the Western Highlands, for example, pigs can comprise the most valuable commodity (as contrasted with shells in the Eastern Highlands). Here, 'Big Men' are invariably those with the largest herds of pigs, and those who can ceremoniously display the longest line of staked-out pigs at a major ceremonial exchange festival are the biggest Big Men of all. Ceremonial exchanges in the Mount Hagen region see the various categories of participants – that is, the donors, aides and recipients – bodily adorning themselves in a way characteristic to each, to allow easy clan and role identification and to create a sense of social unity.

The famous *kula* ceremonial exchange network of Papua New Guinea's southeastern Massim region of the Solomon Sea has linked, for perhaps as long as 500 years, Melanesians of separate languages and customs in a voyaging circle approximately 350 kilometres in diameter. *Soulava* shell necklaces are exchanged for *mwali* armshells or bracelets in the D'Entrecasteaux Islands, the Trobriands, the Marshall Bennetts, Woodlark, the Laughlan Islands, the Louisiade Archipelago, the Engineer Group and all inner-circle smaller islands. The red shell-disk necklaces move clockwise, the white armshells or bracelets anti-clockwise. Traders maintain exchange partners for a lifetime, both in their home islands and in linked islands of the *kula* ring. In olden days, the men of one village – or of neighbouring villages – would pay a ceremonial visit to the village of their *kula* link on a distant island, presenting formal gifts and renewing pledges of loyalty which maintained the network. Later, the visited village, and perhaps also their neighbours, would pay a return visit, similarly bearing gifts. Though this custom no longer obtains, the network itself still continues. For the voyages, specially built and decorated outrigger canoes have always been used, brightly painted in red, black and white designs. The quality and number of *kula* shells acquired and exchanged by one individual determined that individual's status in the network. Alongside the formal *kula* exchanges other, more practical commodities were also traded.

In Micronesia, exchange networks connected neighbouring islands of a group, or even neighbouring archipelagos, to a degree and frequency seen perhaps nowhere else on Earth. The Caroline Islands had two internal networks. One was the localized commodity network connecting Lamotrek, Elato and Satawal in an exchange of sea turtles, coconuts and bread-fruit for resource permissions and assurances of famine relief. The other was the much greater *sawei* system.

The *sawei* was a ceremonial network among most of the 2000-kilometre, east-to-west chain of the Carolines. Up until around a century ago, two villages on western Yap annually received an expedition bringing canoe tributes of shell valuables, coconut oil, sennit twine (for canoes and build-ings), woven skirts and mats, and holy tributes of religious artefacts as well as titles to land from eastern leaders or their representatives. The expedition grew in its numbers of canoes as it progressed westwards, stopping at traditional *sawei* land-falls where higher-ranking chiefs would each time assume authority. Beginning already at the pre-penultimate landfall of Fais, both canoe tribute and religious tribute were presented to the local chief. At Ulithi, the penultimate island of *sawei*, more of both were given to this island's chief. The last paramount leader of the expedition there, at Mogmog on Ulithi, then led all the canoes to Gatjapar on Yap and presented all remaining canoe and religious tribute to the local chief there. Expedition representatives then presented to their *sawei* partners on Yap their land tribute. On departure from Yap, they received in return from their hosts the Yapese flint, wood (scarce on Micronesian atolls) for canoes and building, various foodstuffs and the prized powdered turmeric of the *Curcuma longa* plant, valued throughout Pacific Islands for its yellow flowers for colouring and dying and its aromatic stem for chewing. Though local tradition insists that *sawei* had been maintained to preclude the Yapese turning harmful magic against their neighbours, the network probably began after a Yapese conquest and demand for tribute. This had then developed over the centuries into a paternalistic, then purely ritualistic relationship whose true origins had long been forgotten.

The dual networks of the Carolines encouraged trade and discouraged internal conflict. It also ensured survival on resource-poor, low-lying atolls which were often visited by devastating typhoons: the goodwill of neighbours and the access to foodstuffs and building supplies often meant the difference between life and death. In the antithesis of the Carolines' *sawei* system, the westernmost Ralik chain of islands in the Marshalls had a paramount chief who sailed with his retainers throughout the chain at regular intervals – much like a mediæval European emperor – to collect tribute of sur-plus foodstuffs. It is believed Ralik's chief then redistributed his wealth, however, to needy subjects when typhoons or drought struck, in this way again ensuring human survival... and the chief's legitimization.

In emphasizing inherited rank, Micronesia followed Polynesia. But in acquiring status, Micronesia followed Melanesia. Power and status were to be had through warfare and/or the demonstration and distribution of wealth. The greatest show came at feasting, when the individual competing for chief-tancy, or his kinship group, freely gave of quality foodstuffs and valuables in public demonstrations of largesse.

On Palau in western Micronesia, wealth also consisted of 'bead money'. This was beads containing glass and ceramics otherwise unknown in Pacific Islands. The presence of these suggests trade with the European-influenced Philippines of the sixteenth century, though some scholars have put forward that it demonstrates early Micronesian trading links with mainland Asia, which had access to such glass and ceramic objects from ancient Rome.

On Yap, only 500 kilometres northeast of Palau, stone disks called *fae*, some as large as four metres in diameter, 'financed' marriages. The *fae* were presented by the bride's kinship group to the groom's, who reciprocated with 'shell money'. The *fae*'s argonite stone was quarried 250 kilometres to the southwest and transported in canoes to Yap. Holes for carrying were drilled through the centre of all but the largest *fae*. Once accepted by the groom's kin, the *fae* decorated the precinct of the men's house as a display of the group's wealth. This custom survived for many centuries.

Micronesia's exchange networks and trading routes depended on quality canoes and superb navigational skills. At this time in history Micronesia probably led the world in both. On the one island of Woleai in the Carolines, an ancient sailing centre, there were no fewer than 12 different types of sailing canoe, each with a specific purpose: one ceremonial canoe, two types of canoe for ocean-fishing, two for lagoon-fishing, two for voyaging, and the remainder various paddling canoes for local purposes.

In Polynesia, by the time of European contact only the largest islands which lay close together still maintained voyaging spheres. There were two. Fiji, Tonga and Samoa in Western Polynesia were experiencing a period of sudden expansion under Tonga's policy of aggression, actively engaging one another as well as Rotuma, Niue, East 'Uvea, East Futuna and even more distant islands. The other voyaging sphere lay in the Society Islands, which at that time included the North-western Tuamotus; this network was as active and dynamic as that in Western Polynesia, and similarly troubled by warfare.

However, there is growing evidence that extensive networking took place in prehistoric Eastern Polynesia. That the prehistoric Rapanui people, inhabiting the most isolated of all Pacific

Islands, were familiar with cut and dressed stone architecture, humanoid stone statuary, stone *poi* pounders, stone one-piece fishhooks and many other common features of the region argues that they once participated in the Southeastern Polynesian voyaging sphere. Active from *c*. 700 to 1600, this sphere would have included the Gambiers (Mangareva), Oeno, Ducie, Pitcairn and Henderson. Pitcairn was evidently a quarry island for its neighbours, providing top-quality basalt adzes; it perhaps also supplied high-quality timber for canoe building. Its position between Mangareva and Rapanui made Pitcairn pivotal within the Southeastern Polynesian voyaging sphere. Mangareva itself was linked to the distant north-northwest, procuring adzes also from the prehistoric adze-making centre on the now uninhabited island of 'Ei 'A'o in the Northwest Marquesas. Such trade could never have occurred without the active involvement of the Eastern Tuamotuans. The Marquesas itself maintained an active internal exchange system for many centuries, as did the Australs south of Tahiti, which also long maintained contacts with their ancestral Society Islands in the north. The islands of the Hawaiian chain similarly enjoyed an internal trading network for many centuries, as did the Cook Islands.

However, most larger networks began breaking up around 1500, if not two centuries earlier. Archæoclimatologists have established that a warm and generally settled climate characterized the globe between AD 900 and 1300; after this, great climatic fluctuations, the so-called Little Ice Age, began, unsettling entire regions of the planet. Large areas of the Pacific appear to have been adversely affected by this change. The Southeastern Polynesian voyaging sphere, for example, appears to have ceased altogether by 1600 at the latest. Maintenance of communication had become too difficult by then, and so Ducie was abandoned, then Henderson, Oeno, and finally Pitcairn. Rapanui was thereupon cut off entirely from Mangareva. The date also marks the start of Rapanui's environmental collapse, the end of *ahu* building and *moai* carving and transporting, and the beginning of societal chaos.

Without robust networking, survival on smaller, isolated Pacific islands was always uncertain.

GENDER ROLES

Division of labour between the sexes varied widely from region to region in prehistoric Pacific Islands. Men were commonly responsible for the physically more demanding and dangerous tasks, such as initial land clearance, house and boat construction, terrace building and deep-sea fishing. Day-to-day agricultural maintenance was generally left to women. This included shellfish and other marine resource gathering, water fetching, garment-making and most food preparation. In some Pacific societies, household gardens were the province of women, but their harvest, storage and redistribution the responsibility of men.

Women were universally considered to be polluters, especially during menstruation and childbirth. Most Pacific Islands communities either sequestered them at these times or banned them to special huts beyond the community precinct. If banned, women had to remain topographically lower than the community – downhill and downstream from the men's and sacred relics' houses – lest their blood flow near these and pollute them, bringing supernatural harm to the community.

Some regional generalizations obtained regarding gender obligations and restrictions. Melanesian women, for example, contributed more to food production than did women in Polynesia, where their primary task lay in the manufacture of mats and cloth for both domestic and ceremonial use. Melanesia also stressed more strongly the surbordination of women, upheld by the utter conviction of female danger and pollution. (The belief persists today, especially in New Guinea and parts of the Solomon Islands.) Though Polynesian women often figured as the targets of taboo linked with pollution, they still remained the social equal of men, with the same, or frequently an even higher, status. Between the two extremes lies Micronesia, with a wide spectrum of gender differences, not only between the more Melanesian west and more Polynesian east, but also within an individual island chain. For example, the men of Chuuk Lagoon garden, but the men of Chuuk District hold that this is women's work.

Melanesia has also displayed a remarkable diversity of attitudes about women and their status in society. Women's labour was needed in all Melanesian communities, and women actively contributed to wealth accumulation, whose purpose, however, was to elevate the males who dominated public office. Only rarely in Melanesia have women competed among themselves for prestige. In the Trobriands, for example, mortuary ceremonies demand the giving away of skirts and banana-leaf bundles, traditionally items of women's wealth; women's status there is measured by the quality and quantity they are able to part with. However, husbands also actively contribute to this store, lest they lose face. Similar to what has developed in Muslim societies, Melanesian women have created their own domestic subculture, with its specific prestige and status among other women. Here, men have no place or say. In nearly all aspects of Melanesian society, men and women occupy separate, mutually exclusive domains of activity. Even traditional self-adornment, which is a characteristic extravagance of Papua New Guinea's Highlanders, is mostly a male prerogative. But at important festivals of ceremonial gift exchange and at cult performances, women will decorate themselves with bright and profuse feather headdresses and facial reds and yellows as garish as any men's adornment. Most common throughout Melanesia is the belief that women pollute male power and therefore must be kept from approaching sacred items or rituals. The separation of male and female items and activities there has thus always been ritually regulated.

Common to all Melanesians have been separate men's houses. Here the clan's sacred objects were kept; here the initiated males gathered to talk, work, chew and sleep. Initiation to a men's house was one of the greatest events in

a young man's life, comprising the learning of male comport-
ment and secret lore and objects. In many Melanesian societies,
initiation was not a single event but a long series of graded
stages, whereby a young man was introduced to ever profounder
clan truths. On the island of South Pentecost in Vanuatu, for
example, young men paid and sacrificed to participate in
increasingly more complicated rituals which would see them
ascend through the ten grades of the *warsangul*. (Significantly,
the women of South Pentecost had a secret society, too,
though only of three grades.)

Micronesia was different, in that its generally matrilineal
systems allowed women to also exert strong influence in community activities. However, clan leaders were almost always
men. Young Micronesian women were believed to be ritually
impure. Only childbirth and age allowed them to become
purer and gain in status, especially through an advantageous
marriage. Middle-aged women with male children and lands
possessed influence in the day-to-day business of their estate.
Still, they had to follow the decisions of male superiors.

In Polynesia, the role of women was significant in the
scheme of absolute male authority. Women frequently ranked
higher than their brothers, but usually abstained from political
power. Their higher rank allowed them to influence community
issues through their son, brother and/or husband – indeed,
even to accede to paramount chieftaincy as happened in the
recent histories of Tonga, Tahiti and Hawai'i. However,
formal political titles were almost always held by men. The
women of Polynesia wielded more communal power than all
other Islander women, playing active parts in crucial political
processes such as links in marriage alliances between competing
descent groups, islands and archipelagos.

In Western Polynesia, male and female lines of descent
developed a complementary relationship. For example, in
Tonga brothers were below sisters when it came to ritual
authority and honour: Tonga's paramount chief, the Tu'i
Tonga, therefore owed deference to his sister and her sons,
as they embodied the higher-ranking lineage. As this posed

a threat to the succession of the Tu'i Tonga, the chief's sister was traditionally married off to a non-Tongan, customarily to a Fijian leader.

The only gender constant in prehistoric Pacific Islands appears, then, to be the universal belief in the supernatural danger and pollution emanating from women. This belief was traditional and unquestioned, perhaps not so much out of ignorance as out of conceit: men wielded the power and naturally wished to keep it.

SOCIAL STRUCTURES AND WARFARE

Pacific Islands' leaders stood out by their ability to accumulate food surpluses, either through family power and support of other groupings, or through personal tribute and wealth generated through offerings. This developed differently within each region, from New Guinea's absence of stratification to Polynesia's extreme hierarchies.

Melanesia still preserves a good deal of its prehistoric society, in contrast to Micronesia and especially Polynesia where very little remains of the old ways. Melanesia displays Pacific Islands' greatest cultural diversity because of three factors: the region's largest landmass (New Guinea); most profound time depth (probably more than 50 000 years); and two separate ethnic origins (Papuan, Austronesian), with many degrees of mixture between New Guinea and Fiji. Melanesia has always been characterized by small communities who place little value on social rank; individual status was gained only by the personal acquisition and application of private wealth.

However, in New Guinea's Highland societies and Fiji's largest communities, which include thousands of members, hierarchical structures did develop which more closely resembled those of prehistoric Polynesia. Melanesia experienced various forms of political leadership, each determined by the size of population and available resources. Typical is the possibly quite recent phenomenon of the relatively localized

'Big Man', a particularly influential member of a community who assumes leadership, his position assured through ceremonial exchange and feast-giving. In small societies, the Big Man holds sway in the men's house, influencing communal decisions. In societies of thousands, however, the Big Man very much resembles a paramount chief.

Melanesian descent groups are usually patrilineal, deriving power from a father's influence. The group acquires prestige by memorializing their influential male deaths with elaborate wakes, whereby wealth in the form of pigs as well as other valuables like shell bead strings are distributed to relatives of the deceased. All giving has two purposes: to prove one's status and to ensure future receiving. When a death occurs among the same relatives, gifts of equal if not of greater value are expected in return. Such exchanges of material wealth fire the engine of community competition about which all traditional Melanesian social life revolves.

It is the role of the Big Man to lead and direct such displays and exchanges. He is also paramount in providing the means required for marriage feasts and in arranging alliances beneficial to the descent group. This creates an entire network of obligations, whose centre is the Big Man. His own returns are manifested as political support. The position of Big Man is not hereditary, bears no title and usually lacks any outward display of social eminence. But everyone in the community is fundamentally aware of the importance of this 'invisible chieftaincy'.

Sometimes heredity plays a role. Eldest sons of the Kwaio people of New Guinea seem to enjoy more success if their fathers were already Big Men; but the succession is not assured. Indeed, Big Men often groom successors from more distantly related candidates, particularly if this promises a powerful new alliance. Other groups, such as the Highlands' Melpa, sometimes bred Big Men from among local 'mafia' monopolizing main resources, in which case their true social status was titular rather than proven. The Purari of Papua New Guinea's south coast had social ranking and hereditary chiefs (who were, though, upheld by competitive exchange). In the Trobriand Islands leaders of high-ranking subgroups derived authority from a common female ancestor. Proceeding eastwards the ancient Austronesian substrate becomes ever more evident. Succession of eldest males was common in New Caledonia, where entire descent groups formed confederations under the leadership of paramount chiefs. And in Fiji, Melanesia's threshold to Polynesia, a hierarchical structure emerged which was virtually indistinguishable from Western Polynesian chiefdoms.

As most prehistoric Melanesian communities comprised very small kinship groups, warfare with neighbouring groups was actively discouraged through exogamy, linking neighbours as kin. None the less, warfare took place often, because of injury, competition, ambition, brides and many other things, including the anathema of sorcery. Fighting was generally light and ritualistic, with a minimum of bloodshed. Melanesian warfare was usually restricted to small skirmishes or raids. To repay an earlier injury it often sufficed to score one wound. War was not over conquest or land, but most often involved the restitution of real or imagined grievances. Inter-tribal feuds and wars are still common today, at times broken by formal exchanges of commodities maintained by tradition, ensuring an uninterrupted flow of goods. Such traditional exchanges even help to restore peace and cement alliances. There were also formalized encounters on traditional warring fields, the number of allowed casualties a matter of military protocol.

A particularly unpleasant variety of warfare still plagues Melanesia today. In New Guinea's Sepik River region and among the Asmat of the west, as well as in several of the Solomon Islands, hunting for prestige trophy heads incites bitter conflict. Such heads are believed to imbue a community with spiritual force. Indeed, the Asmat hold them to be indispensible requisites for young men's initiation rituals.

On the Fijian islands of prehistory, competing chiefs used warfare and diplomacy in combination on a large scale to acquire intertribal allies and create ever larger alliances of widely dispersed descent groups. A clever chief who used war and diplomacy in this way could rise to paramount chief, just as in Polynesia.

In Micronesia, inherited rank determined one's place in society. However, the ranking system was highly complex, permitting no two individuals to be ranked on the same level. Some islands had paramount chiefs, others had power invested in councils of high-ranking elders. Apart from social ranking, most Micronesian communities acknowledged two or three social grades (not classes). One of two separate lineages identified each member of a community by descent: more typical was the mother's lineage, which also assigned property inheritance (patrilineal and mixed also existed, though these were not as typical). This social system produced intense rivalry and competition between neighbouring communities. Micronesia was thus fraught with warfare.

Inheritance also characterized leadership. On larger Micronesian islands such as Pohnpei, Yap and Palau more complex social hierarchies emerged over time, each ruler inheriting from his predecessor. On Pohnpei, for example, the Saudeleur Dynasty of high chiefs erected and ruled from their stone 'palace' complex of Nan Madol. Later, Pohnpei was divided into five districts. Each held two parallel lineages of ranked titles, inheriting authority through 'matri-clans'. The paramount chief, the *nanmariki*, whose person was sacred, led one of these lineages. Another was headed by the *naniken*, the paramount chief's spokesman and personal adviser, who also wielded all day-to-day authority over the five districts. This separation of ritual and applied power, which emerged in the last centuries of Pohnpei's prehistory, resembles similar developments occurring in Polynesia at the same time.

Landholding groups in Micronesia frequently inherited authority through matrilineal kinship. This was a component of that larger alliance, the so-called matri-clan, whereby only members of different matri-clans could wed. Some islanders, like the Yaps, were influenced into changing to male-only inheritance; however, the female lineage still determined descent-group membership there. Yapese marriages occurred outside the matri-clan, so the sons of a landholding male did not belong to their father's but to their mother's clan. When they inherited, their lands then passed from one matri-clan to another. This effected a largely harmonious sharing of landed resources among the small island societies.

Western Micronesian clans wished their daughters to marry into higher-ranking landholdings, so that for the following generation the land would be theirs. Eastern Micronesia was different, resembling Polynesian practices. In southern Kiribati, for example, the Gilbertese traced descent through their fathers and mothers, all rights to land being inherited from either lineage. But most Gilbertese preferred to occupy their fathers' lands.

Gilbertese came together regularly at the *maneaba* – the large, thatched, rectangular meeting house with open sides – where each clan elder occupied a traditional seat to discuss conflicts and arrive at a consensus. A 'democratic parliament', the *maneaba* also served as community centre for all ceremonies and feasts. The Gilbertese of northern Kiribati were different in this regard, in that their powerful chiefs and high-ranking landowners dominated everyone below them in rank; they competed for power, they did not share it. However, when southern Gilbertese invaded and conquered the northern Gilbertese, perhaps in the seventeenth century, they forced them to adopt their *maneaba* system of equality and consensus. Northern high chiefs resisted, maintaining traditional prerogatives, and conflicts over land and power structures continued for two centuries. Excellent at settling disputes at local level, the *maneaba* system was ineffectual at resolving larger conflicts.

Social organization in Polynesia was founded on kinship. Once settling populations had grown and divided, island communities remained grouped together in named descent groups or kin assemblages, usually called tribes or clans. Experts chanted long, revered genealogies, sometimes reaching back to mythical eras, not only to document descent group 'history', but also to legitimize blood lines of authority and important land claims upholding those in power. (Indeed, most Polynesian oral 'histories' consisted of such plastically reconstituted legitimizations.) Linguistic reconstructions suggest that Polynesian societies consisted of landholding groups which were based on descent from a shared ancestor. It is assumed that Archaic Polynesian society already held the foundations of the later rank-differentiated hierarchical societies the first Europeans encountered in the region. It was a society of mutual obligations, with kinship the cement. As a rule, political power derived from the father's, rank and status from the mother's line. However, heredity was subject to suitability, with warfare often the decisive factor. Hereditary chiefs wielded absolute power, risking revolt or assassination if too autocratic: the warrior-king had to maintain a fine balance between authority and pragmatism.

Prehistoric Polynesian polities varied greatly. Small atolls checked a warrior-chief's absolutism and encouraged consensus within the community. The Marquesas, Tahiti and New Zealand experienced numerous warring tribes unable ever to achieve unification under a single paramount chief. The large societies of Tonga and Hawai'i experienced absolute rulers who commanded thousands of warriors in a highly stratified and complex system held together by ritual, taboo and protocol. With severe punishment for infringement, these Polynesian 'police states' maintained social cohesion through fear and internal coercion, leaving only a small hereditary élite, as in Europe, exempt from most injunctions and restrictions.

Though patrilineal descent was favoured in Polynesia, matrilineal descent was also important as the basis of descent-group membership. Yet this depended on one's place in the social hierarchy. Rights to land were upheld by living on the land and working its resources. Wedge-like zones stretching down to the shore, allowing a range of sustainable resources, were alotted to each descent subgroup of a clan occupying high-island valleys. Descent groups on atolls, such as those in the Tuamotus, dominated an individual islet, island or local group of islands in the archipelago as a way of maintaining social cohesion.

Members of a clan might wish to regard status in their choice of subgroup affiliation, if a matrilineal link might bring them closer to those in power – that is, to those of highest rank. As in mediæval Europe, rank derived from proximity to a revered ancestor as traced by seniority of birth. The senior son of a senior son was principal in seniority, with the progeny of younger sons and daughters being of lower rank. Growing island populations meant further branching of this seniority ramage, the branches themselves ranked in relation to one another. The leader of the entire descent group – whether valley clan, islet tribe or entire island population – was the chief, the group's focus of ritual and political power. Though this is the general framework of prehistoric Polynesian society, many variations existed.

Rank itself had great variety. On small atolls like Tokelau and Pukapuka a handful of chiefs and priests might be indistinguishable from everyone else; there, village councils generally made decisions by consensus, and individual family heads oversaw food production. Even in heavily populated New Zealand there were only two 'classes', the *rangatira* or 'chiefly families' and the *tuatua* or 'commoners'; captured enemies became slaves, with no rights. Simple stratification – the division of a society into status groups – characterized most of ancient Polynesia.

In contrast, Hawai'i, Tonga and Tahiti developed highly elaborate social hierarchies with ranking, probably due to large populations which early turned to centralization to maintain social cohesion. In Hawai'i, for example, the *ali'i* or 'chiefs' kept aloof from lower-ranking tribal members; highest-ranking chiefs controlled as many as 30 000 subjects. To avoid contamination of royal lineages, marriages between full brothers and sisters, as in Ancient Egypt, were common among those of paramount rank. Chiefs selected aristocratic stewards to manage land use, oversee irrigation networks and organize tribute while they themselves delegated and performed ritual tasks. All productive labour fell to the commoners, whose rights to their land came by grace of higher-ranking 'betters', again as in Europe. Redistribution of surpluses and other accumulated tributes was made by high chiefs often, in feasting. Keeping surpluses circulating to satisfy each level of society, wise paramount chiefs similarly redistributed tribute among high chiefs, also ensuring their loyalty. It was for this reason that Hawaiians regarded their paramount *ali'i* as the source of all wealth.

Throughout Polynesia's prehistory, lower-ranking younger brothers were forever challenging the authority of elder brothers; heroes of low birth attained to status and wealth through extraordinary feats; and exceptional women of low birth became rich and powerful wives of paramount chiefs. It is the stuff that fills the oral literature of Polynesia. Still, the ancient society was uncompromisingly rigid. Classes became castes. Valley clans seldom had members marrying out, or outsiders marrying in. Atoll dwellers rarely moved to islets or islands outside their descent group's control. In contrast, chiefly marriages for political and social gain outside of the immediate descent group and even outside the archipelago – such as between the chiefly families of Tonga and Fiji – were surprisingly frequent in ancient times.

Almost as frequent was warfare, the customary method of settling major disputes in prehistoric Polynesia. In April 1774 Captain Cook witnessed the Tahitian war fleet setting off to attack the paramount chief of nearby Mo'orea: some 160 large war canoes, complemented by 170 smaller ones, holding an attack force of around 8000. When the twenty-third Tu'i Tonga was assassinated in the fifteenth century, as Tongan legend relates, his sons pursued the assassins and, in the process, conquered other islands of the archipelago; this would have involved thousands of warriors as well. And sometime in the twelfth century, it appears, a fleet of Marquesans invaded and conquered the Eastern Tuamotus and the Gambiers, including Mangareva.

Polynesian warfare was of three types: small raids and skirmishes as the restitution of real or imagined grievances (such as a cannibalistic kidnapping); inter-valley battles over land and dominion; and inter-insular or inter-archipelagic invasion and conquest. Only rarely did the latter occur. As *to'a* ('warrior') is a reconstructed Proto-Polynesian word, warfare has evidently been endemic in Polynesia since its settlement. Every island preserves oral traditions of fierce conflicts over land and status, both insular and inter-insular. As we have seen, some islands even developed the concept of the warrior-chief. Rapanui's 'Birdman', for example, was just such an individual, who had relegated the island's hereditary paramount chief or *'ariki mau* to a ritualistic anachronism. A similar thing had occurred on Mangaia in the Cook Islands, where political control ultimately lay with the clan leader who held military strength, while a second *ariki* performed all ritual functions; here, the *mangaia* or 'temporal power' would pass from one descent group to another only as the spoil of war.

New Zealand provides an informative example of social disintegration in prehistoric Polynesia. The fundamental social unit of the Māori was the *hapū*, the sub-tribe whose members occupied discrete villages. Many such sub-tribes were then united into a larger *iwi* ('nation'), and various *iwi* could unite, too, to form a confederation of nations under a higher-ranking chief. Just before European contact, a combination of factors had caused increased intertribal rivalry in New Zealand, which had led to fierce warfare. The climate had turned colder, forests and hunting grounds had been depleted, resources were scarcer, and neighbouring *hapū* began competing for the same valuable agricultural lands. Once fighting became endemic, the Māori raised *pā* or settlement stockades – like the forts of America's Wild West – of wooden palisades defended by deep ditches and steep banks: the North Island alone counts some 5500 erstwhile fortified *pā*. The enormous *pā* at One Tree Hill south of Auckland, for example, with massive terracing, ditches, earthworks, storage pits and many houses – much of it still visible 500 years after first construction – might have accommodated up to 5000 people. Such *pā* were frequently raided by neighbouring tribes.

Captured enemies were often ritualistically cooked and eaten, their flesh passed out to the entire community. Ritualistic cannibalism was practised in most of prehistoric Polynesia. It was infrequent, highly charged with *mana* or sociospiritual power... and almost invariably repugnant to its participants, frequently requiring them, before ingesting, to imbibe a mild narcotic such as kava to endure the ritual. Here cannibalism was a formal display of group superiority, governed by ancient Polynesia's strictest *tapu*. However, several variations of cannibalism existed throughout prehistoric Pacific Islands, and persists in New Guinea even today. Among the Hua people, for example, sons eat the corpses of their fathers and daughters eat those of their mothers as it is believed that this allows the deceased's *nu*, or vital essence, to be transferred to the next generation.

TRADITIONAL PRODUCTION AND ECONOMIES

For the Pacific Islanders of Remote Oceania, the sea was a primary source of food and other important resources. Deep-sea fishing with elaborate lures and hooks provided food surpluses. Sea urchins, sea cucumbers, sea slugs, seaweed and shellfish of every sort enriched the insular diet. All seabirds were easy game. Turtles, though often regarded as gods in Pacific myths, were cruelly slaughtered and even eaten alive whenever encountered, though frequently reserved for chiefs' palates. Most types of shells were artistically fashioned into bodily ornamentation. Melanesia and Micronesia were both familiar with 'shell money' – commonly comprising shell-disk strings – for exchange and status. On coral atolls, shells also served as adzes, diggers, scrapers and knives.

Pacific Islands' economies were founded from the beginning on such bountiful marine resources and on subsistence farming. Whenever possible Islanders also hunted. Pigs, dogs and fowl usually supplemented the diet. Shifting agriculture often saw island plots stripped of vegetation, planted for up to three years, then left fallow for up to 20. Prehistoric Rapanui even used lithic mulch – with an individual stone for each seedling – in order to trap and conserve precious moisture in poor, barren topsoil; the Easter Islanders also used small stone enclosures called *manavai* to plant in, retaining moisture and guarding against wind damage. New Zealand displays evidence of ancient stone-walled field systems employed for a similar purpose.

Root crops – such as yams, taro and sweet potato – were principally cultivated. The Chamorros of the Marianas in Micronesia cultivated some rice, the only Pacific Islanders to demonstrate a cereal-growing tradition, evidently introduced from the Philippines.

One of the Islanders' preferred crops was taro, grown everywhere in tropical Pacific Islands but also on subtropical New Zealand and Rapanui. Eaten for the root's starch, some taro species have comestible green tops as well. Taro demands much moisture, so it thrives in swamplands and especially fashioned taro terraces using controlled water management: this latter method is strikingly visible in such places as Tahuata's Vaitahu Valley in the Marquesas, but known from New Guinea to Hawai'i. In Micronesia, taro horticulture was much simpler and on a smaller scale: there the 'atoll taro' best accommodated sandy, rapidly draining soils, whereby atoll dwellers commonly dug taro pits to allow roots to tap below the water-table.

Yams were favoured in Melanesia and Western Polynesia. They thrive in dry, well-drained soils. In the Trobriand Islands of New Guinea, yams are both food and wealth: Islanders possessing yams possess status and power. Yam gardening is done by women; household garden yams are the women's possession, not the men's. But at harvest time, conical piles of yams rise in front of the yam house of each woman's husband and within several days are then carried inside, conveying status and power to the husband. There, the yams are 'banked' and slowly drawn on, in exchange for services and goods.

In this way, yams have traditionally been the 'currency' of the Trobriands. In Polynesia's Tonga, yams were the principal tribute to the Tu'i Tonga, the chain's paramount chief, at the annual first-fruits festival.

The sweet potato or *kūmara*, as noted, entered the Pacific from South America. Uncommonly tolerant of cool conditions, it soon became the most important food resource of those Polynesians living on subtropical islands. It first became the staple crop of the Rapanui of Easter Island, and then that of the Māori of New Zealand. Nearly 400 years ago, the Portuguese and Spaniards introduced the sweet potato to Island Southeast Asia, whereupon it became the main crop of New Guinea's Highlanders once it was discovered that the sweet potato thrived in the region's cool climate – perhaps the greatest contributing factor to the population explosion which soon followed there.

In the tropical lowlands of Pacific Islands, the coconut palm became the most significant tree crop. This is due to its unparalleled versatility: food, drink and oil from its inner kernel; a hand vessel from the dried shell; fibre from the nut's husk; roofing from the fronds; and sealing, wrapping and weaving from the leaves.

The breadfruit tree supplied a green, seedless fruit which became the staple on some islands of Micronesia and in the Society Islands (Tahiti) and the Marquesas. In the Marquesas, it was customary to ferment the breadfruit in huge, circular, covered pits and store it there for future needs, even for decades.

On many atolls the pandanus was preferred over breadfruit, as it could better accommodate an atoll's salty conditions. Small, salty atolls afforded more restricted regimes, turning sea resources into survival resources. New Guinea's swampy lowlands, in contrast, favoured the sago palm. A wide variety of trees and plants sustained communities on the large, high islands of Oceania.

Pigs, dogs and fowl were always reserved for special feasts. The small *Rattus exulans* or Polynesian rat was eaten in times

of famine. However, not all these intentionally – and uninten-
tionally – introduced animals survived island life. In New
Zealand, for example, pigs and fowl apparently disappeared
early, perhaps because of the islands' surfeit of flightless birds.
And in the Marquesas the Polynesian dog became extinct,
while in Rapanui both the dog and pig did not survive.

Food production tasks were generally performed in the
household or extended family environment, and only very
rarely as a community activity. On those islands with strong
social hierarchies, high-ranking individuals like chiefs, nobles
and priests were customarily provided with prepared food.

In Melanesia and Polynesia, barkcloth provided the material for waistcloths, wraps and loose garments with head-holes.
Women wore skirts of shredded leaf strips or inner-bark
strips, or simply of fibre string. Finely woven matting was
made of pandanus and other similar leaves. The Caroline
Islanders of Micronesia fashioned loomed wraps of banana
and hibiscus fibre. Because of differing resources, many Māori
of New Zealand tailored skirts and cloaks from the indigenous
flax. The wide range of personal garments in Pacific Islands
was of course dictated by availability. On some islands of few
resources, such as on Rapanui, men and children generally
went naked, while adolescent girls and women covered their
genitals with a simple barkcloth waist apron.

Most Polynesians, however, dressed in barkcloth, called
tapa. This was made of strips of inner bark, usually that of the
paper mulberry, beaten flat with a wooden mallet on wooden
anvils, creating very thin sheets which women then layered to
form a thick cloth. *Tapa* was not only the stuff of everyday
dress: it also wrapped divine images and figured in ritual
gift-giving. Patterns on *tapa* varied from archipelago to archipelago and from island to island, as did the techniques to
effect these, producing some of Polynesia's loveliest and most
readily identifiable artwork.

As one still finds in some regions of Southeast Asia, most
Western Pacific Islanders – including New Guineans and
Western Micronesians – chew 'betel-nut'. This is actually the

seed of the areca palm, which is chewed together with lime, and only the leaves of the betel plant. It produces a sense of wellbeing, releasing alkaloids, it is believed, which have a similar effect to nicotine. It also reduces hunger. Chewers stain their saliva red, and frequent chewers show stained teeth and lips as well.

In Fiji and Western Polynesia, kava drinking is the social equivalent of 'betel-nut' chewing, but with much greater social scope and ritual expression. Calling it *yaqona*, Fijians have included kava in holy ritual since time immemorial, though its social drinking was probably introduced to Fiji from Tonga in the eighteenth century. Kava drinking in Tonga and Samoa – and now also in Fiji – comprises a formal etiquette of seating, order and actions (such as clapping on returning the emptied cup) which reflects social rank and respect in the community. Intimate, informal kava drinking invariably retains some of the etiquette of formal occasions. Kava was drunk on Pohnpei and Kosrae in the Caroline Islands of Micronesia, where it was called *sakau*. Kava was generally known in Western Melanesia, too, imbibed in areas where 'betel-nut' chewing was not as favoured.

Micronesia had special pottery and looms used for weaving which attest to early contacts with the Philippines or Indonesia. Palau, in Micronesia's far west, was known for manufacturing in wood: its craftsmen created bowls and boxes inlaid with intricate shellwork. Pohnpei and Kosrae were noted for their fabrics woven from banana and hibiscus flowers. However, Micronesia was especially known for its canoes. Experts claim these were the best in the Pacific, showing the widest variety for many different purposes. It appears atoll-dwelling Micronesians depended far more on immediate sea transport than did the Polynesians, most of whom occupied much larger high islands. This dependency honed seafaring skills which the Micronesians have reverently preserved up to the present day, long after Polynesians lost all their voyaging traditions. Whereas Melanesians and Polynesians on the whole harvested the resources of either reef or ocean, Micronesians nearly always exploited both equally, possessing for this Pacific Islands' most extensive maritime toolkit.

There were few degenerative diseases in prehistoric Pacific Islands: few people lived long enough to develop them. Nevertheless, ancient Islanders generally lived better than the rest of their contemporaries on the planet. Apart from New Guinea, they had no dangerous animals, insects or infectious diseases, and their environments held no extremes. Indeed, these environments – apart from the atolls – provided nearly everything needed to live. The price for this bounty: intensive labour. Pacific Islanders spent a large amount of their time at open sea, fishing. They built and managed taro terraces in high valley steeps. They raised irrigation aqueducts, often of stone and up to several kilometres in length. They planted, tended, harvested, nursed, cooked, wove, carved and continually rebuilt damaged or destroyed structures. As a result, premature ageing saw most Islanders elderly by 40. Life was constant work under the perpetual scrutiny of absolute warrior-kings, powerful priests or one's own immediate relations. And the threat of a sudden raid from a neighbouring valley or island always loomed.

BELIEF SYSTEMS AND ART

Melanesian supernaturalism consisted of a vast number of predominately malevolent spirits to be feared and placated. 'Religion' was social pragmatics: one performed rituals to ward off harm and win success. There was no worship. Just as with everyone else in society, spirits were there to be manipulated. Often this manipulation could be accomplished through magic and sorcery, by men who practised this secretly for personal gain. There were few public sorcerers in Melanesia, few shamans or priests. Only a limited number of Melanesians lived by virtue of special knowledge and/or skills. Each member of a descent group usually fulfilled the same tasks and roles.

As everywhere in Pacific Islands, art in Melanesia expressed the indigenous belief system, immediately supporting, legitimizing and maintaining those in authority. Artistic creation often focused on ritual. Decoration both beautified and dignified cult houses. Spirit paintings depicting clan deities of the Abelam people of the Sepik region of Papua New Guinea, for example, covered the high house fronts connected with the *tambaran* cult. Colourful headdresses of bright feathers and elaborate body paintings and ornamentation, as well as vivid costumes, empowered all Melanesian ceremonial meetings and exchanges, even warfare. Ritual canoes were brightly painted and decorated. Carved slit-gong drums, brilliantly painted wooden masks and costumes highlighted song and dance festivals, some of these items to be destroyed at the festival's conclusion. They would then be recreated for the next festival, their designs the private property of individual carvers. Melanesia still enjoys hundreds of regional art styles, many characterized by their use of indigenous materials: feathers, woods, barkcloth, plaited rattan and other specialties.

Micronesia refrained from the magic and sorcery of Melanesia. Like Western Polynesia, Micronesia held an array of ghosts and spirits. Some of these, as deified ancestors, could be 'departmental gods' called upon to assist in specific crafts and activities. In their artwork the Micronesians were sober utilitarians, reflecting the sparse resources of their island world. None of Melanesia's flamboyant colours, headdresses and body paintings, none of Polynesia's complex carvings of stone and wood are to be found in Micronesia. Bodily ornamentation – necklaces, bracelets, gorgets, belts – often consisted of simple shells, sharks' teeth, flowers, coconut leaves and other perishables. However, Micronesian basket and mat weavers are still celebrated today for their geometric designs, achieving the felicitous marriage of controlled uniformity and resourceful creativity.

Prehistoric Polynesia similarly never held 'religion' to be the separate social domain it has been, for example, in the West since the Reformation. Religion in ancient Polynesia was yet another expression of the ruling class's hold on the commoners, promoted to maintain and legitimize those in authority. Eastern Polynesian deities, in particular, resembled the ancient Greek pantheon in being departmental entities who sometimes appeared to mix with mortals and exert specific influences on nature and human activity. However, unlike the Greek gods these were deified human ancestors who stood not remotely, but in 'traceable' lineages to the living. This is the essential characteristic of all Polynesian deities, who were more ancestral than divine. The word 'gods' is actually misleading for prehistoric Polynesia, as it suggests Western analogies which do not obtain. The oldest of these deified ancestors, reaching back into myth, was the most greatly venerated, shared by all Polynesians: Tangaloa (Tangaroa, Ta'aroa, Kanaloa and so on). Others were the assemblage of only Eastern Polynesians. Western Polynesians had fewer powerful deities but, for that, many more spirits, as in Tonga and Samoa; these spirits were identified not with specific roles, but with kinship groups and even individuals. Some islands valued both departmental gods and family spirits: in Rapanui, for example, the *akuaku* or ghosts came out at night to guard family land from intruders.

Similar to the European religions which predated Christianity, ancient Polynesian belief focused not on righteousness, morality and goodness, but on success, strength and influence. The deified ancestors were not ideals, but tools to be used to benefit oneself and one's descent group, and to guard from storm, drought and attack. Religion offered no scheme for personal 'salvation' or proper social behaviour – it offered protection, power and wealth. Those who sacrificed to the gods, received in return. Ancient Polynesian 'religion' was thus the same as society itself, as nothing separated the two realms: 'religion' was merely the supernatural extension of the descent group's lineage.

Two fundamental concepts defined Polynesian socio-religious life: *mana* and *tapu*. Only high-ranking individuals possessed *mana*, sociospiritual power, which ultimately derived from the ancestors but became evident through an individual's remarkable deeds and successful undertakings. The creation of a confederation, the conquest of an enemy, the bountiful harvest – all these things demonstrated a chief's *mana*, which then also empowered those who supported him. The concept of *mana* maintained the hierarchy of authority, as it also channelled community efforts towards stratified remuneration, combining the secular and divine (a Western dichotomy).

To maintain uncontaminated *mana* and ensure continued success, Polynesian society devised very early on a ritual restrictive complex or *tapu*, often called 'taboo' in English but much more profound than the word's conventional significance. Varying in its implications from island to island, the *tapu* affected use of land, crops, buildings, precincts and the sanctity of individuals, but also behaviour, speech, diet, sexual practices, beliefs and attitudes. *Tapu* was more than a mere rule. The *tapu* set aside and elevated from the common domain some sacred function, station, its holder and his or her person, tools, prerogatives and possessions. It could obtain for generations. The *tapu* complex embraced a way of thinking, a philosophy of life. It was a rigorously enforced social code against which the position and actions of each member of the island community were daily defined. There is no true equivalent to *tapu* in the English language.

Some Polynesian islands had more stringent *tapu* than others. On Rapanui, for example, only the royal steward could touch the paramount chief's food and possessions. Hawaiians had to prostrate themselves on the ground before their paramount chiefs. A powerful Māori chief's shadow could not fall on a food store lest it became inedible for everyone but the highest ranking. These are all expressions of the *tapu*. Breaking a *tapu* could bring swift death.

Many myths were shared throughout Polynesia, such as several surrounding the trickster-hero Maui who gave humankind fire and fished up important islands (such as New Zealand's North Island, according to some Māori tribes). Most similarity is found among Eastern Polynesians. Nearly all of these myths tell of a sky father and an earth mother – in New Zealand: Rangi Nui and Papa Tū a Nuku; in the Cook Islands: Avatea and Papa; and so on – who were the parents of lesser deities, each of these related to certain activities. As first-order anthropomorphic deities who were 'traceable' ancestors, their names usually differed from island to island because of respective phonological changes in the evolving languages.

The Māori of New Zealand, for example, knew Tangaroa as the patron of winds, ocean and fish. Tāne was the patron of forests and its bounty. Rongo was the patron of cultivations. Tū was the patron of war. And so forth. (Of these four, Tonga and Samoa were familiar only with 'Tangaloa' and 'Longo'.) In Hawai'i these were known as Kanaloa, Kāne, Lono and Kū. In addition, each island had local deities: Rapanui venerated Makemake, Mangarevans 'Atu Motua, later Tahitians 'Oro, son of Ta'aroa. Female deities were also prominent, emphasizing Polynesian women's meaningful role in society: Hina, the 'moon goddess' and patron of womenkind, was venerated by most Eastern Polynesians. Pele, on the other hand, was the patron of Hawai'i's volcanoes (Big Island only), though known elsewhere in other guises.

Offerings were given to the appropriate deity before any undertaking of significance: a war expedition (Tu'u), a fishing voyage (Tangaroa), a plot clearance for planting (Rongo), or a new settlement (Tāne). Dedicating a new house or canoe, priests would chant long series of procreations to commemorate the begets and begats of Polynesia, in this way ensuring a supernatural blessing.

Polynesian priests – the *tohunga* (Marquesas and Rapanui *tuhunga*, Hawaiian *kahuna*) – advised chiefs on matters of *tapu* and *mana*. These were not 'priests' in the Western clerical or ancient Egyptian caste sense: they were experts (navigators, tool-makers, carvers, architects, physicians and so forth), men of knowledge, soothsayers, shamans, who interpreted deceased ancestors' desires, officiated at rituals, chanted the holy liturgies and genealogies, and safeguarded the descent group's traditions. They ensured protocols were observed, lest ancestors take offence; in this, they were a pillar of the ruling class's authority. They inducted *mana* into temporal projects and steered chiefs towards traditional solutions. *Tohunga* were no community leaders or paragons of 'virtue': they were agents of earthly-cum-otherworldly power. Paramount chiefs themselves would fear the authority of certain high *tohunga*, who stood in immediate relationship with powerful ancestors.

Descent groups venerated objects which were from or of deceased leaders whose supernatural power was sought. These were often skulls, bones, small stones or carved figurines. Such objects were kept in special wooden god-houses, as those on Tonga and Samoa. When Eastern Polynesian rituals eventually came to be practised outdoors for the entire community to observe, sacred sites of open courtyards or walled enclosures developed, called *marae* or *tohua*. Sometimes they featured raised platforms (*ahu*) at one end, for special rituals and the display of ancestral figures or deities who were thought to dwell therein. The *marae* of New Zealand were like a simple village green, but in Tahiti and other Society Islands the *marae* comprised large stone 'temples' of several layered platforms. On Rapanui it was the *ahu* itself, the platform, which developed.

Polynesian artwork often involved carving deities'/ancestors' images in wood or, less frequently, stone. These were erected as highly stylized torsos or squat phallus-bearing likenesses on a ceremonial platform or along its wings. An internationally recognized icon of ancient Polynesia is the Rapanui *moai* or ancestral figure which evolved out of this tradition. Similar statuary adorned the *marae* of the Society and Austral Islands, the *tohua* of the Marquesas and the *heiau* of Hawai'i. Wood and stone carving features prominently in all Polynesian art, particularly in Eastern Polynesia. It can even relate clan history, as the Māori 'read' in the intricate architectural carvings of the *whare runanga* or meeting house of New Zealand.

Samoans were expert mat weavers. Hawaiians excelled in fashioning cloaks of thousands of red and yellow feathers worn by high chiefs. Rarotongans carved intricate genealogical staffs, similar to the abstract, phallus-like genealogical *ti'i* (*tiki* or figurine) of Rurutu in the Austral Islands. The South Island greenstone or nephrite jade of New Zealand was fashioned into powerful symbols of authority (Māori chiefs' ceremonial adzes and clubs) as well as elaborate personal ornaments like small *hei tiki* figures, *hei matau* hooks, *pekapeka* ornaments and other things. Possession of such portable objects increased one's *mana* in ancient Polynesian societies. Certain portable objects in time came to be identified as necessary paraphernalia of rank, such as the Māori chiefs' *mere pounamu* club or the Rapanui orators' *'ua* staff. Such pieces now adorn the world's museums, acknowledged to rank among the finest indigenous artwork on Earth.

All Polynesian art was an impersonal expression upholding the sacredness of the ruling authority. In this, it was 'political art'. No names attached to Polynesian productions, as the individual was insignificant: art was the expression not of one person, but of an entire community. Free creativity was discouraged and rigid conformity encouraged; even the accidental slip of a chisel or scraper could result in an artist's severe punishment. Religion, art, politics – all occupied the same space in the prehistoric Polynesian psyche, which was yet spared the West's compartmentalization and personalization.

A special domain of Pacific Islands art was occupied by the *tatau*. Islanders always practised *tatau*, that wonderfully versatile bodily decoration encountered in the eighteenth century by Europeans who called it 'tattoo'. It is assumed that the Lapita people were already wearing *tatau* over 3500 years ago, who then carried the practice with them wherever they settled in Oceania. Melanesian tattooing was known from Papua New Guinea to Fiji. Micronesia's Caroline and Marshall Islanders tattooed themselves. Pacific Islands' most elaborate *tatau*, however, occurred in Polynesia, where each island over time developed readily identifiable designs. A *tatau* in itself never signalled rank, but brought great status to those who bore especially elaborate, high-quality designs covering much of their body.

Polynesian *tatau* implements included fine bone chisels with teeth which were set like tiny adzes. These were dipped in pigment – such as the charcoal of burnt ti mixed with oil – then tapped underneath the skin with a light tapping mallet which left the pigment behind in puncture holes. Each puncture stung like a needle, and the *tatau* process involved thousands of punctures. Sessions lasted days, months, even years. Ritual surrounded each step; family members often attended to console the patient who, in the tropical climate, sometimes died of wound infection. Men's tattoos covered more body area than women's, which sometimes were traditionally located on one spot only – such as Māori women's *moko* on the chin and lips. Marquesan women, in contrast, had tattoos on their arms, hands, stomach and lower back; Marquesan men often had full-body tattoos, including the face. (Indeed, Marquesan women thought it shameful to have sex with a man who was 'naked' – that is, without a tattoo.) Rapanui experts of the *rongorongo* writing in the first half of the nineteenth century sometimes had their chests and even both cheeks tattooed with sacred inscriptions in Oceania's only indigenous script.

Some Melanesian communities eschewed the bone tattooing chisel and instead punctured the skin with stone flakes, shells or thorns. In Fiji, only women were tattooed, and only by other women. Indeed, the *qiā* – as the *tatau* was called in Fiji – was an important stage in a girl's initiation to adulthood. The tattoo was limited to the pubic region, occasionally stretching from midriff to upper thighs. It was then concealed by the girl's new *liku*, the 'womanhood attire'. To publicly signal her advancement to adulthood, the girl would then be tattooed around the mouth or hands.

Throughout Pacific Islands, the *tatau* represented 'worn wealth': that is, portable artwork which no one could steal. This fact held great significance in small island societies where

communal possession was the rule and personal possession
had few safeguards.

ON THE EVE OF EUROPEAN INCURSION

Austronesians entered Remote Oceania 3300 years ago much
in the same way as we are entering the Solar System today:
that is, with little awareness of the entry's impact on finely
balanced systems. Successful human adaptation to island habitats did not include successful island adaptation to humans.
The rats, dogs and pigs the settlers introduced, for example,
annihilated most ground-dwelling birds which until then had
known no predators. Rats were particularly destructive of
nature. The loss of Rapanui's tall palm forests, for example,
can largely be attributed to the unchecked proliferation of the
Polynesian rat there: these devoured the palms' tiny coconuts,
preventing regrowth; in time this denuded the island, with
calamitous consequences for nature and humans. Greatest
depredation, however, was caused by the settlers themselves;
one should toss out any notion of 'happy Pacific Islanders'
living in harmony with nature. The resources of the Mystery
Islands described above were probably abused to such a
degree that their inhabitants had to leave or perish. To their
credit most Micronesians on small atolls have maintained low
populations who have carefully nurtured their limited
resources. Most prehistoric Melanesian and Polynesian populations soared, however, exterminating entire biosystems as
a result.

Earth's most isolated group of islands, Hawai'i, is a perfect
example of this. In contrast to continents, islands are particularly vulnerable to human depredation. Hawai'i once had
the greatest collection of unique animals and plants of any
group of islands on Earth. Following Hawai'i's settlement by
seafaring colonists from the Marquesas around AD 700, the
collection was lost. Polynesians were among the planet's most
ravenous 'switching predators', eminent at exploiting newly

found fauna and flora for personal survival. At least 1000 species of animals have disappeared in Hawai'i as a direct result of Polynesian (and later European) intrusion: they were simply unequipped to withstand the newcomers, especially the feral pig. Among the first to go were 20 species of flightless birds, reminiscent of the disappearance of the *moa* very soon after the Māori had landed in New Zealand.

By the time these predators of the Pacific had degraded most island habitats, voyaging itself survived in only three areas: the Society Islands and Northwest Tuamotus (perhaps in decline from a much larger erstwhile sphere); Micronesia, where voyaging was everywhere essential for survival; and Western Polynesia (Fiji, Tonga, Samoa and neighbours), where voyaging thrived under Tongan dominion. In general, voyaging spheres were no longer the rule. A fundamental change had taken place in Remote Oceania. By the sixteenth century most inter-insular and inter-archipelagic networking had collapsed, perhaps because of the Little Ice Age. Former kinsfolk and affiliates were becoming myth and legend.

At Polynesia's northern extremity, Hawai'i had no more canoes which could cross the vast ocean. In the far southeast, Rapanui was left with only reed rafts and tiny canoes of patched-together planks barely suitable for offshore fishing. In the far southwest, New Zealand's double-hulled sailing canoes were a rare item. Throughout Polynesia many Islanders were hardly subsisting on islands unrecognizable as those they had settled centuries earlier; other Islanders had already emigrated or died. Yet in other places – the Society Islands, Samoa, Tonga – Polynesians were thriving in large, powerful and culturally rich societies. Again, the fate of an island in Remote Oceania was principally determined by its size and location. Centrally located islands and groups tended to fare better than marginalized isolates.

By the fifteenth century AD the 'nautical revolution' had peopled all the Pacific. Islanders were still drawing from their vast store of skills, traditions and resources stretching back many thousands of years. Carried to new environments, this store had mutated because of climatic variation, population growth, social evolution and geographical location. With the ancestral past allowing a sense of continuity to bind and empower, the Islanders continued to elaborate ever more innovative ways to procure food and other things, cope with collapsing networks, survive recent conquests and endure exploding or imploding populations. Given time, they would doubtless have mastered all these challenges, too.

But a new people arrived in Pacific Islands.

3

The European Trespass

FIRST OUTSIDERS

A little over 500 years ago Europeans were still aware of only three landmasses on Earth: Europe, Africa and Asia. But since the world had to be round, or so Greek and Roman geographers had already reasoned in antiquity, the northern lands had to be balanced by an equal portion of southern lands. In the second century AD the Alexandrian mathematician and geographer Ptolemy had even depicted on his maps such a *Terra Australis Incognita* ('unknown southern land') covering the globe some 10 degrees south of the equator. Arab, Indian and Chinese geographers were similarly convinced that the round Earth held vast lands in the south. But no one sought these southern lands, because of era, dogma, economy, climate and – most particularly – lack of appropriate maritime technology.

The first probes into the Pacific were tenuous. For many centuries Chinese and Mongol trading ships plied the South China Sea to the Sunda Islands, and beyond. Accompanying a Mongol expedition from Quanzhou to Sumatra in 1291, Marco Polo heard about a 'great spice-producing island to the south, called Java. And out there, too, were exactly 7448 more islands'. Between 1405 and 1431 China's Ming Dynasty sent out expeditions under the command of Zheng He through the Western Pacific and into the Indian Ocean. Though China at the time exerted considerable influence in Sumatra and else-where in Indonesia, no Pacific settlements resulted.

Europe's arrival in the Pacific emerged from the same dynamic which had brought Christopher Columbus to the Americas in 1492. The time was ripe for European expansion. Because of improved ship design and sail-rigging, vessels could now undertake longer voyages. Accumulated capital invited the financing of foreign enterprises. Above all, a new move-ment in Europe – the Renaissance – was inspiring far-sighted Europeans to reach out beyond traditional boundaries: to discover, claim and Christianize. Paramount in the European 'discovery' of Pacific Islands was the Americas' role as the stepping stone to the riches of the 'Indies'.

After Columbus's discovery of the New World, Pope Alexander VI divided, through the Treaty of Tordesillas (1494), all known and unknown discoveries into equal halves: every-thing east of an imaginary line in the mid-Atlantic fell to Por-tugal, everything west to Spain. Crucial to Spanish foreign policy was a communications route which would lead the Spaniards as quickly as possible to the 'Indies', whose location was still disputed; indeed, that there was a difference between the East Indies and the West Indies was then still unknown. In 1513, Vasco Nuñez de Balboa crossed the Isthmus of Panama to become the first European to view the Pacific Ocean. Balboa immediately 'took possession' of it on behalf of the Spanish monarchy, unaware of its immensity and geographical location. In fact, it was thought at the time that the Indian Ocean reached to the Americas.

The Portuguese were becoming active near the Pacific, too, having arrived in Indonesia. Already in 1512 they had occupied the Moluccan Sea (Maluku, Indonesia) and eventually took control of the 'Spice Islands' there. Europe's primary source of spice, the Spice Islands promised to become Europe's treasure-house.

Spain then wanted what Portugal was claiming. Intending to seize for itself these Spice Islands which, Spain was alleging, lay within its jurisdiction as defined by the Treaty of Tordesillas,

Spain inaugurated its exploration of the Pacific with three so-called 'Moluccas Voyages'. Searching for a Western Passage to the Spice Islands, the Portuguese Ferdinand Magellan (Fernão de Magalhães), sailing for Spanish Emperor Charles V, set off in 1519 in five ships. Whereupon he and his crews became the first Europeans to enter the *Mar Pacífico* (named for its deceptive calm), by way of the strait separating Tierra del Fuego and other islands from South America's southern tip. Unaware of the Pacific's vastness, Magellan's five crews all but starved, finally hailing land in 1521 at Guam in Micronesia, where chronicler Antonio de Pigafetta recorded the earliest ethnographic data about Pacific Islanders, in this case the Chamorros.

First contact between Europeans and Pacific Islanders on Guam demonstrated their fundamental incompatibility. Both met in curiosity, but when the Chamorros attempted to seize a skiff – a matter of life or death to the Spaniards – Magellan's 40-strong landing force attacked, killing many Chamorros. The Spaniards then proceeded to burn between 40 and 50 houses and destroy several canoes. Whereupon Magellan sailed on to the Philippines, where he was murdered. Only one Spanish vessel managed, via the Spice Islands, the return voyage to Spain, arriving in 1522 and thus completing history's first circumnavigation.

The four ships of the second Spanish 'Moluccas Voyage' (1525–27), commanded by García Jofre de Loaysa, were soon scattered after clearing the Strait of Magellan. The *San Lesmes* was lost, but three vessels survived, two of them successfully crossing the Pacific to Mindanao, second largest island of the Philippines, and to the Spice Islands. (The *San Lesmes* ran aground at Amanu Atoll in the Tuamotus in Eastern Polynesia; it has been argued that its crew survived to intermix with locals, significantly influencing Polynesia's languages, cultures and genetic pool already at this early date.) Spain's third 'Moluccas Voyage' (1527–29) was planned from Mexico, but only one ship, led by Alvaro de Saavedra, ever reached the Spice Islands. Saavedra had sailed via the Philippines, travelling north of the equator and raising some of the Marshall Islands. When Saavedra twice tried, unsuccessfully, to return from the Spice Islands, he discovered the Schouten Islands, ranged New Guinea's coastline, and discovered the Admiralties and several islands in the Carolines.

The Portuguese Jorge de Meneses had been the first European 'discoverer' of New Guinea (1526), whereupon the Portuguese laid claim to this entire region of the Pacific, threatening the Spaniards with dire consequences if they did not withdraw. As a direct result of this international affair, the Treaty of Zaragoza, signed in 1529, extended the principle of the Treaty of Tordesillas to the entire Pacific: the Eastern Pacific now 'belonged' to Spain, the Western to Portugal. Thus Portugal finally won European 'jurisdiction' over the Spice Islands.

But the Pacific was still unknown territory. As latitudes and longitudes were unclear, even the Pacific's size was unknown. Magellan's trip had largely been meant to prove that the Spice Islands lay within Spain's jurisdiction. Later voyages proved this to be wrong. Still, Hernando de Grijalva led two vessels into the Pacific in 1536–37 to explore for Spain – one ship returning to Mexico after sighting the Galápagos – and made the first European crossing of the Pacific north of the equator, discovering en route the Line Islands and Kiribati before being wrecked off New Guinea.

Though Spain played a major role in opening up Pacific Islands, its interests there were minimal. Subsequent treaties granted the Philippines to Spain – finally settled in 1565 – though these islands clearly lay in Portugal's hemisphere. Beginning in the same year, Spain's galleons annually sailed the 'Acapulco Run' between Acapulco, Mexico and the Philippines (Manila, on the South China Sea, was founded in 1571). This rendered the Pacific the 'Spanish Highway' for many centuries, leading to greatly increased European recognition of this part of the globe.

Whereupon a new series of Spanish explorations south of the equator began. Once the Viceroyalty of Peru in Lima saw

Spain secure in the North Pacific, it explored the possibility of opening up the South Pacific to Spanish colonization and the Roman Catholic faith. In 1567–69, departing from Lima's port of Callao, Alvaro de Mendaña de Neira led two ships south of the equator across the Pacific in search of the fabled Terra Australis, sighting one of the Tuvalu Islands in Polynesia before discovering the Solomon Islands in Melanesia, which the fleet then explored for half a year. Mendaña returned to the Pacific nearly 30 years later, in 1595–96, in search of his Solomons again, but this time failed, discovering instead the Marquesas in Eastern Polynesia (providing the earliest ethnographic data about Polynesians), Pukapuka in the northern Cooks, and the Santa Cruz Islands in Melanesia. Mendaña was killed, and his crew sailed on to the Philippines then back to Peru. The third and last Peruvian expedition (1605–07) was led by Mendaña's former pilot Pedro Fernandes de Queirós who, in his attempt to find the Terra Australis, sighted new islands in the Tuamotus, Lines and Cooks, and 'took possession' of Espiritu Santo in the New Hebrides (Vanuatu), which he believed was the Terra Australis. After his violent expulsion from Espiritu Santo in 1606, Queirós was summoned to Alcapulco, but Luis Váez de Torres assumed command of the expedition and sailed southwest to discover the strait separating New Guinea from Australia – now called Torres Strait – proving New Guinea is an island.

Queirós urged the organization of a new expedition, but the Viceroyalty of Peru was not inclined. Disheartened by Queirós's failure in the New Hebrides, the Spanish Crown thereafter limited its colonizing activities to the Americas. Spain's historical opportunity in the South Pacific was lost.

Throughout this time, the galleons of the 'Acapulco Run' – the last sailed in 1815 – still regularly called at Guam for water and provisions. The several archipelagos of Micronesia were encountered very early, such as Magellan's landing at Guam, which by 1600 had become a staging post. Jesuit missionaries arrived there in 1668 to establish a mission once Spanish forces had seized control. The Jesuits estimated the Chamorro population at 70 000, approximately half of them resident on Guam. In the 1680s Spanish troops and Jesuit priests removed the Chamorros by force from scattered villages on Guam, Rota and Saipan to settlements within earshot of the mission bells: within 30 years, 70 per cent of all Chamorros were dead, most having succumbed to Old World diseases which Austronesians had never encountered. (One of the Mariana Islands which escaped death was Chuuk: its people violently repelled all outsiders.) The Carolines then became the focus of Jesuit activity, beginning in 1710 in western Palau then extending throughout the archipelago. 'European' Micronesia began under Spanish hegemony. It remained the last Pacific territory in Spanish possession, until the end of the nineteenth century.

Both the Dutch and British were also active in the sixteenth-century Pacific, exploring as they preyed on Spanish shipping and settlements there. In 1577–80 Francis Drake, for example, became the first Briton to circumnavigate the globe during his infamous quest for Spanish booty, which included the Pacific. These 'buccaneers' waged the first foreign warfare in Pacific Islands; until then, each atrocity had always involved Islanders, too, in some way. The Dutch took the lead in Pacific exploration in the seventeenth, the British in the eighteenth century.

In 1602 the Dutch East India Company was established, as of the 1670s permanently located at Batavia (Jakarta, on the island of Java). Having wrested jurisdiction from the Portuguese, the Dutch used the Company to exert sole right to grant licences in the region. This was done in order to protect the Company's private trading interests there, an early form of corporate monopoly. Within the Company's monopoly – then virtually the entire Pacific except the Spanish Philippines – no Dutchman was allowed to trade privately or deal with Pacific Islanders. Only the Company held these rights. Four years after the Company's founding, Willem Jansz left Batavia to explore New Guinea's southern coastline as far as the Torres Strait, which he did not enter. In 1615, the Dutch navigators Isaac Le Maire and Willem Schouten voyaged westwards from Holland to accomplish the first rounding of Cape Horn. They then crossed the Pacific through the Tuamotus to Tonga, Futuna, Alofi, New Ireland and New Guinea to Batavia, where they arrived in 1616. Yet the Company did not welcome their countrymen, despite their many historic discoveries: they were not Company men.

In 1642 Batavia's Dutch Governor-General Van Diemen, the Company's resident administrator, personally encharged his employee Abel Tasman to explore the Pacific and find the Terra Australis for the Company. Tasman sailed south of Australia to discover Van Diemen's Land (later renamed Tasmania), then east to discover New Zealand which he named after a Dutch province. Whereupon Tasman sailed on to Tonga, Fiji and New Guinea before returning to Batavia. Once back, Tasman was reprimanded for having failed to return with 'riches or things of profit'. The Company kept the discovery of New Zealand a house secret: Tasman had so extolled the land's commercial potential that the Company suspected it might be the Terra Australis. Tasman undertook a second expedition for the Company in 1644, sailing from Batavia to western New Guinea and to northwestern Australia. After this, the Company failed to venture out again into Pacific Islands, and the real potential of New Zealand was never realized. (European visits to Pacific Islands were so infrequent that New Zealand was not sighted again until James Cook arrived in 1769.)

Three generations after Tasman, in 1722, the Company actually confiscated Jacob Roggeveen's two surviving ships – after the Dutchman had sailed from Holland with three vessels to discover Rapanui, Bora Bora and Maupiti in the Societies, and Samoa – because Roggeveen's voyage had not been a Company venture.

Holland in general showed no further interest in Pacific Islands after Roggeveen's historic voyage. Batavia had become Europe's greatest port in the East Indies (whereas Manila was long Europe's principal port nearest the Western Pacific). Its pre-eminence continued well into the nineteenth century, long after the first Australian and Pacific Islands ports were founded. The Company and the Crown were both content to collect the massive revenues of the Dutch East Indies, where the Dutch presence remained strong until the founding of the modern Indonesian state in 1950.

BRITAIN AND FRANCE

Britain came late to regular Pacific exploration. In 1687–88 William Dampier had voyaged to the Marianas, Philippines, Spice Islands, then on to the northwest coast of Australia; in 1700 he had discovered New Britain, off the coast of New Guinea. But only towards the middle of the eighteenth century did Britain actively turn its attentions to the Pacific, initially with the primary aim of wresting control from Spain. Towards this end, George Anson was sent in 1742–43 to conquer the Spaniards in Manila. Britain later controlled the Philippines from Manila (1762–64), but then abandoned the difficult islands. Within a generation, France was similarly increasing its trade with Spain's South American settlements along the Pacific coastline. By then the competition had become intolerable for Britain.

The lords at Whitehall concluded that anyone who discovered and colonized the Terra Australis would win strategic advantages over Spain and France in the still largely unexplored region. Perhaps, over time, profit might be had as well. The naval competition between Britain and France during the Seven Years' War (1756–63), which delayed further exploration of the Pacific, nevertheless brought great advances in maritime technology and navigation. After 1763, both Britain and France were firmly committed to expanding their international influence while exploiting these new innovations before others.

For these reasons, in 1765 Britain dispatched John Byron to secure the Falkland Islands east of South America's southern tip. At the same time he was instructed to search for the southern continent as well as the Northwest Passage which was rumoured to link the Northern Atlantic to the Pacific; in the latter two ventures Byron failed. In 1767 the Admiralty sent Philip Carteret and Samuel Wallis in two vessels to discover the Terra Australis once and for all. The two ships became separated near the Strait of Magellan. Carteret sailed on to Pitcairn, the Tuamotus, Cooks, Santa Cruz Islands, then continued on to New Britain. Wallis raised the Tuamotus, then became the first European to sight Tahiti, in June 1767. Just before his departure Wallis 'annexed' Tahiti in the name of King George III, a ritual accompanied by the hoisting of the Union Jack and the firing of a volley of musketry. Wallis then voyaged on to Niuatoputapu in the Tongan archipelago, followed by Wallis Island, the Marshalls, Marianas, then Batavia on Java.

By this time France had already joined in the race. Only months after Wallis had left Tahiti, Louis Antoine de Bougainville arrived there, having safely navigated his way through the Tuamotus. Bougainville had received from the French Crown virtually the same instructions as Byron had received from the British: secure the Falklands and explore the Pacific for the Terra Australis. Now Bougainville 'annexed' Tahiti, too, but in the name of Louis XV. (Neither Britain nor France could defend their respective claim, the Pacific being too far away from Europe.) Whereupon Bougainville sailed to Samoa, Pentecost in the New Hebrides, the Great Barrier Reef of Australia, then north to New Guinea, discovering several further islands there, including Bougainville.

Britain received the news of Bougainville's successful voyage with concern, appreciating that the search for the Terra Australis was now becoming a strategic contest between Britain and France, with possibly the entire Pacific as the reward to its discoverer. In addition, the English Royal Society and the Royal Navy had long deliberated enhancing navigators' ability to fix longitude more precisely in order to give Britain a decisive advantage over its maritime rivals. Yet only astronomical observations could achieve this. The transit of Venus across the Sun, as seen from Earth, could supply valuable information that would allow the calculation of the respective distances between the Earth, Sun and Venus, helping in fixing longitude. Such a transit would occur in 1769 and not come again until 1874. For viewing this transit properly, astronomers would require triangulated observations from points as far from each other as possible. Wallis's Tahiti sounded like the perfect candidate for one of these points... if the voyage could be combined with an exhaustive search for the southern continent.

To lead the expedition, the Royal Navy selected its finest cartographer, the 40-year-old Yorkshireman James Cook. Selecting his own vessel, the North Sea collier *Endeavour*, Cook directed her refitting personally. Almost uniquely for an eighteenth-century navigator, he also oversaw all provisions for his crew, intent on avoiding at sea the familiar ravages of scurvy. Equally remarkable, Cook also permitted the natural scientist Joseph Banks, with assistants, to join the expedition in order to record and preserve what they might find in the Pacific. Cook's secret dispatch included instructions that, should he indeed raise the Terra Australis, he was to 'take possession of convenient situations in the country in the name of the King of Great Britain'.

James Cook arrived at Tahiti on 13 April 1769. With nearly two months before Venus's transit on 3 June, he expeditiously mapped the area and gathered many specimens of animals and plants. After the transit, he set off again – not west as others before him, but south and southwest. On 7 October Cook sighted New Zealand, where he then spent six months mapping all 3860 kilometres of its coastline. On the last day of March 1770, Cook sailed west and within two and a half weeks reached Australia's southeastern coast which he then surveyed. Perhaps to compensate for his failure to discover the southern continent for the Admiralty as instructed, Cook declared that this 'New Holland' (Australia), known since 1606, was actually the only great land mass in this part of the globe. Its southeastern region, which he named New South Wales, could well support a British colony, Cook propounded, writing in his log: 'The coast of this country... abounds with a great number of bays and harbours.' The appraisal encouraged Britain's greater role in the region. It was to have an historic reverberation.

Whereupon Cook ranged north, surveying the 5000 kilometres of Australia's eastern seaboard. (He landed shortly at Botany Bay, today the southern half of greater Sydney.) Sailing through the Torres Strait, he came to Batavia, where six of his crew died of 'nostalgia' (malaria). One of them was Tupaia, the priest and navigator Cook had taken on board in Tahiti whom Cook was bringing back to Britain as the finest example of his 'race'. Tupaia had learnt sufficient English to pass along to Cook and Banks such important cultural information as elements of Tahitian navigation and geography. He also served as 'translator' in New Zealand: the Māori language is as close to Tahitian as German is to English. Tupaia's death in Batavia was thus a great blow to the entire expedition. However, during the 11 weeks from there to Cape Town in South Africa, 23 more crewmen died of 'the gripes' (dysentery). And several more perished on the last leg home to Britain. Land's End was finally sighted on 10 July 1771, nearly three years after departure.

James Cook was celebrated as a national hero. But he had little time to bask in the glory: France was again venturing into the Pacific just as the *Endeavour* was returning. A second, similar British expedition was immediately organized for Cook, who left in July 1772 in the *Resolution*. Cook used Tasman's route this time, sailing by way of Cape Town from west to east. He penetrated into the southernmost waters, disproving the existence of rumoured lands in the southern Indian Ocean. Then he voyaged to New Zealand for more detailed knowledge of the Māori and their land. After this he sailed again down into southern latitudes to disprove the existence of a southern continent south of the Society Islands. Whereupon Cook visited the Societies again, the Cook Islands (named this later by the German-born Russian navigator Adam Johann von Krusenstern) and Tonga, then back to New Zealand. During the southern summer of 1773–74 Cook searched the southernmost latitudes for the Terra Australis: by summer's end he was convinced it did not exist. Ranging the Eastern Pacific Cook became the third European visitor to Rapanui, reached the Marquesas (first/last visited in 1596), then sailed again to Tahiti, Tonga, past Fiji, then confirmed and charted in the Western Pacific those 'lost' islands of the Spaniards Mendaña, Queirós and Torres, naming them the New Hebrides. South of the New Hebrides, Cook sighted a large island which he named New Caledonia. Back in New Zealand, he replenished his stores, then voyaged into southern latitudes yet again to disprove earlier 'sightings' there before calling at Cape Town, then heading home. On his return to Britain in 1775, Cook was hailed a greater national hero than before.

The Royal Navy was already planning a third voyage. However, this time James Cook was not to search for the Terra Australis, whose existence he had disproven, but rather for the fabled Northwest Passage which Elizabeth I's buccaneers had sought two centuries earlier. In 1776 Cook again sailed Tasman's route through the Indian Ocean, stopping once more at New Zealand, Tonga, the Cooks and Tahiti before heading into the North Pacific. On 18 January 1778 he sighted Hawai'i, possibly aware of an alleged Spanish visit there in 1555. Cook sailed north to map the North American coastline as far as Bering Strait and into the Bering Sea, but then returned to warmer latitudes to winter in Hawai'i, which he named the Sandwich Islands. On 14 February 1779 he was killed in a minor skirmish on the Big Island.

No explorer in human history has contributed more to geographical knowledge than James Cook in his ten years (1769–79) of Pacific exploration. Cook penned in the Pacific's boundaries; verified and mapped most major island groups; bequeathed to science an unparalleled wealth of information, specimens and artefacts; and defined the discipline of healthy long-voyage sailing. Cook's own journals are also the point of departure for any investigation into the early cultures of four main Polynesian groups: Societies, New Zealand, Tonga and Hawai'i; the New Hebrides (Vanuatu); New Caledonia; and eastern Australia.

After Cook, exploring continued despite the fact that the search for the Terra Australis had now been abandoned by all nations. It is a worthy testimonial to James Cook that in their Pacific peregrinations, nearly all explorers closely followed his characteristic methods and procedures.

In 1785, Louis XVI of France personally commissioned and financed a major expedition to the Pacific to be led by nobleman Jean-François Galaup de La Pérouse in two ships, the *Boussole* ('compass') and the *Astrolabe*. The race was now on between Britain and France to discover the Northwest Passage. However, prominent among La Pérouse's further instructions was the collection of scientific and ethnographic information about the Pacific and the gathering of specimens of animals and plants. La Pérouse's two vessels sailed first to Hawai'i, then ranged north to seek the Passage. Unsuccessful in their chief mission, they then voyaged southwest to visit Japan's Kuril Islands, then further south to Japan's Ryukyu Islands. Whereupon they sailed into the South Pacific to visit Samoa, Tonga and then Botany Bay (Sydney) in Australia where, in March 1788, they encountered the First Fleet – Australia's first convict-colonists – who had just arrived. The French soon sailed on to New Caledonia and finally to Vanikoro in the Solomons...where both vessels wrecked on the reef in a terrible storm with the loss of the entire expedition.

France was frantic with worry when La Pérouse failed to return. In 1791 Bruni d'Entrecasteaux was sent to search for the expedition, accompanied by the natural scientist Labillardière who was a good friend of Joseph Banks. D'Entrecasteaux searched throughout the South Pacific, but failed to find any trace of La Pérouse and his men. (Irish sea captain Peter Dillon eventually stumbled upon the expedition's remains in 1826; Jules Sebastien César Dumont d'Urville recovered some cannons and anchors in 1828.) On D'Entrecasteaux's voyage back to France, Britain's Royal Navy, at war with France, seized Labillardière's botanical collection – some 10000 specimens in all – but Joseph Banks mediated with the Admiralty to ensure the collection's return to France.

Alarmed by Britain's and France's increasing attentions in 'its' sphere of influence, Spain was similarly prompted to explore the Pacific for the sciences. While James Cook was in the Pacific on his first voyage, an expedition led by Felipe González de Haedo in 1770 relocated Rapanui, of which it 'took possession' for the Spanish Crown (again without consequence). The Viceroyalty of Peru then sent out three further fleets. Domingo de Boenechea established a Spanish presence in Tahiti and other Society Islands in 1772–73, during Cook's second voyage. On a subsequent expedition, Boenechea and José Andía set up a Franciscan mission on Tahiti. The third voyage, led by Cayetano de Lángara in 1775–76, then dissolved the Viceroy's Tahitian mission, whose maintenance and defence were too difficult. A subsequent expedition, led for the Spanish Crown by the Italian Alessandro Malaspina in 1789–94, focused on the scientific exploration of many parts of the Pacific. This expedition also carried out a detailed exploration of Tonga – which Malaspina similarly 'annexed' for the Spanish Crown (without consequence) – as well as seeking out New Zealand.

Exploration of Micronesia remained meagre at this time. At the start of the eighteenth century the Jesuits had established missions on Palau and Ulithi in the Western Carolines; most missionaries were soon murdered, however, and so the Jesuits withdrew. The British East India Company was regularly passing through the Western Carolines by the second half of the century. In 1788, two Company captains named Gilbert and Marshall, who had transported the first British convict-colonists to New South Wales then had sailed up to China to collect a return cargo for Britain, happened upon Micronesia's two major eastern groups of islands, which the two British captains now named after themselves: the Gilbert Islands and the Marshall Islands. One of the Company ships was later wrecked in Palau, whereupon its crew, aided by the Palauans, constructed a small vessel and returned to civilization; as a result, the Company conducted a survey of Palau in 1791.

Again in search of the Northwest Passage, in 1791–95 British navigator George Vancouver sailed to New Zealand, Rēkohu

(Chatham Islands), Tahiti, Hawaiʻi, then north to the North American coastline from where, failing in his chief objective, he then returned to Hawaiʻi. Vancouver's was Europe's last great Pacific expedition of the eighteenth century.

James Cook had all but covered the Pacific's canvas, leaving only a small number of blank spaces. In the nineteenth century Britain withdrew from active exploration in the region, concentrating instead on specific tasks such as surveying islands or observing astronomical events. At this time French and Imperial Russian explorers assumed a greater role there. The Americans mounted their first scientific exploration of the Pacific with the Wilkes Expedition of 1838–42. However, most nineteenth-century geographical discoveries in the Pacific were made by sealers, traders and whalers who ultimately transformed the European trespass into an invasion.

SEALERS, TRADERS AND WHALERS

James Cook's third expedition had discovered fur seals along America's northwest coast. Once news of this spread in the 1780s, sealers began voyaging from Canton (Guangzhou), the first Chinese port open to European trade, to hunt the seals, then replenish and winter over in Hawaiʻi. Whereupon they would return to Canton to sell their sealskins for small fortunes.

At Hawaiʻi the sealers sought water, provisions, alcohol and women. At first the Hawaiians were happy to provide whatever and whomever they could in exchange for nails, hoop-iron (for adzes) and cloth. However, by the 1790s they were also demanding gunpowder, muskets, small cannon and ships' boats. These the Hawaiian chiefs then used to intimidate rivals and wrest greater power on their own and neighbouring islands, making Hawaiian society ever more unsafe for Hawaiians and visitors alike.

Seal-fur traders also discovered sandalwood in Hawaiʻi, which the sealers from Canton knew the Chinese highly valued for their joss sticks of incense. A brisk sandalwood trade ensued, but Hawaiian sandalwood was of poor quality and so the trade ceased early. For the next 30 years, Hawai'i meant provisions and women and that was sufficient for most North Pacific hunters. Small trading settlements appeared on the islands of Maui, Hawai'i and O'ahu.

The establishment of the first British colony in Australia at Port Jackson (Sydney) in 1788 meant increased shipping and more intruders to the region. It took only a decade before the British of New South Wales were turning to Pacific Islands for sustenance. Tahiti quickly became a focus for such visits because of Wallis, Bougainville, Cook, Bligh and the Spaniards, and because it was the largest island in Eastern Polynesia, at the crossroads of trans-Pacific voyaging. As Hawai'i was becoming the hub of North Pacific commerce, Tahiti was becoming this for the South Pacific. Already by 1792 the increasing number of visitors there had led the Tahitians, as Vancouver noted, to depend so much on the foreigners' iron, implements and cloth that the Tahitians' own equivalents were hardly to be seen any longer.

In 1800 whalers began calling at Tahiti. In 1801, Britain's Royal Navy at Port Jackson sent the *Porpoise* to Tahiti for a shipment of salt pork, as New South Wales's small colony had already outgrown the capacity of local production. The trade continued on a regular basis with Tahiti for some 30 years: between 1801 and 1826 Tahiti supplied New South Wales with more than 1 500 000 kilos of salt pork. Founded as a mission station by the Rev. William Crook in 1818, Pape'ete became the whalers' chief port for supply and refit in the area, rapidly growing in the first half of the nineteenth century from a small Polynesian village into a bustling European town. The salt pork and supply/refitting trades soon became the Society Islands' main source of foreign goods.

One of the 'Mystery Islands' was also chosen to sustain Port Jackson. Situated 1500 kilometres east of Australia, Norfolk Island, once home to an Eastern Polynesian society which had abandoned it hundreds of years earlier, was settled by Britain in the first few years of the 1800s to supply timber and flax to New South Wales. But then Norfolk was abandoned for the second time, in 1814. Eleven years later, New South Wales established a penal colony there, Pacific Islands' first, as an extension of the penal colonies of New South Wales (1788) and Van Diemen's Land (Tasmania, 1803). Norfolk soon became one of the cruelest places on Earth.

In most instances, however, it was the Pacific Islanders themselves who supplied the earliest European ships in the region, providing fresh water, meat, fruit and vegetables in exchange for nails, knives, axes, trinkets and cloth. Pacific Islanders were always expert traders. They were most anxious to acquire metals: European knives, axes, and iron and steel nails were infinitely more valuable than their native equivalents in stone and shell. The first store of metal in Islander hands might possibly have entered the Eastern Polynesian network in 1525 with the wreck of the *San Lesmes*, but certainly in 1722 with the wreck of Roggeveen's *Afrikaansche Galei* on Takapoto in the Tuamotus.

James Cook had traded a hatchet for a pig in Tahiti. Because Cook and others had introduced the larger European pig – as well as goats, cattle and sheep – on to some of the islands, these animals became endemic to most, but not all, of the visited isles. (The Rapanui, for example, ate up their four-footed introductions before these could breed). In addition, European visitors introduced vines, citrus trees, pineapples, papaya, root vegetables and cereals (hitherto known only in Western Micronesia) which then provided those European supplies the Islanders could trade more readily. Of special importance was the white potato, which kept well in the sealing and whaling ships and was therefore in high demand in the stations.

Tahitians, too, at first wanted only metal objects. As trade increased, they especially valued imported red feathers from Samoa and Tonga. But by the 1790s, alcohol also became a desired commodity. It was at this time that Tahitians were receiving firearms, hardware and other manufactured goods which they either amassed as a show of *mana* or traded for traditional goods with neighbouring islands. Tahitians soon became the most materially advantaged of all Pacific Islanders, and the most Europeanized.

In 1800 ships began to visit Tonga as well, but there the intermittent outbreaks of tribal warfare thwarted the establishment of a regular trade. Tonga thus failed to attract the degree of attention Hawai'i and Tahiti were receiving from Europeans, and ultimately maintained its sovereignty as a result.

From 1804 until around 1816, ships called at Fiji for sandalwood, making the northern island of Vanua Levu – especially its Bua district – the archipelago's centre of power and wealth for its European muskets and other trade items. Sea-captains, too, grew wealthy fast in Fiji: 50 American dollars' worth of muskets or trinkets would acquire sandalwood that would sell for $20 000 in Canton. However, Fiji's sandalwood stocks were depleted by 1814 and the trade collapsed completely in 1816.

The sandalwood traders then concentrated their efforts in Eastern Polynesia's distant Marquesas Islands which, since the 1790s, had provisioned small numbers of whaling ships. The United States Navy had its first foothold in Pacific Islands in the Marquesas: it had established a base at Taioha'e on Nuku Hiva during the War of 1812–14 to harass British shipping in the region. (The American commander actually convinced Nuku Hiva's paramount chief to 'cede' the entire island to the US, but the American government subsequently ignored the gift.) It was likely a captured British vessel which had escaped the Americans, reached Port Jackson and told of Marquesan sandalwood, that inspired the traders of New South Wales to import their first cargo of Marquesan sandalwood in 1815. But the forests there were depleted by 1820, whereupon the Marquesans returned to provisioning whaling ships.

In Hawai'i, Kamehameha I's victory over rival chiefs in 1796 had brought the Hawaiian Islands an era of peace almost unparalleled among Pacific Islanders. It arrived just as the fur-seal trade and trading posts were starting to flourish there. The Hawaiians themselves imposed on visiting Europeans and

Americans strict regulations regarding prices and items – particularly firearms – achieving through this a social stability which soon made Hawai'i the most socially advanced of all Pacific Islands societies. Less than 30 years after Cook's murder there, Hawai'i had fledgling towns of tradesmen, artisans, shipfitters and taverners hardly distinguishable from comparable settlements in the Americas or Australia. Though hampered by the War of 1812–14, Hawai'i's renewed sandalwood trade soon became its economic mainstay, as Fiji's stocks dwindled. Kamehameha wisely made the trade a government monopoly, then used his profits to purchase tools, implements and ships to generate his own trade, avoiding the mistake of other Pacific Islanders who acquired only muskets for feuding. But Kamehameha died in 1819. And soon the sandalwood forests of the Hawaiian Islands, too, were disappearing.

When the sandalwood trade was already in decline, the Hawaiian governor of O'ahu, Boki, who had settled Hawai'i's debts to foreign sandalwood traders, set off in two ships to the New Hebrides in 1829 to profit from the sandalwood trade there directly. But Boki's ship sank, and its sister ships' crew were decimated by disease and repeated New Hebridean attacks. Also in 1829, the son of a missionary in Tahiti, Captain Henry, led more than a hundred Tongans to Erromango (New Hebrides) to cut sandalwood while fighting off local tribes. Several similar ventures occurred in the New Hebrides between 1829 and 1830, most of them failing because of poor management and lack of diplomacy. Melanesia was not Polynesia: enlisting the aid of one tribe invited wrath from neighbours. With a depressed market for sandalwood in Canton, the Melanesian trade soon folded, only to be revived in the 1840s (see Chapter 4).

It was the end of an era. The fur-seal trade was over. Sandalwood was in sharp decline. Tahiti's salt-pork trade to Sydney (formerly Port Jackson) had all but ceased, as the New South Wales colony was now self-sufficient in pork. Pacific Islands might have easily been forgotten by the rest of the world at this time, its resources depleted and its people possessing nothing of value the world desired. The region stood at a crossroads.

Yet a new dynamic was already pointing the way to the future. Generations of whalers in the North Atlantic had all but eradicated entire populations of sperm whales, whose oil was the developed world's most valuable and applicable source of oil for lighting and industrial lubricants (until the discovery of petroleum in the 1850s). Both Americans and Europeans realized that the only way to maintain a steady supply of whale oil was to turn to the Pacific. Until the early nineteenth century only occasional whalers had ventured into the Pacific – it had simply been too far away from American and European markets to make the trade financially practicable. But now, with the demand for whale oil soaring as Atlantic sperm whales dwindled, whalers descended in droves ... and stayed for decades.

New Englanders from the new United States eventually dominated whaling in the Pacific. But the earliest whalers had sailed out of Port Jackson in New South Wales, establishing tiny stations along the coasts of Australia, Tasmania and New Zealand for ship repair and the processing of blubber to render it down for oil, which was then shipped elsewhere in barrels. The Pacific's whaling trade had been interrupted by the War of 1812–14, but then increased dramatically at exactly the same time that the sandalwood trade was starting to decline. There was also great profit to be made in provisioning, shipfitting, ship and boat building, milling and all sorts of associated activities, such as 'entertainment'.

In Pacific Islands the whaling trade became the whaling industry, for 40 years (1820–60) the backbone of Pacific commerce. It was also the chief reason for the founding of foreign settlements there which later became nuclei of foreign colonization. Whaling did not affect all of Pacific Islands, only those islands nearest the major whaling grounds. (Islands and groups ignored by the whaling trade have generally remained in a backwater ever since.) Whaling poured the cast for the Europeanized Pacific. In most places this cast was New England

American: 200 US whaling vessels ranged the Pacific in 1828, and 571 by 1844. In contrast, both Britain and France had only a few dozen whaling ships in the Pacific in the 1840s. Each whaling voyage lasted an average of three years. The industry fundamentally, and permanently, altered the life styles of all affected Islanders (see below).

Already in the first years of the 1800s Kamehameha I of Hawai'i, planning to establish a modern navy in the European fashion, had offered his Hawaiians as crewmen to work the sealers bound for North America. By the 1830s, Hawaiian sailors – known as 'kanaks' from Hawaiian *kanaka* for 'person', among the most expert crewmen in the Pacific – were so ubiquitous on American, colonial (Australian) and European vessels throughout Pacific Islands, and even further afield, that New England whalers found it more lucrative to leave the US with a skeleton crew and sign on 'kanaks' on their arrival in Honolulu. As many as 3000 Hawaiians (men and women) were crewing whaling ships in the 1830s. Tahitians and Māori (men and women) were especially popular among British/colonial and French whalers. In all, Polynesians accounted for as much as one-fifth of 'American' and 'European' crews. And they subtly affected nearly every Pacific population they encountered.

Melanesia was only infrequently visited by whalers, Polynesia being preferred because of its climate and 'hospitality'. (Between the 1820s and 1850s the largest foreign contribution to Polynesia's genetic profile came from New England Americans.) Fiji was generally avoided because of cannibalism and reefs, though its neighbours Rotuma and East 'Uvea were major whaling ports by the 1830s. Instead, Fiji became the focus of the trade in *bêche-de-mer*, the black or brown sea 'slug' of tidal reefs exported to Canton as a delicacy in Chinese soups. Thriving from 1828 to 1835, and again from 1842 to 1850, the trade in *bêche-de-mer* required small numbers of outsiders using a large Fijian labour force organized and overseen by a local chief: the reverse of the whaling communities' power structure. This perfectly suited Fiji where, from the early 1800s until 1854, warfare ravaged the land and

Europeans had to fear for their lives. Labour-intensive, the work was hazardous (because of attacks and sabotage by neighbours), time-consuming and greatly resented by the 'indentured' Fijians. Europeans could make enormous profits; however, most suffered and died. In return for the *bêche-de-mer*, Fijian chiefs received muskets, implements, cloth and trinkets. Most wanted only muskets. Since there was no stability or security in Fiji, the trade was dead by 1851.

Micronesia was largely ignored by the outside world in the first half of the nineteenth century, with only rare callings and the first tenuous attempts at rudimentary trade. Vessels voyaging between Canton and Hawai'i traversed Micronesia, but did not stop. Because of this, several Caroline Islands communities regularly sailed to Guam to acquire the rare manufactured goods they had already become familiar with. Micronesia was only drawn into the greater Pacific Islands with increased numbers of whalers appearing in the 1820s and 1830s, its two principal ports being located on Kusaie (now Kosrae) and Ponape (Pohnpei). Like many ports in Pacific Islands at this time, both festered with deserters, escapees, arms traders, taverns, prostitutes and every vice the West could import. By the 1840s, both islands were suffering from population loss, social instability, cultural degradation and anarchy. But almost all other Micronesian communities maintained traditional lifestyles, experiencing little or no contact with outsiders. Americans and Europeans of the day generally held most Micronesians to be 'savages' and avoided them at all costs.

MISSIONARIES

The first missionaries in Pacific Islands were Spaniards whose Roman Catholic missions failed when all Spanish attempts to colonize Pacific Islands failed. Guam's seventeenth-century mission alone 'succeeded', through ethnic relocation and mass deaths. Only at the end of the eighteenth century did a new missionizing dynamic emerge, the first and most influential being that of Protestant Evangelists whose literal interpret-ation of the Bible, they believed, would 'save' those souls James Cook and others had so recently described in the highly popular accounts of their Pacific voyages.

The Missionary Society (later London Missionary Society or LMS) attempted missions in Tahiti, the Marquesas and Tonga in 1797. Only the Tahiti mission survived, and was reinforced in 1801. Eight frugal years passed before Tahiti's dismal plight – population loss and anarchy – led to the first conversions among the low-born. Higher-ranking Tahitians turned to the missonaries two years later and, following the civil wars in 1815, mass conversions took place, with the missionaries even called upon to advise the new government. However, there were many setbacks.

In New Zealand, the Anglican Church's own Church Missionary Society landed the first missionaries in 1814 when Samuel Marsden, Chaplain of New South Wales, established a mission in the Bay of Islands on the North Island. Māori resisted conversion for many years, but further Anglican, Wesleyan (Methodist) and Roman Catholic missionaries arrived who then actively mediated throughout the protracted Māori Wars, also serving as physicians and teachers. Once the Church Missionary Society developed a written form of the Māori language which was acknowledged by leading Māori chiefs to lend their people *mana*, conversions increased and by the 1830s and 1840s Christianity was successfully challenging tribal warfare, cannibalism and *tapu*. Many prophetic cults – which often mixed Christianity and tradition – enthused rural Māori, a characteristic feature of New Zealand's conversion which continued into the twentieth century.

Tonga experienced a troubled conversion. The murder of three missionaries of the (London) Missionary Society in 1799 as civil war raged in the islands forced the seven surviving missionaries to flee for their lives. The Methodists' Wesleyan Missionary Society (WMS) sent a mission in 1822, but it soon failed. In 1826, two further WMS missionaries from Tahiti – John Thomas and a colleague – fared just as miserably, but were reinforced in 1828, rescuing the mission. The conversion of the Tongans then proceeded rapidly, chiefly the result of Thomas's dedication. In 1831 the WMS Methodists managed to convert Tonga's chief Tāufa'āhau, who then used the Methodists to end the tribal wars. In 1845 Tāufa'āhau changed his name to King George Tupou I (demonstrating his respect for the late King George IV of England) and set up the Methodist faith almost as a 'state religion' as he ruled a united Tonga. His family still rules Tonga today.

John Thomas remained a missionary in the Tongan Islands for 30 years, his notes on local oral traditions comprising the greatest store of island history before 1860. The new unified Christian Tonga maintained Polynesian hegemony while profiting from Western advantages (see Chapter 4). Later missionaries continued to influence the new royal family: the king's subsequent adviser was the Wesleyan missionary Shirley Baker, who even became prime minister of Tonga in the 1880s.

Samoa first learnt of Christianity from the LMS missionary John Williams of Ra'iatea in the Society Islands, who arrived at Savai'i – Polynesia's largest island after New Zealand and Hawai'i – with other teachers in 1830. During the voyage he had proposed to Tonga's Wesleyan missionaries an arrangement – Samoa for the LMS and Fiji for the WMS – but the Wesleyans subsequently denied any arrangement had been agreed upon. Greeted at Savai'i by Malietoa Vainu'upō, the island's paramount chief, Williams promised that LMS missionaries from Europe would arrive to instruct the Samoans in the Christian faith. Williams then left, and several years passed. When no European missionaries arrived the Samoans turned to the WMS on Tonga, and in 1835 Peter Turner landed on Samoa to establish a Wesleyan mission. Within a year, the LMS missionaries finally appeared. Most Samoans allowed themselves to be converted from both groups in 1835–36, but sectarianism then tore Samoan communities apart. The Wesleyans ordered Turner to close the WMS mission in 1839. Their eventual return to Samoa two decades later infuriated the LMS.

Perhaps because traditional 'religion' was less developed there than on other islands, Samoans were open to Christianity like few people in the Pacific. Great social changes came quickly after conversion. As the missionaries taught that nakedness was sinful, the Samoans were soon allowing European traders to settle there who then sold them cotton cloth for 'Mother Hubbard' gowns and other European attire unsuitable for the hot climate. Williams's own son, John Chauner Williams, became the island's first coconut-oil trader, exporting six tonnes already by 1842. The missionaries even sold books for coconut oil: one gallon in 1843 would buy 'a portion of Scripture'. Two years later the LMS built Malua College, the Protestant secondary school for boys, on the island of 'Upolu. The following year the paramount chief's rival – in true Samoan fashion – converted to the competing Roman Catholic faith and was baptized 'Iosefo'. By 1850, John Chauner Williams was already exporting 1000 gallons of coconut oil as Christianity spread rapidly throughout all the Samoan Islands. Traditional cults sometimes emerged in protest at this sudden foreign intrusion, which Samoans often perceived as a strange combination of creed and commercialism.

While the LMS and similar British and French societies were thriving in the South Pacific – bringing their faith to the Tuamotus, Australs and Cooks – the Americans chose the North Pacific as their pulpit. Shortly after the formation of the American Board of Commissioners for Foreign Missions, in imitation of the British-based organizations, the Board sent a small group of missionaries and their wives in 1820 to establish missions on several of the Hawaiian Islands. It was fruitful soil for the Americans: only one year after Kamehameha I's death peace still reigned, manufactured goods were desired more than ever, and the old Hawaiian ways and gods had already largely been discarded. At first, the Hawaiians displayed suspicion, but by 1822 a printing press was already turning out Hawaiian-language primers and catechisms. Four years later Hawai'i's highest-ranking chiefs chose public conversion and by the 1830s all of Hawai'i was a Christian archipelago – the most sweeping conversion anywhere in Pacific Islands. Early in the 1830s the Board attempted to convert the Marquesans, too, but with them they failed. (The British LMS made three separate attempts to convert the Marquesans, but finally abandoned their aim once France declared its 'possession' of the archipelago in 1842.)

The French eventually succeeded in converting the Marquesans – who today still remain largely Roman Catholic – after having established the archipelago's first mission of the Paris-based Congregation of the Sacred Hearts (SSCC) on Tahuata in 1838. Roman Catholicism thrived in Eastern Polynesia. At first rivalled by British (South Pacific) and American (Hawai'i) sects, it gained a foothold especially in Tahiti, Mangareva and the Marquesas in the 1830s through the Valparaíso diocese of the Roman Catholic Church. Father Honoré Laval, for example, established the first SSCC mission at Rikitea on Mangareva in 1834, where he missioned until his forced removal in 1871 to facilitate France's political agenda in the region. It was also from Valparaíso that Florentin Étienne 'Tepano' Jaussen arrived at the SSCC's Ha'apape mission – now named Mission, a suburb of Pape'ete – in 1849 as Polynesia's first Apostolic Vicar of Tahiti and titular Bishop of Axiéri *in partibus infidelium*. From there 'Tepano' Jaussen then courageously championed Islanders' rights against French absolutism for the next 42 years.

The missionaries' general success in Polynesia in the 1830s was followed by financial straits, disillusionment and desertions in the 1840s. One contributing factor was the enormous number of Islanders' deaths at this time (see below). Polynesians had desperately turned to stories of salvation as they died in their thousands; in many cases, few 'saved' souls were then left to shepherd. Whereupon numerous Protestant missionaries abandoned their calling to become traders or planters, their children often becoming Pacific Islands' wealthiest and most powerful personalities.

Fiji's first Christian instructors were LMS missionaries who were dispatched on a short visit from the LMS mission at

Tahiti in 1827. In the 1830s, Fijian chiefs requested Wesleyans from Tonga, just as the Samoans had done. As a result, David Cargill and William Cross arrived with their families in 1835. Conversion of the Fijians, however, took nearly 20 years, as the missionaries encountered not the general welcome they had been expecting but protracted intertribal fighting.

In the 1840s, the Roman Catholic Marist Order attempted to establish missions in the New Hebrides and the Solomons, but were driven out. The Marists eventually returned later in the century, when they succeeded in establishing permanent missions there.

It is true that missionaries almost everywhere in Pacific Islands forbade and eliminated traditional dress, dancing and many 'non-Christian' customs and forms of behaviour. Included among their targets was the *tatau* – tattooing – which all missionaries regarded as a 'heathen' vestige; between *c.* 1850 and 1970 indigenous tattooing nearly died out in Pacific Islands, though popular among European and American sailors (it is now again popular not only in Pacific Islands, but throughout the world). Yet missionaries counterbalanced the harm of the whalers, traders and publicans, one should appreciate, in that they brought a different face of European civilization to Pacific Islands. Missionaries actively mediated in local conflicts, they physicked, negotiated between Europeans/colonists/Americans and Islanders, taught ethical conduct and introduced those cultured aspects of European life which the other foreigners lacked. They showed Islanders that not all outsiders were avaricious and insidious. The Pacific languages were given their first writing system, script and orthography; these languages were then printed and widely read. The languages had their first grammars and lexicons, too, all the work of dedicated resident missionaries. The oral histories and traditions of much of Pacific Islands were preserved by committed, intelligent, sensitive missionaries. Trusting these unusual white people over others, the Islanders turned more to them for advice and guidance…as other Europeans and Americans turned away even more to create their own 'white' Pacific Islands.

THE OUTSIDERS' PACIFIC ISLANDS

Mythical island societies have always fascinated Europeans: classical Greeks wrote of Atlantis and Hesperides, Celts sang of Avalon. The Portuguese traveller and poet Luís de Camões published *The Lusiads* (1572), telling of explorer Vasco da Gama's voyages and recounting how his men had dallied with naked nymphs on an 'island of love' in the southern seas; in a vision, the book further claimed, da Gama learnt that Europeans would extend their influence throughout this southern ocean. Such tales thrilled and inspired generations of readers. In 1719, Daniel Defoe's immensely popular *Robinson Crusoe* – based on the true-life story of Alexander Selkirk's five-year sojourn (1704–09) in the Islas Juan Fernández west of Chile – inspired a host of 'desert island' imitations in many languages. It also created a false image of a pristine environment in the Pacific, far removed from Europe's taint, where idyllic nature would allow one to live a life of Christian virtue. The fable was reinforced by such novels as Jonathan Swift's *Gulliver's Travels* (1726) which told of antipodean lands peopled by any number of remarkable societies of all sizes (and heights).

Here in the Pacific lay a region awaiting the civilizing hand of European Christians whose duty was to stamp out savagery – or so read the repeated message of these fashionable works. Indeed, in the eighteenth century the notion of the 'Pacific savage' became a fixture in the European imagination. As promulgated in the publication of Englishman William Dampier's four voyages around the world, if first understood as meaning the brute awaiting the civilized European, later the notion of the 'noble savage' offered an equally attractive conceit.

The 'noble savage' is just as ancient. The idea can be found in Homer, Pliny the Elder and Xenophon. Europe's earliest authors frequently enjoyed invoking idealized primitives – such as Tacitus's Germanic tribes (who were real) or the 'Arcadians' (imagined) – in order to hold up a mirror to their own corrupt societies. Idealizing primitivism was revived as a literary motif in the Renaissance and greatly influenced

Europe's early conceptualization of the newly discovered Pacific. In particular, Polynesian societies' sexual licentiousness was so shocking yet at the same time so appealing – as no social harm was apparent in the custom – that European voyagers had to draw classical analogies to deflect the injury to Christian morality.

To imagine that people existed elsewhere whose lives were uncorrupted by civilization and unencumbered by toil was especially attractive to oppressed Europeans of the sixteenth and seventeenth centuries. As the English poet John Dryden (1631–1700) wrote: 'I am free as Nature first made man, / Ere the base laws of servitude began, / When wild in the woods the noble savage ran.' Many writers of the age took up the theme, chief among them the founders of the Age of Enlightenment, such as the Swiss philosopher Jean-Jacques Rousseau: 'man is naturally good and only by institutions is he made bad'. The popular notion explains why such sons of the Enlightenment as James Cook, Joseph Banks and Louis Antoine de Bougainville were admiring among Pacific Islanders only what they had brought with them from Europe.

Cook wrote of the Antipodeans: 'They live in a tranquillity which is not disturbed by the inequality of condition: the earth and the sea of their own accord furnishes them with all the things necessary for life.' Banks penned of the Tahitians: 'These gentlemen, like Homer of old, must be poets as well as musicians.' And Bougainville, who called Tahiti the 'New Cythera' (after the Greek isle once dedicated to Aphrodite, goddess of love): 'I never saw people better made and whose limbs were more proportionate', while Tahitian women were like Aphrodite herself, bearing the 'celestial form of that goddess'. He had to conclude of Tahiti: 'I thought I was walking in the Garden of Eden.' Such impressions filled expeditions' logs and travel accounts, and the paintings and watercolours of artists accompanying these voyages glow with Enlightenment sentiments, honouring, dignifying and beautifying Pacific Islands.

Particularly evident in mid to late eighteenth-century accounts is the Europeans' desire to 'classicize' Pacific Islanders, in particular Polynesians because of racial preference: that is, to compare them with ancient Greeks and Romans and their pantheon of gods and goddesses. This distancing and categorizing seemingly allowed these outsiders to accept what was otherwise a wholly inscrutable human experience. Indeed, the semantic impact of the word 'Tahiti' today, in many of the world's languages, still invokes romantic images far removed from the smog, traffic and congestion which is the modern reality. This phenomenon, too, is a legacy of the eighteenth-century mythification of Pacific Islands.

Several Islanders came to Europe, strengthening the noble fancy. What few Europeans realized was that these Pacific exiles had been rare individuals in their own societies, already excelling in birth, talent and intelligence. In 1774 Tobias Furneaux brought from the Society Islands to England the 21-year-old Ra'iatean Omai, who was then courted by London society and received by King George III. In 1770 the Tahitian Aotourou had already been introduced to Parisian salons by Bougainville – who then had been publicly chastised for having removed the 'noble savage' from his Eden to the corruption of France!

Not all navigators viewed Islanders through the rose-tinted spectacles of the Enlightenment. French explorer Jean-François Galaup de La Pérouse, reaching Samoa in 1787 and experiencing there the brutal murder of the commander of the *Astrolabe* and several crewmembers, concluded that 'despite the academies which award the crown to the paradoxes of philosophers, the almost savage man, living in anarchy, is a being more malicious than the wolves and tigers of the forest'. Others managed a more balanced perspective, though these were certainly the rarest voices of all. In 1809 William Lockerby found of the Fijians that 'in war they are fearless and savage to the utmost degree, but in peace their disposition is mild and generous to their friends, and the affection they bear towards their relations is very seldom found among Europeans'.

This latter view in particular became the general impression of those outsiders who later settled in Pacific Islands and became best acquainted with the Islanders themselves and their ways. But Europeans and Americans continued to maintain the dichotomy – the 'Pacific brute' versus the 'noble savage' – in the popular imagination. In fact, Europe and America exploited both according to need well into the nineteenth century. By the twenty-first century both fancies have of course disappeared, long superseded by the equally unrealistic image of nubile Polynesian maidens and handsome Polynesian bucks in grass skirts dallying under high palms alongside golden beaches and turquoise lagoons. This has furnished the masquerade of such popular novelists as America's Herman Melville and France's Pierre Loti, but also the pageantry of the paintings of Paul Gauguin.

Such tales and artwork inspired others to search the South Pacific for this newest conceit. Most were soon disillusioned and left. Having sought Melville's Typee in the Marquesas in 1907, for example, American novelist Jack London had to conclude that 'the white race flourishes on impurities and corruption'. Yet the myth still endures today, expressing not what is the South Pacific but what people in other parts of the globe wish it to be. Like Cook, Banks and Bougainville, most of us carry our own Pacific Islands with us.

There were also the so-called 'beachcombers', those Europeans and Americans who chose to become Islanders. Almost all of these lived in Polynesia and were wholly dependent on their hosts, having been abandoned by their captains, shipwrecked, deserted or simply 'crossed the beach' to call the native village home. Most survived the grim realities of everyday life there for only several weeks or months. Very few remained as 'adopted Polynesians'. Such beachcombers often mediated between visiting captains and local chiefs. Most brought valuable European skills to their community: carpentry, blacksmithing and musket maintenance were greatest in demand. A few beachcombers rose to prominence in their respective societies – in the 1790s John Young, for example, became steward to the great chief Kamehameha I of Hawai'i. They had Islander families and changed the way many Polynesians thought and felt about outsiders, long before the arrival of missionaries.

But Pacific Islanders themselves were adapting more and more to the changing realities effected by the European trespass. The beachcombers soon disappeared, their unique place in island society assumed by mercantile middlemen whose hosts had become Europeanized consumers. The merchants acquired property and, with it, power in local island affairs. They soon appreciated that greater growth in the region – that is, increased international trade which would swell their profits – could come only with a larger European and American representation there. This demanded an influx of capital, goods and, above all, permanent settlers. The process would eventually force the merchants themselves to defer to company representatives...who then opened the floodgates.

PACIFIC ISLANDERS AND OUTSIDERS

With the exception of those Western Micronesians who had enjoyed protracted contact with the Philippines, and the Rapanui who had sailed to South America (it is assumed), Pacific Islanders had never encountered outsiders before. White men, when first encountered, were thus believed to be supernatural beings or spirits returning from the ancestral dead, whom one met with wonder and fear. It was one of the great ironies of history that it was the outsiders who, in the end, enabled the Islanders to transcend atemporal super-stition and to visualize the true extent of their ancestors' achievements in, as well as their profound claim to, this part of the globe.

Most characteristic of first contact were skirmishes between nervous European landing parties and curious and rapacious Islanders defending descent-group territory (while abusing local rules against theft). It was the clash of two worlds, neither able to understand the intention and protocol of the other.

The consequences for both were frequently farcical and nearly always tragic.

When Schouten and Le Maire, for example, were approaching Tonga in 1616, they encountered a party of Tongans in a double-hulled canoe. Mistaking the large unknown vessel for a European barque, the Dutch fired two warning shots across her bows then sent out marines in a ship's boat. Terrified, the Tongans blackened their faces with charcoal; some leapt into the water while others prostrated themselves before the marines and kissed their feet and arms. A few Tongans were hauled out of the water (several of the others had drowned), to whom the Dutch then gave trinkets and knives. When the Dutch left, the Tongans fled southeast ... towards empty ocean.

The following day, the Dutch raised Tafahi, one of the Tongan Islands, and were met there by many double-hulled canoes. No aggression was apparent and so goods were harmoniously exchanged. But when the Dutch sent out a boat to reconnoitre a safer anchorage, some 14 canoes descended on it. The Dutch opened fire. At least one Tongan was struck in the chest. On the morrow, the exchange of goods resumed without incident. The paramount chief of Tonga arrived at Tafahi from the nearby island of Niuatoputapu, bringing with him 35 canoes of armed retinue. Le Maire accepted the chief's gift of a pig but refused his kava, fearing poison. Seriously offended by this injury to high protocol, around a thousand Tongans attacked the Dutch the following day. The Dutch muskets succeeded in repelling the Tongans with much bloodshed but, resolving the Islanders could not be trusted, the Dutch fled, designating the place 'Traitors' Island'.

Something similar occurred at Europe's first encounter with the Māori of New Zealand. In December 1642 Abel Tasman sailed his two ships into Golden Bay on the South Island's northern coast where the local *iwi* ('nation'), the Ngāti Tīmata Kokire, came out to greet them in canoes with a 'Moorish-like trumpet'. When the Dutch flagship returned the call in salutation, the Māori understood the gesture to be a formal challenge and so they of course attacked. Four Europeans were slain. Tasman immediately sailed off, naming the place 'Murderers' Bay'.

All Islanders at first believed these strangers were supernatural beings of some kind: they were white, their physiognomy and dress were radically different, and they came in ships as large as islets. When James Cook arrived in New Zealand 127 years later – as one Māori eyewitness, then a child, later recalled – the Māori called his ship an *atua* ('deity') and the strange people on board were for them *tupua* ('goblins'): 'There was one supreme man in that ship. We knew he was the lord of the whole by his perfect gentlemanly and noble demeanour. He seldom spoke but some of the goblins spoke much. But this man did not utter many words...He was a very good man, and came to us – the children – and patted our cheeks, and gently touched our heads. His language was a hissing sound ....'

The Islanders' reception of European visitors in general was one of initial fear and awe, possibly hostility, then caution and, finally, ceremonial welcoming. Pacific Islanders harboured nothing of those European preconceptions based on ancient traditions. There were no preconceptions: the Islanders' attitude was immediate, subjective and conditioned by circumstance. Both Islanders and Europeans alike ordinarily behaved at first encounter with heightened restraint, insisting on observance of neither *tapu* nor etiquette. Violence only ensued when the Islanders' tolerance was strained beyond limit, when something was stolen or when someone was direly threatened.

Earliest encounters sometimes had enormous repercussions for small island societies once the outsiders had disappeared. Rapanui's 'Birdman Cult' which annually installed a warrior-chief to rival the island's traditional '*ariki mau*, for example, appears to have started just after the island's discovery by Roggeveen in 1722. In time, frequent and intimate contact with Europeans and Americans brought calamitous consequences to all Islanders, the ultimate losers in the sad saga of historical conveyance in the Pacific. It meant in most, but certainly not all, cases social instability, diminished health, huge population loss, economic dependence and, finally, political subservience.

During the whaling era, especially from the 1820s to the 1840s, great numbers of Islanders were lured from villages to harbour settlements. Islander men performed hard labour, some skilled work and, as we have seen, shipped out as sailors, crisscrossing the Pacific and learning of other, related Islanders. Islander women went into domestic service and prostitution; thousands sailed on whaling ships as concubines, domestics and, rarely, wives. In the tribal villages, less attention was given to community needs and more to whalers' needs. In exchange, the Islanders received trade items, cloth, alcohol, gunpowder and muskets. In time they learnt the advantages of cash economics and were accepting paper money, silver and gold.

The whaling era also altered the Islands' structures of authority. Nullifying the *tapu*, Polynesian chiefs became capitalists, exploiting their tribe's labour for commercial gain. No longer committed to a community identity even their elders were denying, young Polynesians became individualistic, prioritizing foreign values. Many Polynesian women bore children of mixed heritage; these children then married among themselves or with other Europeans and Americans, diluting the Polynesian patrimony. A new people of the Pacific was rapidly emerging, of two bloods and two cultures...and forced to live European to survive.

Relatively minor acts of violence had characterized first contact. But now began a dynamic era of trade which, by providing Islanders with muskets and powder, introduced into the region a frequency, savagery and mortality of conflict Pacific Islands had never before witnessed. New Zealand's fate was typical of this tragic process.

The Māori of New Zealand had learnt from James Cook that Europeans chiefly sought water and provisions, things for which the Māori could receive highly prized metal and cloth. And so the initial phase of caution and hostility eventually turned into a more protracted and intimate one of mutually satisfying relations. A disturbing exception was the French expedition of 1772 led by Marion du Fresne, who arrived at the Bay of Islands and clashed with the local *iwi* there: du Fresne and 15 crewmen were killed; in reprisal, the French burnt down three villages and slew many Māori. Cook's two subsequent voyages profited again from peaceful relations with the Māori. In the 1790s New Zealand became celebrated among visiting sealers and whalers as the place for trading in tattooed human heads. But the land's bountiful natural resources soon saw sealers and onshore bay whalers from New South Wales establishing small settlements along eastern and southern coastlines. By the end of the decade deep-sea whalers were also regularly calling at Kororareka (later renamed Russell) in the Bay of Islands for water, provisions, women and alcohol. Māori men and women were soon being taken on as crewmembers. An entire shipping industry quickly developed in the Bay of Islands, and Kororareka became New Zealand's major port.

Most Europeans in New Zealand remained either in the Bay of Islands or occupied the *c.* 45 whaling stations which lay chiefly along Cook Strait – between the North and South Islands – and on the southern and southeastern coast of the South Island. The Māori, eager to maintain the supply of axes, knives, cloth, fishhooks and other manufactured goods, strove to accommodate the trespassers. It was not that the Māori people had suddenly embraced Western commerce: above all, the Māori wanted Western muskets. Once an inordinately large number of Māori in the Bay of Islands owned muskets a point of criticality had been reached, and local chiefs began brutally driving rival *iwi* from their ancestral lands, sending them southwards in a domino-like felling of Māori nations. The extremely savage tribal warfare, New Zealand's 'Musket Wars', lasted from 1818 until the 1830s and the resultant migration caused a major population redistribution in the country. Scholars have estimated that as many as one-quarter of adult Māori males fell at this time, victims of their Māori neighbours. Only the missionaries offered a 'civilizing' alternative during the almost two decades of ceaseless inter-*iwi* slaughter.

In the 1820s New South Wales, already boasting a population of several thousands, started encouraging the Māori to produce flax as well. A decade later they had Māori felling timber and growing cereal crops for the Australian colony's exploding population. Many Māori adopted European farming methods, growing wheat and white potatoes; others herded cattle and sheep. By the early 1830s, around 200 Europeans resided permanently in New Zealand, most of them in the Bay of Islands. But by 1840 there were already 2000, all of them British but for 50 Americans and 20 French.

Unprecedented changes were taking place throughout Pacific Islands by this time. Many communities were no longer producing traditional Pacific Islands foods at all. Islander marriages were no longer being forged as before. *Tapu* had lost its social effectiveness, while *mana* had assumed new, commercial forms. A foreign god now ruled the Pacific, and his name was profit. Only the missionaries preserved a semblance of order and meaning among the perceived chaos and senselessness of the many changes, and so Pacific Islanders increasingly turned to the missionaries' new religion with a fervour, sincerity and dedication Europe itself had not known since the Middle Ages. (The new faith still joins and empowers most Pacific Islanders today, indeed their 'saviour' in the sense of ethnic identity and social cohesion.)

And still Islanders perished in their tens of thousands.

Populations crashed primarily, but not exclusively, because of diseases the Europeans and Americans had unwittingly introduced: measles, chickenpox, whooping cough, influenza, virulent tuberculosis, venereal diseases, leprosy and elephantiasis – and these in repeated waves of infection. Pacific Islanders had never been exposed to Old World diseases and so carried no immunity against them. The first recorded mass deaths in Pacific Islands had occurred with the Chamorros of the Marianas in the 1680s, whereby within 30 years only around one in four Chamorros was still alive.

Human losses in Polynesia were staggering. In the Australs, Ra'ivavae's population in one year alone (1826) fell from 3200 to 120 because of an epidemic of malignant fever. A similar tragedy struck Rapanui, whose 1863 population of *c.* 3000 fell to 111 by 1877. At the end of the eighteenth century the Marquesas had over 80 000 people; by the 1920s only 1500 remained. The *c.* 142 000 Hawaiians in 1823 numbered only 39 000 in 1896. The *c.* 35 000 Tahitians before James Cook's visits there numbered only around 7000 to 8000 by the beginning of the twentieth century. Tonga suffered fewer deaths, its total of *c.* 20 000 people in the nineteenth century being only a quarter lower than that before the civil wars had erupted (1799–1820s), though it is believed that a much larger population there had been decimated by European diseases in the eighteenth century. Samoa had a population of *c.* 50 000 at the beginning of the nineteenth century and only half this number by the century's end.

In Melanesia, Fiji's estimated population of *c.* 150 000 was reduced by several epidemics (especially 1791–92, 1802–03 and 1875) to *c.* 100 000; it continued to decline into the 1920s. It appears that many Western Melanesian islands lost around 90 per cent of their people. The Solomons and New Hebrides were depopulated in the second half of the nineteenth century by labour recruiters who took most of the young men. Aneityum in the New Hebrides had around 4000 people in 1848, and only 186 in 1940. All of the New Hebrides lost half its population. There were around 100 000 indigenous New Caledonians in 1800 but only *c.* 34 000 in 1900.

In Micronesia, the overall loss approached 50 per cent, though some islands also experienced 90 per cent. Kosraeans, for example, numbered *c.* 3000 in the 1820s but only around 300 in the 1880s.

Large populations with good nutrition survived pandemics better and recovered more quickly. Though pandemics were by far the most frequent cause of population loss, they were certainly not the only cause. Sterility caused by disease was a major factor, as well as the loss of young men to the sealers and whalers, and later to copra and cane plantations, removing them from the genetic pool. Populations which suffered greatest were often those demographically overwhelmed by foreign settlers, though also unsettled islands (Rapanui, Ra'ivavae, Kosrae) suffered terribly. Population loss in general must be ascribed to a variety of factors, chief among them disease (and its repercussions), loss of young men, and the greater colonial context. Murder by Europeans and Americans was, it appears, the rarest cause of all.

Pacific Islanders' contact with outsiders brought tragedy to the Marquesas, Hawai'i, the Australs, parts of New Zealand and dozens of small island societies throughout the region. However, most Island group populations survived, meeting the European and American trespass in a variety of ways and creating in the process the new hybrid culture which still survives today.

We can finally shelve certain twentieth-century myths about this era. Not all whalers and traders were drunken debauchers pushing arms, alcohol, tobacco and girls. Not all missionaries were Bible-beating sex-police. And not all Islanders were innocents from the Garden of Eden. Each person did her or his best to survive and thrive in that difficult time: most in relative harmony, more than a few in violence.

None the less, tragic loss for the one meant fortuitous gain for the other. Many Europeans and Americans perceived the Islanders' mass deaths and crumbling societies as the 'triumph of European superiority', seemingly a divine confirmation of their destiny in the Pacific. The judgment opened the door to total colonization, and tens of thousands of outsiders walked in. By the middle of the nineteenth century, the European trespass in Pacific Islands had become the European invasion.

4

The Second Colonization

A CENTURY OF DISPLACEMENT

For the first time in more than 3000 years a different people had begun to colonize Pacific Islands. The governments of Europe and the US had still not woven primary plans for the region, and so well into the nineteenth century the Pacific remained the arena of solitary traders, shipmasters and missionaries. But as shipping increased more foreign settlers arrived, too, and with more settlers came even more traders, more missionaries and then larger commercial ventures, many from established concerns in Australia, the US and South America (Peru and Chile).

Foreign stations and settlements quickly changed. No longer did Europe and Pacific Islands quaintly reconcile both cultures: the European prerogative began to prevail. Large numbers of white women started arriving who, as legal wives, replaced common-law Islander women. Soon the 'civilizing' affect of these white women – in behaviour, dress, material ostentation, civil decorum and other things – transformed muddy settlements into colonial towns. The European domestication also displaced Islanders in general who, when not relegated to domestic servitude, were banned to ghettos or satellite villages, rudely denied a decent status in the new urbanized Pacific. By then Europeans and Americans were no longer outsiders: they had become the new lords of the 'White Pacific'.

Trade had been the chief reason for the British/colonial, French and American presence. For many decades the region's most profitable trade had been sperm-whale oil. However, once petroleum was discovered in the US in the 1850s the market in sperm-whale oil collapsed, to be largely replaced by that of coconut oil which was soon supplying most of Europe's and America's soap and candles. For this and other industries in the Pacific – like cotton and sugar-cane – many large plantations were needed, requiring land and cheap labour. In time, these two issues – land and labour – came to lead the Pacific Islands agenda. And in order to guarantee their nationals these two essentials, foreign governments started taking a more direct and active interest in the region.

Having once acquired Islanders' land, however, foreign settlers grew bolder and began challenging not only the local authority, but also the indigenous franchise itself. The new-comers required European-style laws – and their local implementation with punitive safeguarding – in order to protect their acquired property and augment their wealth. This meant establishing a new power structure: a European power structure. Throughout Pacific Islands, settlers began demanding the European form of governance which trad-itional systems and new indigenous governments could hardly provide. When Islanders' traditional political orders failed, the settlers – including many influential missionaries – frequently saw no other recourse but to take the matter into their own hands. They started appealing to their govern-ments directly, who then intervened in protection, litigation or gun-boat intimidation. As a result, international rivalries in Pacific Islands heightened European and American competition there, the primary policy of these foreign powers now being to prevent a rival from securing an advantage in the Pacific. The eminent success of numerous treaties, which largely disadvantaged Islanders, encouraged foreign powers to elaborate ever greater schemes in the region. In the end, the native prerogative was the lowest of priorities.

Labour 'recruitment' – often a euphemism for brutal kidnapping – was another industry which fundamentally altered Pacific Islands in the second half of the nineteenth century. For example, in search of cheap labour for Peru's plantations, haciendas and guano islands a small fleet of vessels belonging to international entrepreneurs, most of them Peruvian, sailed in 1862–64 from Lima's port of Callao into the South Pacific and as far north as the Gilberts in Micronesia where they removed around 3500 Polynesians (around 1000 from Rapanui alone) and Micronesians mostly by deceit or violence. Human loss on affected islands, already decimated by Western diseases, ranged between 25 and 50 per cent. Outraged when they learnt of the trade, foreign nations demanded Peru return the 'slaves'. By the time Peru acquiesced, the harm had already been done: by 1866 only 257 'blackbirded' Islanders were still alive, the rest having died of smallpox and other diseases. Only 37 were ever returned directly to their home islands, some introducing pandemics upon landing. Still today, Peru is anathema to many Islanders, particularly in southeastern Polynesia where descendants frequently recount the atrocity as family lore. However, the later labour trade proper wreaked far greater havoc on Pacific populations than this, affecting tens of thousands of Islanders.

Of prime concern to most of the major players in the Pacific for the greater part of the nineteenth century was the establishment of a rule of law to control traditional violence and to regulate transactions between peoples in a generally peaceful and mutually agreeable fashion. Foreign powers in themselves were rarely brutal ogres, as Pacific Islanders were rarely unshorn lambs. In truth, for most of the century leading colonial contenders such as Britain and France harboured little real interest in Pacific Islands, which was too poor and too far away to be of any true advantage to them in the greater power game.

However, this situation changed with the entry of Germany into the Pacific, which occurred after the unification of the German state under Bismarck in the 1870s. Especially after 1881, Germany embarked on an aggressive campaign to 'collect' large parts of Pacific Islands for the Kaiser, obliging Britain and France – then Spain, the US and Chile – to conceive and enact their own Pacific designs, sometimes despite themselves.

In this way, Britain assumed control over most of the southwestern Pacific, France dominated most of Eastern Polynesia, while Germany extended its authority over most of the equatorial and northern regions of the Western Pacific. Secondary powers seized last 'tidbits' at the end of the century. However, once all rivals had declared and ratified their possessions – as with Chile on Rapanui (1888); the US in the Hawaiian Islands (1898), Guam (1898) and Samoa (1899); or even France in its numerous island groups in both the Western (New Caledonia, Loyalties) and Eastern Pacific (Societies, Marquesas, Tuamotus, Australs and Gambiers) – it appears most governments thereafter took little real interest in the region, generally, but not exclusively, leaving their newly gained colonies to languish in an economic backwater.

NEW ZEALAND BECOMES BRITISH

Polynesia's largest landmass received its first flock of 100 sheep in 1834. Over the following decades great swathes of forest fell to create the grazing land which characterized New Zealand by the end of the 1800s. During this same period introduced European domestic animals, pests, birds and plants ravaged the indigenous fauna and flora to an extent that far exceeded the extinctions the Māori had initiated around 500 years earlier. By 1900, New Zealand was British in both blood and soil.

European settlement of New Zealand exploded with the founding, in 1837, of the New Zealand Company, whose express purpose was the creation of a British colony in the South Pacific. The Company implemented the scheme of land grant purchases as devised by Edward Gibbon Wakefield in 1827 while a prisoner in London's Newgate jail: selling land above market value to would-be migrants then using the earned surplus to subsidize passages, the Company allowed migrants to work off their assisted passages as hired labour and then to purchase their own land in the colony. The scheme proved to be very successful in New Zealand, where it brought settlers to the North Island's Wellington, Wanganui and New Plymouth regions and to the South Island's Nelson area.

France's sudden interest in New Zealand and the New Zealand Company's success were the two main reasons why Britain decided to annex the country, which act would render all land sales there a monopoly of the British Crown. In the early 1830s the government of New South Wales was already exerting *de facto* authority over all non-Māori in New Zealand. In 1833 James Busby was appointed the British Representative there and championed annexation as he united British settlers in the common cause. Britain's Colonial Office then sent William Hobson to New Zealand to negotiate a treaty with the Māori chiefs, whereby Hobson was to convince them to cede the North Island's sovereignty to the British Crown.

Hobson arrived in the Bay of Islands in January 1840. Already on 6 February he formally presented his written treaty – in both English and Māori – to the many Māori chiefs who had gathered at Waitangi, across the bay from Russell (formerly Kororareka). Hobson's treaty specified that the Māori were ceding their sovereignty over the North Island to Great Britain; any sale of land thereafter would extinguish the original title and all further claims; and all sales of land would transpire only between Māori and representatives of the British Crown. In exchange, the Māori were guaranteed proprietorship and full use over their lands, protection by the Crown, and the same rights and privileges as all British subjects.

However, the Māori were unaware of substantial differences between the English- and Māori-language versions of what came to be known as the Treaty of Waitangi. The Māori-language treaty guaranteed *te tino rangatiratanga*: full chiefly authority. But the English-language version had the Māori ceding all rights to law and government. The 45 Māori chiefs who signed both the English- and Māori-language treaties that day at Waitangi were being deceived, as the British government subsequently enacted only the English-language version. More than 500 Māori eventually signed the Treaty of Waitangi, none of them aware of the deception. Though not all the Māori *hapū* ('sub-tribes') had signed the treaty, in May 1840 William Hobson proclaimed Britain's sovereignty over the North Island 'by virtue of cession' as well as over the South Island 'by right of discovery'.

From 1840 to 1841 New Zealand was 'legally' (in a Western sense) part of New South Wales, its capital Russell. In 1841 the capital moved south to Auckland and the land became a separate Crown Colony, its first Governor being Hobson himself. Abuses of the Treaty of Waitangi abounded in New Zealand Company territories: the Company in the Cook Strait region, for example, frequently failed to identify the true owners of lands it purchased or whether proprietorial rights to them were in dispute. Many conflicts ensued, and Māori became ever more disgruntled with the permanent foreign presence.

The Northern War of 1845–46 erupted when northern chiefs Hone Heke and Kawiti of the Ngā Puhi begrudged the loss of their guns, clothing, sugar and rum, and the sharp decline in their timber and whaling revenues when New Zealand's capital moved from Russell down to Auckland. Hone Heke, in symbolic defiance, three times cut down Russell's governmental flag-pole; three times the Crown re-erected it. On his fourth felling, Hone Heke and his men plundered Russell and murdered 19 foreigners there. The British retaliated with an attack on Hone Heke's and Kawiti's *pā* ('fortified stockades'), but were repelled. Though the

Crown eventually declared its 'victory' over Hone Heke, he was actually defeated by an alliance of Ngā Puhi chiefs in 1846.

After this, relations between Māori and colonists worsened. At the same time, however, George Grey's governorship (1845–53) marked a period of great economic growth and general stability: the foreign population actually quadrupled to 100 000. New Zealand was becoming British, a wholly new land which now held more Britons than Māori. In 1852, the Constitution Act of New Zealand divided the colony into six provinces: Auckland, New Plymouth and Wellington on the North Island; and Nelson, Canterbury and Otago on the South Island. Though granting colonists more representation, the Act still left the Governor and dual-chamber General Assembly in control of the Crown Colony. The colonists never developed keen provincial allegiances, but generally saw themselves simply as New Zealanders. (A strong egalitarianism characterized white New Zealand society until the end of the twentieth century.)

The colonists' demand for land in the 1850s had forced the Māori to extreme measures, uniting normally hostile factions. These groupings of Māori now called for a halt to land sales to all non-Māori. From 1858, the factions south of Auckland coalesced into the King Movement, which strove to guarantee Māori independence. Organized by the self-styled 'King' Te Wherowhero and later led by his son Tawhiao, the King Movement won large support among nearly all the *iwi* ('nations') in the land, as the government continued to ignore all opportunities to reach a compromise solution on the issue of land sales. It came to an impass, then war.

Labelling the Māori the 'aggressors', the British waged the so-called 'Māori Wars' between 1860 and around 1865, at the same time as the US Civil War. The Māori proved how resourceful Islanders could be in military tactics and defence: constructing bunkers and erecting earthen barricades, the Māori saw their *pā* easily withstand British artillery bombardment. The Māori were redoubtable fighters; losses on both sides were formidable. But the British comprised an organized army of 14 000 professionals, with a corresponding infrastructure; the Māori warriors could only sustain battle for several days at a time, then pause to collect water and food. Because of this, the British were successful in mounting a counter-offensive which weakened the Māori drive. No decisive battle ever occurred during the wars; for this there were too many small numbers of individual Māori units and over a thousand impregnable *pā*. By the mid-1860s the war had dwindled to intermittent local conflicts, then by the end of the decade to sporadic skirmishes. However, it was only in 1881 that the final peace agreement was concluded with the prominent guerrilla leader Te Kooti, who had also founded a religious cult on the North Island's eastern coast.

After the Māori Wars, Chief Justice Prendergast ruled that the Treaty of Waitangi was 'a simple nullity'. Whereupon great tracts of the best Māori lands were then confiscated by the Crown and sold to colonists. Māori retained lands of inferior value, much of it far from regions of colonial settlement and active trade. In 1867, the Māori were given the vote in a highly contentious attempt to assimilate them into the land's new European society. Few Māori made use of suffrage, however, and their numbers continued to rapidly decline.

The South Island had a different history of dispossession, where first pastoral farming, then gold mining altered traditional proprietorships. Between 1856 and 1860 ten Crown purchases acquired the tribal lands of the Ngai Tahu. The Native Land Act of 1862 then legalized all conveyances of land between Māori and colonists everywhere in New Zealand. After the early 1870s, when virtually all Māori resistance had collapsed, most of the Māori's remaining titles were bought up in individual conveyances.

A great boost to the white settlement of New Zealand came when gold was discovered in Otago Province on the South Island in 1861. The population of Otago's largest town, Dunedin, doubled to 30 000 when Australian and Chinese prospectors and miners descended in thousands almost overnight. The gold-rush brought great wealth to the South Island, making

Dunedin the colony's most prosperous town and the cultural capital in the 1860s and 1870s. New Zealand's first (and finest) monumental architecture in stone rose there at this time, along with the colony's first university and medical school. The sudden influx of revenue allowed railways and roads to be built, opening up the land to even greater settlement. But by the end of the 1860s the gold-rush was over, and from Otago's gold fields the miners moved to the South Island's west coast, turning the small hamlet of Hokitika for a short period into a thriving port town. Thereafter, commercial leadership slowly shifted northward once more, to Auckland and Wellington (New Zealand's capital since 1865). By 1873, four more provinces had been added to the Colony: Hawke's Bay on the North Island, and Marlborough, Westland and Southland on the South Island.

By 1890 the British colonists owned 22 of the 26 million hectares of New Zealand. Most of the remaining 4 million were isolated North Island Māori holdings. The many Māori with no land at all became tenant croppers and day labourers. Villages vanished. Shanty towns sprang up where Māori lived a life of poverty and disease. By 1900 only c. 45 000 Māori remained, who still resisted complete assimilation. Māori held their own unofficial Parliament (1892–1907) as they also generated several cults predicting the ruin and departure of the British. The Young Māori Party, led by the first Māori graduate Apirana Ngata, exploited the foreign system to improve the Māori's lot. At last, the Māori population decline reversed and tribal leaders began to endorse the new generation of Western-educated Māori spokesmen.

Sheep farming has been the mainstay of New Zealand since the mid 1800s, bringing sudden wealth to the colony when the introduction of refrigerated ships in 1882 allowed colonists to sell New Zealand's mutton in Europe. The colony's high country became 'merino territory' for wool production; lamb breeding took place in hill country; and fat-lamb farms were started for the breeding of lambs destined for export. New Zealand exported mutton, wool, sheepskins and dairy products in exchange for European manufactured goods. By 1900, New Zealand was one of the world's leading food producers, its isolation ensuring its relative independence and self-sufficiency.

At this time, New Zealand also experienced sweeping social changes introduced by such dynamic politicians as John 'King Dick' Seddon who, with his Liberal Party, introduced many of the reforms: minimum wage structures, child health services, old-age pensions and other things hardly found anywhere else in the world at the time. New Zealand was also the first country in the world to give women the vote, in 1893.

New Zealand's population increased through a highly selective immigration policy which introduced chiefly British and Irish but also German, Dalmatian, Italian and other selected immigrants. By 1900 the colony's population was nearing 700 000 (but only around 42 000 Māori). It had taken decades before the settlers' stone cottages had yielded to the white-collar workers' bungalows with verandahs. The longing for Home – the Britain usually only heard or read about – was only a short-lived phase for second- and third-generation colonists who were now calling themselves 'Kiwis' but remained uncertain what this was. Though the British- and Irish-dominated society was still dependent on the European Britons – who were called 'Poms' by the end of the nineteenth century – it could take pride in its unique achievements. Out of this a national patriotism was born.

Characteristic of New Zealand's settlement had been pockets of uprooted British communities congregated in one locale, so that New Plymouth farmers, for example, were West Country Anglicans, and Dunedin merchants were Scots Presbyterians. Because of New Zealand's agricultural settlement and restricted mobility, the distinctions have remained. (Only now is it disappearing.) In contrast to Australia which was principally settled by convicts, New Zealand began with ready-made families pre-selected by immigration agents, already creating in Britain the society of Smiths, Kellys, Stewarts and Evanses which has since characterized European New

Zealand. Most settlers had been rural farmers in Britain and Ireland; these had simply transported their culture which they then had to adapt because of New Zealand's dense bush, heavy rains, strong winds and lack of infrastructure. A resilient, energetic and resourceful people was the result of this historical process. The transformation of the country was complete by 1900, resulting in a European-like nation of small rural communities and townships with only a handful of larger towns: Auckland, Wellington, Christchurch and Dunedin.

By then most New Zealanders had been born and bred in the colony, though Britain was still very much Home. Success was often perceived as something to be had only by returning to Britain or Ireland to lead the gentleman's or gentlewoman's life or otherwise attain to consequence – as experienced by writer Katherine Mansfield, physicist Ernest Rutherford, painter Frances Hodgkins and other luminaries. Others were content to use their wealth to turn the colony into a British ideal. It was these latter Kiwis who determined New Zealand's history in the twentieth century.

TAHITI AND THE FRENCH

Pomare, chief of Matavai Bay, had welcomed Tahiti's first missionaries but resisted personal conversion. After he died in 1803, his son Pomare II attempted to conquer all of Tahiti, but failed and fled to nearby Mo'orea in 1808 with the London Missionary Society's Henry Nott. In 1812 Pomare II, whom LMS missionaries still refused to baptize for his 'non-Christian' behaviour, used the missionaries to regain power and allowed his Mo'orean subjects to be converted. Within three years, Pomare II had conquered all of Tahiti, whereupon he then enforced mass conversions there.

From then on, LMS missionaries dictated all social behaviour on the island: banned was dancing, singing of everything but Christian hymns, traditional dress, even the wearing of flowers in the hair. Morality police scoured Tahiti's communities in search of 'sin'. In 1821 Pomare II died at 40 of drink-related disease. He was first succeeded by his infant son Pomare III then, upon the boy's early death only six years later, by Pomare II's half-sister Aimata who became Queen Pomare Vahine IV.

Astute and talented, Queen Pomare also worked closely with the LMS. Their assistance was of particular need when it came to the French. With the 1830s, France found its whaling fleet in the Pacific rivalling Britain's, while its vesssels traded profitably out of Chile's Valparaíso and Peru's Callao on South America's Pacific coast. French Roman Catholic missionaries of the Congregation of the Sacred Heart (SSCC) were even beginning to compete with Britain's LMS and WMS missionaries in the South Pacific, and it was these Roman Catholic missions which later became cells for initial French governmental activities in the area.

In 1836, two priests of the SSCC, Honoré Laval and François Caret, arrived on Tahiti from their two-year-old mission on Mangareva but were immediately expelled by Queen Pomare, who resented any competition to her LMS friends' missions. At the same time Belgian Jacques-Antoine Moerenhout was creating for himself a comfortable trading empire there and had been the US consul. He was appointed French consul to Tahiti's Queen just as the French government was prepared to support French and allied entrepreneurs who sought to colonize Pacific Islands for France. (One vessel actually sailed to New Zealand in 1839 towards this end, but its effect was minimal as British colonization there had grown too strong for rivals.) Moerenhout intervened in the affair of the two SSCC priests, convincing French Admiral Abel du Petit-Thouars, along with other French naval officers, to insist on Tahitian reparations for this affront to the French nation.

A French frigate arrived at Pape'ete in 1838 and, threatening immediate violence, demanded $2000 in compensation and a salute to the French flag. The Queen complied, but then appealed to the new Queen Victoria of Great Britain, on the throne for only one year, for assistance: however, Queen

Victoria chose to remain silent on the issue. Witnessing Queen Pomare's submission to France, the few European traders in Tahiti were prompted to individual acts of insubordination towards the Tahitian throne.

In 1839, a French gunboat arrived at Pape'ete and declared it would bombard the town unless Queen Pomare paid 2000 Spanish dollars and allowed free entry to Roman Catholic missionaries. Again the Queen had to comply, which then encouraged the European traders' further insubordination.

Shortly after this, Admiral Du Petit-Thouars proposed the Marquesas Islands to the French government as a strategic colony: situated between Cape Horn and Hawai'i and between Chile's and Peru's profitable ports and the Asian markets, the islands were a favourite haunt of whalers; in addition, Britain's LMS had twice failed to establish a mission there, leaving the group free for Roman Catholicism. The French government was approving, as the idea agreed with existing foreign policy which prioritized the countering of any British advances in the Pacific. Paris dispatched Du Petit-Thouars himself to carry out the annexation of the Marquesas, and in May and June of 1842 the Admiral violently seized control of the archipelago for France. Outraged Marquesans long resisted the appropriation, but in the end all resistance was brutally crushed.

The Marquesas' sudden and violent annexation by France was, after New Zealand, Europe's second imperialistic seizure in Pacific Islands. However, it led to a unique and unplanned 'domino-effect' which, in time, saw a large portion of Eastern Polynesia becoming French national territory, a situation which has lasted to the present day.

After succeeding so eminently in the Marquesas, Du Petit-Thouars was certain Britain would retaliate by annexing Tahiti. (Neither young Queen Victoria nor her government entertained the notion.) So he led his fleet from the Marquesas, through the Tuamotus and directly to Tahiti. In the meantime, while Queen Pomare and her trusted advisor, the former missionary and present British consul George Pritchard, were away, the French consul Moerenhout coerced four Tahitian chiefs to sign a petition requesting that France grant Tahiti its 'protection'. Once arrived at Tahiti, Du Petit-Thouars accepted the petition for France then used it as legitimization for declaring, on 9 September 1842, Tahiti a French protectorate. Again with her back to the wall, Queen Pomare was forced to accept the indignity.

But Tahiti's Queen thereafter kept her red-and-white royal flag and refused to cede actual governance. So Du Petit-Thouars overthrew the monarchy on 8 November 1843 and militarily occupied Tahiti, in essence single-handedly annexing Tahiti to France. In physical danger, the Queen fled to the island of Ra'iatea. France then deported Consul Pritchard to Britain. This last act finally wakened Britain to the seriousness of its position in the Eastern Pacific. In fact, Britain and France actually stood on the brink of war over the infamous 'Tahitian Affair'.

But France was interested in the Marquesas – not in Tahiti – as a potential strategic crossroads in Pacific commerce. Concerned by the international outcry and its harm to French international prestige and trade, King Louis Philippe I of France re-established Tahiti's protectorate status in 1844. From then until 1847, the Tahitians violently resisted the belligerent occupation of their island; the French erected military stockades; much blood was spilt on both sides. Finally, Queen Pomare realized that her peer Queen Victoria, now ten years on Britain's throne, had no intention of ever responding to Queen Pomare's many letters pleading for support, and so she reached an agreement with France: Queen Pomare would submit to France's protectorate so long as Britain agreed to guarantee France's promise not to annex the Leeward Islands (Huahine, Ra'iatea and Bora Bora). The three parties consented to this in writing.

In 1848, Tahiti's first Apostolic Vicariate was established at Ha'apape (now Mission, a suburb of Pape'ete). Many French missionaries arrived after this to convert the Tahitians to Roman Catholicism, but this proved to be successful only in the Marquesas as no LMS missions had been established there.

The imposition of French authority was still strongly resisted in both Tahiti and the Marquesas for many years. Once Tahiti settled into its protectorate status, it enjoyed some measure of native government: most traditional laws were maintained, such as that forbidding foreigners from purchasing land. However, French authorities became increasingly autocratic. Native participation in local affairs declined and the LMS missionaries exerted less influence in Tahitian communities until, in 1852, they were wholly replaced by French Prostestants who had pledged loyalty to the French authorities. This now left the Tahitians without foreign mediators.

Once established in Tahiti, however, the French authorities appeared diffident about actual day-to-day governance. In contrast to New Zealand, where the Māori had lost almost all of their lands after mainly British and Irish colonists had inundated the country, native Tahitians continued to retain their lands as very few French colonists ever arrived in Tahiti. There was little economic development there, and thus little incentive to colonization. Once the whaling industry had collapsed, the local economy turned to coconut oil (later only copra) and pearl-shell. All social services lay not with the French government, but with the Christian missions; however, these, too, were in French hands.

Queen Pomare died in 1878. Her son and successor, Pomare V, was weak, given to personal pleasures. It was then that France assumed total power over its protectorate. Prompted by France's growing concern over a Panama canal and its possible significance for Tahiti, the colonial administrators contrived to have Pomare V relinquish his kingdom in return for a governmental pension. On 29 June 1880 the Protectorate of Tahiti officially became the 'Établissements français de l'Océanie', an annex of the French state. Unlike Britain's system of indirect rule through local chiefs, France ruled absolutely from Paris. In 1885, an 18-member Conseil Générale was created to regulate specific financial affairs, but in 1899 it was weakened and four years later replaced by an advisory council of French civil servants. Tahiti had only one democratically elected official with authority and a budget: the mayor of Pape'ete.

Even with Tahiti's formal annexation to France, things had hardly changed there. Economic incentives were still lacking, and so few colonists arrived. The French administration hit upon the idea of stimulating the economy by selling land – still a difficult process as land titles were unclear – and to facilitate this declared that all Tahitians had to register their titles. But no one did. French administration was a ramshackle business of local feuds between resident tradesmen and of Paris' ineffectual foreign policy which lacked vision and guidance. Between 1882 and 1914 no fewer than 24 governors led Tahiti, their main concern later being the profits from the phosphate deposits on Makatea in the Tuamotus. But these profits brought little to Tahiti itself; the phosphate was simply exported elsewhere unprocessed and the labourers were not Tuamotuans or Tahitians but Cook Islanders in the main. French Polynesian life resembled very much what it had been before the French had arrived: traditional subsistence and a governance dominated, in all daily practical matters, by village elders and missionaries.

However, France soon consolidated its claims throughout Eastern Polynesia. Most islands of the Austral group were declared to be French protectorates in the 1880s; annexation of the entire group was not complete until 1900. The Tuamotus had been declared a protectorate in 1844 after Tahiti's seizure, and was annexed to France in 1881. The Gambiers (Mangareva) were made a protectorate in 1871 and were formally annexed in 1881. Wallis (East 'Uvea) became a protectorate in 1886 and was annexed in 1924, Futuna in 1887/ 1924. The sacrosanct Leeward Islands, whose independence Queen Pomare had had Britain guarantee before she had finally bowed to France, were annexed to France in 1887, nine years after the Queen's death.

France was about to annex the Cook Islands in 1888, but failed. During the 1880s the chiefs of Rarotonga had looked on with anxiety at France's encroaching annexations. In 1885 they had even appealed directly to the British government for protection. Three years passed before Britain responded favourably. After also having witnessed France's rash of annexations in the region, Britain declared Rarotonga its protectorate, and the eight other islands of the Southern Cooks soon followed. In 1889, when a French warship approached Manihiki to claim the Northern Cooks for France after an appeal from Islanders there who had fallen out with their local British missionaries, these latter hoisted the Union Jack and the French warship sailed off without landing. In August of the same year Britain declared a protectorate over Manihiki and all six islands of the Northern Cooks were soon included.

Over the next decade the local chiefs of Rarotonga, aware of France's poor colonial treatment of Tahitians, along with local British missionaries petitioned the British government to have both groups formally annexed to the British Crown, and finally on 11 June 1901 both were included in the boundaries of New Zealand. This occurred after a number of political experiments on several of the Cook Islands had clearly demonstrated that only colonial rule could provide the necessary governance to guarantee the Cooks' economic and social stability. The Cooks have remained closely aligned to New Zealand, in various legal relationships, ever since.

HAWAI'I

Already during the reign of Kamehameha I (†1819) the Hawaiian Islands, then known as the Sandwich Islands, were recognized by all foreign powers as a sovereign nation. In 1843 both Britain and France issued a joint declaration which acknowledged Hawai'i's independence and pledged to abstain from annexation of the group. The US was invited to join the declaration, whereupon US Secretary of State John Calhoun announced that President John Tyler 'adhered completely to the disinterested spirit which breathed in it'. Hawai'i was clearly inviolate.

Kamehameha I's establishment of a government of unity –
in Hawaiian hands but along European models – was, after his
death, long successful in thwarting all attempts by settlers
there in creating their own European and American entities
which would favour foreign interests to the disadvantage of
native Hawaiians. Kamehameha I had been succeeded by his
son Liholiho who abolished *kapu* (*tapu*) and traditional
religious practices and ruled virtually with no legitimization
but his father's military victories. In 1822, he had posted
notices prohibiting the visiting sailors' uncivil conduct:
Hawai'i's first 'laws'. By 1824, with the new missionaries' advice,
the Christian chiefs drafted a list of injunctions modelled on
the Ten Commandments. Liholiho, hoping to encourage
Britain's patronage and protection, sailed to England. But he
suddenly died there.

In the following years new laws were added to the old,
principally on the advice of missionaries and visiting naval
officers, and in 1835 a new code of laws was announced. But
there still lacked a constitution prescribing how Hawaiian laws
were to be made and who were the Hawaiians to make them.
The old traditional system was gone and something of value
was urgently needed to fill the lacuna. Land tenure had
become the urgent issue by the mid-1830s, as foreign investors
and merchants held the traditional tenure to be no guarantee.
For two years the chiefs begged the missionaries to help them
in constitutional and other matters of Western legality.
Finally, in 1838, the missionary William Richards resigned his
appointment and drafted the historic Declaration of Rights
and Code of Civil Law (1839) which attached to existing
criminal codes and became Hawai'i's first Constitution.

The latter formally defined Hawai'i's government as
consisting of civil rights, procedures for constitutional amendment, a House of Representatives and a Supreme Court.
Haole ('non-Hawaiian') planters and merchants resisted this
response to their entreaties because they believed it was a
direct or indirect missionary manoeuvre. What they desired
was a European- or American-style system of law controlled

by *haole* in order to guarantee their interests and maximize their profits. So the pressures continued to mount between the Hawaiians, who had discarded their past and were creating as best they knew a new European-influenced Hawaiian society, and the Americans, Germans, British and French who simply wanted the Hawaiian Islands for themselves.

Already in the 1820s and 1830s the merchants and consuls Richard Charlton of Britain and John C. Jones of the US had attacked native Hawaiian authority, even prompting foreign intervention as a result of slander and violence. In 1835 the first sugar-cane plantations were established by US investors; soon Germans were establishing their own plantations. In 1836 Charlton's outrages had forced the Hawaiian government to sign a disadvantageous treaty with Britain, and in 1843 Charlton's infamous litigation led Lord George Parlet to 'annex' Hawai'i to Britain. However, the 'annexation' was never ratified by the British parliament.

The Hawaiian government began the protracted process of standardizing land leases as it also issued a code of civil law. The whaling industry thereafter reached its pinnacle of profitability, which drained the population of several thousands of young Hawaiian men who served as crewmen (even into the 1850s). The upshot of this was that the plantation owners, chiefly Americans and Germans, feared the loss of their investments through a labour shortage, another epidemic in the late 1840s further reducing what was evidently a rapidly declining population of native Hawaiians. At the same time, those Hawaiians available to work the plantations did not exhibit the reliability the planters needed to turn a profit. As of 1848, the US influence in Hawai'i increased when America won the Mexican-American War and California became a principal centre for the expanding Asian trade. The planters of Hawai'i appealed directly to the Hawaiian government for modern legislation on land tenure and foreign labour. The act presented a dilemma to the government, which did not want to be dictated to by foreigners but which nevertheless saw this as an opportunity to allow the foreigners to bring prosperity to the Islands and ensure the survival of the indigenous government.

In 1848 the Hawaiian government individualized land holdings, with one stroke destroying time-honoured land tenure relationships. This at once imposed great hardship on many Hawaiians. However, because of the greatly reduced population of the Hawaiian Islands the act also rendered idle land productive, accessible and the key to future growth. In 1852, the government allowed *haole* fee-simple (unrestricted rights of disposal) ownership of land, opening up the market to even greater foreign investment.

Yet US tariff policies prevented profitable access to the nearest markets in California, though the 1849 gold-rush there helped to stay the negative impact of the declining whaling industry which was generating an economic depression in the Islands. Hawai'i's history in the second half of the 1800s involved its tug-and-pull with the US to solve economic impasses in a complex series of negotiations whereby Hawaiians wavered between compliance and defiance. It took 25 years for Hawai'i to achieve a trade reciprocity with the US, at the same time that Hawaiians were insisting on maintaining their sovereignty while US residents there were demanding US annexation.

The Hawaiian government, in the meantime, had finally acceded to the plantation owners' demands for the recruitment of labourers from outside the Islands. It authorized the importation of foreign labour in very restricted numbers, fearing foreign contamination. The planters then abused the authorization over successive decades by bringing in, as indentured labourers, tens of thousands of chiefly Japanese (mostly disadvantaged Okinawans), Koreans, Philippinos, Chinese (whom, along with blacks, the Hawaiian monarchy at first rejected for racial reasons), Puerto Ricans and Portuguese. Almost at once, this influx of new peoples radically altered the Islands' ethnic profile and created innumerable new difficulties for the Hawaiians and their beleaguered government.

Four main issues then determined Hawai'i's political destiny: labour recruitment free of racial repercussions and social imbalance; the attraction of foreign investment, particularly in Hawaiian plantations; the maintenance of a strong monarchy; and the acquisition and guarantee of access to US markets.

King Kamehameha III died young in 1854 while attempting to resolve all four issues. After him, first Kamehameha IV then Kamehameha V each spent about a decade wrestling unsatisfactorily with these same issues. The next king, Luna-lilo, was given to drink and did not last a year on the throne. The colourful Kalakaua (1873–91) escorted his people through an era of increasing debt and imminent revolution: Hawaiian conservatives called for the expropriation of foreign holdings, while *haole* whites, many born in the Islands, demanded closer ties with the US. By then the Hawaiian monarchy had assumed the lavish culture of the British royal family, Kalakaua making a celebrated world tour and embarking on a grand building scheme to make Honolulu a 'Pacific London'. By 1887, Kalakaua had amassed treaties and conventions with some 20 nations, at least five treaties or conventions with the US, and approximately 100 diplomatic and consular posts abroad for his sovereign state.

At the same time, the plantation owners and shipping magnates assumed colonial superiority and began secretly planning the violent overthrow of the Hawaiian government. It was that the landed gentry of sugar planters, many of them the children and grandchildren of the earliest missionaries, and their urban colleagues in shipping, had formed a new social stratum. Sugar, not the Hawaiian King, now ruled the Hawaiian Islands. By this time, democratic redress was impossible for injured Hawaiians because non-indigenous voters, as in New Zealand, far outnumbered indigenous voters. At the height of the tensions, in 1891, Kalakaua died, leaving his sister Lili'uokalani to reign as Queen of Hawai'i. She did not stand a chance, as she was pitted against the dynamic of history itself.

In 1892–93, the US consul to Hawai'i secretly encouraged a small group of white revolutionaries who, abetted by a US naval captain, forced the Queen to capitulate. Lili'uokalani did so under protest. The revolutionaries then declared a 'provisional government' whose primary intention was Hawai'i's annexation to the US. They attempted to legitimize their revolutionary regime by drafting a perfunctory 'constitution' and announcing a wealthy planter, Hawaiian-born Sanford J. Dole, son of a missionary, as first President of their self-styled 'Republic of Hawai'i'.

The Queen appealed to Washington, DC, to condemn the revolution by American nationals in the sovereign nation of Hawai'i. Indeed, the entire Western world was denouncing the heinous act. But the US Republican President, Benjamin Harrison, supported both the revolutionaries and their idea of annexation, the legislation for which latter proposition he then negotiated, signed and ratified.

But before the legislation could be forwarded to the US Senate for final approval, Harrison lost his Presidential re-election. When in 1893 the Democrat Grover Cleveland became the new President of the US, he strongly denounced what American nationals had done in Hawai'i. Cleveland told the US Congress that, under international law, the revolution was a 'disgrace' and he refused to forward the legislation. But in 1896 Cleveland himself lost the US Presidential election.

As of January 1897 the new President of the US was the Republican William McKinley who, like the Republican Harrison before him, wholly endorsed the revolutionaries. On 12 August 1898 the US Congress approved the Newlands Resolution which accepted the 'Republic of Hawai'i's' cession of sovereignty to the US and established a US territorial government in Hawai'i. The revolutionary Sanford Dole was appointed first Governor of the Territory of Hawai'i.

With the Organic Act of 1900, each citizen of the former 'Republic of Hawai'i' automatically became a US citizen and subject to US law, though no Hawaiian had ever been asked whether he or she wanted to become an American. Large tracts of land – the former Crown and government holdings – were then transferred to US Federal control. (Most of these so-called 'Ceded Lands' fell to the State of Hawai'i with statehood in 1959, but the US Federal Government kept vast areas for itself as military reservations.) The *haole* oligarchy thereafter commanded the economy and politics of the Hawaiian Islands for the next half century.

SAMOA

Samoa's greatest historical burden was that it lacked a centralized authority, its chiefs with the four-titled status of Tafa'ifa not ruling, but governing often very limited territories with only prestige and status as legitimization. In the 1830s, the murder of Samoa's leading Tafa'ifa had led to a competition between rivals to acquire the four titles necessary to confer Tafa'ifa or paramount status. A principal contender of the island of 'Upolu won and, as a converted Christian, might have revolutionized Samoan society, as the port settlement of 'Apia lay within his territory. But he proved to be a traditionalist, then died in 1841, and the competition for the status of Tafa'ifa led to new rivalries and even warfare from 1848 to 1856. Just at the time when ethnic cohesion was crucial to address the foreign trespass in the Samoan Islands, Samoans bitterly fought among themselves.

British and American settlers and naval officers sought to codify standards of law and land rights in order to protect their interests in the Islands, but there was no Samoan central authority which could help them achieve this. 'Apia, the centre of foreign activity, and Samoa in general direly needed governance of some kind. In this case, the solution came from the outside: from the establishment in 'Apia in 1856 of the company Johann Godeffroy und Sohn (GuS) of Hamburg, Germany, whose remarkable innovations in trading there changed all of Pacific Islands history.

Before GuS, Pacific trade had generally been ephemeral, haphazard and individualistic. GuS brought to the Pacific both corporate capital and a sustained base commodity – coconut oil. The copra or dried coconut flesh was pressed and its oil traded even in the smallest Pacific Islands communities, directly involving extremely isolated island populations for the first time in international Western commerce. There had been little demand for coconut oil before 1840; however, after this date the process of refining the coconut oil to produce soap and candles had reached a stage which at last made the trade profitable. Europeans and Americans then opened their markets to Pacific coconut oil. GuS now replaced small traders with company agents and made 'Apia on 'Upolu its commercial centre which collected the oil in large, unwieldy barrels from its vast network of island suppliers. By the early 1860s, more than 100 Europeans and Americans were living in 'Apia, which was soon to become one of Pacific Islands' main commercial centres.

GuS elaborated a scheme to maximize profitability: Company ownership of coconut tree plantations and Company hiring of labour. To achieve both, a compliant Samoan government was essential. Samoans of course resisted the scheme, reluctant above all to relinquish traditional land titles. But by 1864 a GuS manager had bought up several thousand acres on 'Upolu and had imported wage labourers from China and Melanesia. Whereupon he stopped receiving coconut oil in uneconomical barrels but demanded only the copra itself, which he then collected in 'Apia and shipped in bulk to foreign centres whose more sophisticated machines could more efficiently process the copra to extract the oil. This eliminated costly barrels and extraction stations as it greatly reduced Company shipping costs.

GuS grew rich while Samoans only feuded, missing their historical opportunity. The major issue for most Samoans was not the foreign trespass nor the chance to found a wealthy independent Samoa, but the title of Malietoa – one of the four highest-ranking titles which comprise the Tafa'ila – that was claimed in the 1860s by two rivals who refused to settle. Local Europeans still had no government or code of law to protect them, their only recourse to redress being the might of visiting naval officers. In 1869, Samoa's incipient cotton trade collapsed and the two rival Malietoa went to war. The war lasted four years, and European mediation clouded the final outcome so that Samoans perceived the unsatisfactory political solution as a temporary plaster. But the war had caused two fundamental changes in Samoan society: Europeans were now an inextricable part of it, and land tenure was no longer regarded as solely a Samoan prerogative.

Meanwhile, Germany's interest in Samoa had deepened. Since the mid-1850s GuS had demonstrated that Germany could play a major role in the commercial exploitation of the Central Pacific. The trade in coconut oil, later in copra, had brought more Germans to the large Samoan, Fijian and Tongan coconut plantations owned and managed by Germans. With Germany's unification in 1871, the German Imperial Navy entered the Pacific to protect its nationals and to promote their, and Germany's, interests, as other foreign powers already had been doing in the region for decades.

In 1879, 'Apia's non-Samoan residents, exploiting a civil war, enacted a municipal convention which in effect put control of 'Apia in European and American hands. However, this government, too, failed to satisfy rivals and maintain a lasting peace. As of this time, German interests in the Pacific focused mainly on Samoa, and so the German government eventually re-organized Godeffroy und Sohn into the Deutsche Handels- und Plantagen-Gesellschaft in the 1880s in order to realize imperialistic ambitions there. After Germany's treaty of 1884 provoked further civil unrest in Samoa, the three main foreign contenders, Germany, Britain and America, in 1885 called a series of conferences to resolve the impasse. However, nothing was resolved, and two years later Germany reconvened the series to settle the issue once and for all.

This was when the Deutsche Handels- und Plantagen-Gesellschaft staged a coup, forcing the nominal 'king' of Samoa, the Malietoa Laupepa, to flee. Whereupon the Germans installed their own puppet 'king'. But the new German government of Samoa – sanctioned perhaps by German naval officers but not by Berlin – quickly alienated resident British,

Americans and especially Samoans. In March 1889 the Samoans themselves rebelled in turn. Germany, Britain and the US immediately sent warships to 'Apia. When a hurricane struck, the seven men-of-war in 'Apia Harbour refused to seek the safety of open sea, fearing more that a rival might remain behind to annex Samoa. As a result, four ships were wrecked and 92 Germans and 54 Americans drowned; two further ships were beached and damaged. Samoans hailed the divine intervention, but Berlin, London and Washington were appalled at their nationals' arrogance and stupidity. The 'Samoan Question', all now agreed, had to be resolved permanently.

The military posturing ceased. The three nations, without Samoan participation, returned to the conference table. In June 1889, a Tripartite Treaty was signed by Germany, Britain and the US to form a 'neutral' government of the independent nation of Samoa led by a 'king' and the three respective consuls in 'Apia. Samoa's chief justice and prime minister were to be selected by the neutral King of Sweden. At the final conference the delegates appointed Samoa's 'king': the Malietoa Laupepa. (It was at this time, in 1889, that Robert Louis Stevenson and his wife Fanny settled at 'Apia.) Nevertheless, for ten more years rivalries continued to seethe, and even erupted in open warfare, with the new government proving to be as useless as all earlier ones. Samoa experienced many dynamic movements, but never knew lasting governance.

In Samoa, everyone had failed. The Samoans never appreciated the deeper implications of the foreign trespass. So they never ceased their intertribal feuding, never united and never profited from this trespass. And the Europeans and Americans failed to unite, too: they could not force the Samoans to achieve a stable government, and they could not agree among themselves on a viable foreign alternative. In the end, the solution was a weak government which betrayed the Samoan people's best interests as it polarized non-Samoans' allegiances.

The irrational outcome of this litany of failures was the division of Samoa into two separate legal entities: Germany and the US partitioned Samoa in 1899, each power taking half.

(Preoccupied with its own Boer War in South Africa, Britain bowed out, having received in compensation German concessions on the Tongan and Solomon Islands.) Samoa remains divided today.

TONGA

One man steered Tonga's destiny in the nineteenth century. Born in 1798, Tāufaʻāhau was political authority incarnate there until his death in 1893 at age 95. This personal supremacy, more than anything else, secured Tonga's successful transition to international peerage. Such a historical process was possible, however, only because of Tonga's precontact tradition of highly stratified authority.

Once Tāufaʻāhau had secured his fledgling reign's legitimacy at the end of the 1830s by introducing a Western-style code of laws which borrowed heavily from biblical injunctions, he warred against the island of Tongatapu in 1840 and five years later succeeded his uncle as Tuʻi Kanokupolu, finally achieving a re-united Tonga. It was then, in 1845, that Tāufaʻāhau declared himself to be 'King George Tupou I of Tonga' in imitation of his ideal King George IV of Britain (see Chapter 3). With the considered advice of British Wesleyan (WMS) missionaries, the Chief Justice of New Zealand and his own tribal chiefs, and after familiarizing himself with the Society Islands' legal codes of the 1820s, King George enacted a new code of laws in 1850, proclaiming the King of Tonga to be the solitary form of government and source of all law in the Tongan Islands.

Within two years civil war ravaged Tonga as dissident chiefs challenged the new oligarchy. But King George suppressed all opposition and consolidated his power, whereupon he concentrated his efforts on acquiring, as Hawaiʻi had done, foreign recognition of Tonga as an equal among nations. King George actively aspired to good government and international respect in order to guarantee Tonga's continued independence, purposefully avoiding those pitfalls which had destroyed the native regimes of other Polynesian islands. A direct result of this sophisticated policy was Tonga's highly evolved law code of 1862. For this, King George had sought wide foreign advice and, in 1853, had even travelled to Australia. He was cautious and acutely sensitive to the sentiments of opposing factions, which included Tonga's older WMS missionaries whom his autocratic policies had partially alienated. Of particular concern had been the protests of Roman Catholic priests in Tonga who had been appealing to the French Imperial Navy, as had happened at Tahiti with dire consequences.

Though King George's new code of 1862 essentially upheld the code of 1850 with its declaration of the absolute authority of the King of Tonga, it also introduced regular taxation to finance a budgeted government, compulsory education for children, new principles of land distribution and the emancipation of all Tongan serfs. In this way, Tonga in the 1860s became, with Hawai'i, Pacific Islands' most sophisticated indigenous monarchy. The new code weakened the many chiefs' authority while strengthening that of the King, introducing greater internal stability. In the formulation of the new code King George received substantial assistance from the young WMS missionary Shirley Baker, who then went on to become the King's personal advisor.

Over the next decade King George and Baker focused their efforts on framing Tonga's first formal constitution. Its announcement in 1875 gave Tonga its first legislative assembly, half of its 40 members being popularly elected delegates. The King and Baker also tried to establish a Church of Tonga; though this attempt failed, it resulted nevertheless in the Wesleyans allowing greater autonomy in religious matters in the Islands and diminishing Tonga's financial burden to foreign missions. In 1876 the King and Baker also concluded a treaty of friendship with Germany – a cunning posture to counter French aggression and British indifference – which allowed the Kaiser the use of Vava'u's harbour for a coaling station if, for his part, the Kaiser recognized Tonga as an equal among nations. Britain was then forced to ratify its own treaty with Tonga in 1879 (eventually prompting the US in turn to conclude a treaty with the island nation in 1888).

In 1880, King George appointed Shirley Baker his prime minister, making the ex-missionary one of the most influential statesmen in this transitional era of Pacific Islands history. From this period on, Tonga's government approached ever closer the European model while remaining independent, much to the chagrin of Tonga's white settlers, and also King George's rival chiefs who disdained European-style 'democratic' reforms.

In 1885 the Free Church of Tonga was heralded as an entity independent of the Wesleyans, a move that did nothing to change Tonga's Christian canons but everything to promote the Islands' sense of sovereignty. Many Tongans refused to quit the Wesleyan Church, however. The King, reading this as civil disobedience, had them flogged, dispossessed and dismissed from public office, among other measures. Shirley Baker was nearly assassinated by the King's opponents for his part in the affair.

As a result, many loyal Tongans turned against the Wesleyan Church, whereupon white settlers cried religious persecution. Taking a vociferous stand, Baker publicly accused the British consul of complicity in the foiled assassination attempt. This was what Britain had been waiting for: its High Commissioner for the Western Pacific then convinced King George that Baker had transgressed his authority as prime minister, and the King dismissed Baker from office after nearly 25 years of unparalleled service to Tonga's monarch. Whereupon Britain's High Commissioner then saw that Baker was expelled from the kingdom. Baker finally left in 1890.

With Baker out of the way, Britain used the need for new reforms in law and administration in Tonga as a pretext to directly intervene in local politics, something Baker had always prevented. After a decade of immediate British influence at the highest levels of government, a decade which had also seen the death of King George in 1893, Tonga signed a Treaty of Friendship with Britain which established a British 'protectorate' there in 1900. Yet the monarchy endured.

FIJI

Warfare was raging in the Fiji Islands when WMS missionaries arrived from Tonga in 1835, and it was not until 1849 that they achieved their first conversions of importance: that of the Tui Nayau, paramount chief of the Lau group. When Fijian chief Cakobau of Bau, overlord of the Lau group, learnt of this conversion he threatened war against the Laus. But large numbers of Tongans occupied Lakeba in the Laus, and so Cakobau desisted. Because he did not attack, the Tongan chief Ma'afu – who had come to Fiji in 1847 and who, as of 1853, governed the Tongans there by appointment of his cousin King George Tupou I of Tonga – rose to prominence as Cakobau's chief rival. The Tongan Ma'afu also knew how to use both the Wesleyan mission there and its many Tongan converts, among them mission teachers, to influence and persuade local Fijians to endorse the Tongan cause. Cakobau became embroiled in warfare elsewhere and lost, leading to internal rebellion and insurrection. His chiefdom was on the point of collapse.

In a brilliant move, in April 1854 Cakobau converted to Christianity and within one year commanded the western region of the Koro Sea. But he did not yet control Fiji's main island of Viti Levu, nor the eastern Laus where Ma'afu continued to expand his power base, even up into Fiji's second largest island, Vanua Levu.

However, Europeans had begun settling at the port of Levuka on the island of Ovalau northeast of Bau, purchasing land from local chiefs for cotton and coconut plantations. The USA's 'commercial agent' in Fiji was one John Brown Williams who held Cakobau, as paramount chief of the Bau region, personally responsible for a series of misfortunes which had been the result of Williams's own poor luck and folly. By 1855, other Americans on Fiji made similar claims against other chiefs, and they and Williams asked exorbitantly inflated sums as 'compensation'. A US naval officer commanded Cakobau to pay up, as Cakobau was the Tui Viti or 'King of Fiji'. Cakobau protested to the US consul in Sydney, Williams's superior, but the protest fell on deaf ears.

Williams continued to hound Cakobau for payment and in 1858 another visiting US naval officer again commanded him to pay the alleged 'debt'. Seeing no recourse, Cakobau approached Britain's recently arrived first consul in Fiji, W. T. Pritchard, with a remarkable proposal: Cakobau would 'cede' Fiji to Britain if Britain agreed to settle the so-called 'American debt'. It was an inspired manoeuvre: only Britain's patronage could halt the Tongan Ma'afu's encroachment in northern Fiji while allowing Cakobau to rule as Tui Viti throughout the land.

For the next four years Britain did not respond, however, and Fiji's true power lay with Ma'afu in the north and with Pritchard in the south of the Fiji Islands, both of them promoting stable governance and maintaining peaceful relations between all parties. But then in 1862 Britain refused Cakobau's proposal and terminated Pritchard's exceptional consulship. The Wesleyan missionaries and the new British consul established a confederation of Fijian 'states' in 1865, but this failed two years later when Ma'afu, seeing his power base lost, withdrew to found his own confederation of Northern and Eastern Fiji. Because of internal rivalries, Ma'afu's confederation was short-lived. Ma'afu shrank his demesne voluntarily to the Lau group and introduced there a highly efficient, European-style chiefdom which was eminently successful, profiting from a European secretary and European advisors.

When the southern confederation collapsed, a white-led government was formed, crowning Cakobau 'king' but ruling themselves through a poorly managed white legislature to enact pro-white legislation. Virtually everyone in Fiji, however, simply ignored its rulings. Again the US Navy returned to demand payment of the ludicrous 'American debt'. Now Melbourne entrepreneurs sprang to Cakobau's aid: they would pay the Americans and grant Cakobau an annuity in exchange for 200 000 acres of Fijian land and the right to operate in Fiji as a mercantile monopoly. With no alternative, Cakobau agreed.

The subsequent Polynesia Company brought increased numbers of foreigners to Fiji, a land-rush and a complete loss of law and order. Pressed by complaints from all quarters, Cakobau declared a new government under the old 1867 constitution. Yet this failed to settle the growing civil unrest and racial violence, as the demands of native Fijians were never those of the foreign settlers and their immigrant labourers. In 1874, Cakobau saw the hopelessness of his situation and again offered to cede Fiji to Britain, whereupon Britain now immediately accepted. In October 1874, Fiji was at last declared a British 'possession'.

In 1876, a punitive expedition into central Viti Levu forced the hill tribes to submit to British rule. One year later, Britain's High Commission for the Western Pacific was established in order to protect British interests in all surrounding island groups, which led in 1881 to Rotuma being annexed to Fiji. The following year Fiji's capital moved from Levuka to Suva, from where two British administrators created a modern Fijian state almost single-handedly: the first British Governor, Arthur Gordon; and his colonial secretary and successor, John Thurston.

'Ruling' indirectly through Fijian chiefs, Governor Gordon and Secretary Thurston decreed that no Fijian land could be sold, only leased; this then secured traditional communal lands underlying Fiji's chieftain system. They also ensured that no Fijian could be forced to labour on European plantations. By the 1880s, sugar had replaced cotton as Fiji's economic mainstay. However, since the Pacific Islanders Protection Act of 1872 (see p. 155) Fijian plantation owners were no longer allowed to recruit Solomon Islanders and New Hebrideans as before. With Fijians now exempt from forced labour, the severe labour shortage in the Fiji Islands threatened to bankrupt the local economy.

Governor Gordon, who had earlier served in Trinidad and Mauritius, believed Indian indentured labourers would solve the labour crisis and so, in 1879, the first Indians arrived in Fiji (37 years later, when Indian immigration ceased, there were 63 000 in Fiji). In order to come, the Indians had to indenture themselves to five years in Fiji's sugar-cane plantations, after which they could lease small plots from the Fijians for another five years to plant sugar-cane or raise livestock. Upon expiry of the ten-year contract, they could then return to India or Ceylon (Sri Lanka) with their earned capital or remain in Fiji. Over half chose to remain.

Gordon and Thurston's plan worked eminently well: European capital, Fijian land and Indian labour not only saved the plantations from bankruptcy but generated large profits and preserved the Fijian chieftainships ... yet at the cost of marginalizing the Indians who failed to take part in the country's prosperity. (The same special rights for indigenous Fijians which the British government established in the nineteenth century are still in force in the twenty-first century, continuing to thwart the attainment of stable and equitable governance there.)

When Europeans began colonizing Fiji, there were around 150 000 Fijians. However, Cakobau and two of his sons returned from an Australian consultation infected with measles. Though they recovered, the subsequent epidemic slew nearly one out of every three Fijians. The deaths continued. By 1881, 115 000 Fijians were left; by 1921, 84 000, only slightly higher than the number of Indians in the Fiji Islands.

Fiji had come alarmingly close to becoming a Tongan kingdom in the 1860s, but traditional feuding and the increasing numbers of European settlers thwarted Ma'afu's ascension. In this way Fiji was perhaps saved for the Fijians, but only to come in the end, for the same reasons, under Britain's 'benevolent yoke'. Thereafter, Fiji has ceaselessly struggled to attain its true majority.

GREATER MELANESIA

Apart from Fiji which had always been closer to Polynesia in its social structure and general attractiveness to European settlers and missionaries, greater Melanesia for the most part had escaped the main foreign trespass. Its nineteenth-century history was chiefly dominated by two activities: the sandalwood trade of the 1840s and 1850s and the labour 'recruitment' trade from the 1860s to the early twentieth century. Though in smaller volume than that of its Polynesian counterpart, Melanesia's increasing mercantilism had attracted muskets and other manufactured goods, augmenting competitiveness for public display of wealth, multiplying and intensifying warfare, and introducing European diseases which here, too, ravaged island populations. Changes came more slowly to Melanesia. But they came, and with similar cruelty.

The first sandalwood traders converged on Erromango in the New Hebrides (now Vanuatu) in 1829–30, but halted their enterprise because of mismanagement and native abuse (see Chapter 3). The trade recommenced in 1841 on a much grander scale in the southern New Hebrides, New Caledonia and the Loyalty Islands. It was always a dangerous and treacherous undertaking, rife with violence, fraud and theft. At first Islanders performed all tasks, including onboard delivery, but local wars, ceremonies or harvests too frequently lost valuable working days. Shipmasters therefore soon established shore stations of stockpiled sandalwood where vessels could quickly load then leave. For permanent shore parties, the masters recruited Melanesians from other islands in order to avoid local rivalries and kinship obligations.

The few stations of the 1840s became many by the 1850s. Some large islands had several. This brought Melanesians directly into the international shipping trade; many now signed on as crewmen, just as Hawaiians, Tahitians, Māori and other Polynesians had done in the first decades of the 1800s. The presence of shore stations and increased contact with Europeans helped to reduce the general violence in the region by the mid-1850s. Melanesians also began to appreciate the immediate benefits of regulated commerce, and grew more dependent on it. Though the trade in sandalwood remained dangerous and wrought with vice, it had its humane practitioners, too, who brought wealth and foreign invention to the region. Missionaries often settled only where sandalwood traders had first been successful: in time this led to mass conversions which, in turn, then made Melanesians reject the sandalwood traders and their generally vice-ridden activities.

The sandalwood trade in Melanesia lasted only 20 years. For the Europeans and Americans in the traffic, risks were great and losses were high. Though few in numbers, these non-Melanesian trespassers exposed entire societies for the first time to the fundamentally contrary European way of life. By the 1860s, sandalwood trading had ceased entirely, but new forces were then already in motion which would soon be sapping the very life blood from countless Melanesian islands.

The high price of cotton caused by the American Civil War in the early 1860s led several sandalwood traders and other capitalists in Australia to import Melanesian labourers to work Queensland's new cotton plantations. This commerce in human cargo soon became a lucrative trade in itself, with Erromango and Tanna in the New Hebrides its new arenas. However, the traffic never led to the mass atrocity which Peru had committed in Polynesia in 1862–64: Melanesia's population was much larger, its traders well known, its missionaries well established on most of the islands, with the British Royal Navy regularly patrolling the region and the Australian reading public keeping a watchful eye.

Still, the trafficking in Melanesians grew in the 1860s, as did its agents' ruthlessness. Imported labourers were frequently arriving sick and dying; isolated violent acts occurred which shocked Australia's citizenry. In response, Queensland passed the Polynesian Labourers Act to regulate the trade and reduce the suffering. Nevertheless, little changed. And the Act's jurisdiction did not extend to those Melanesians recruited for the plantations of Fiji and Samoa. Isolated incidents continued to outrage concerned Australians, but nothing was done…until the '*Carl* Incident' in 1871.

When near Bougainville the 180 kidnapped Solomon Islanders crowded into the *Carl's* hold tried to escape, the vessel's crew used them as target practice until 50 were dead and 20 wounded; all 70 were then tossed to the sharks. When the capitals of the world learnt of this atrocity, there was outrage, then loud protestations. The following year saw the British government passing the Pacific Islanders Protection Act, which ensured the active implementation of the Queensland act of 1868. Though the new Protection Act did quell most cases of violence, it also raised the stakes: when the more punitory patrol ships approached, some shipmasters now chained their human cargoes to weighted lines and tossed them overboard.

Between the 1860s and 1900 the labour trade principally brought northern and western Melanesians into contact with Europeans. If the New Hebrides furnished most labourers in the 1860s, cheaper and more recruits were taken from the Solomons in the 1870s. By the 1880s, Germany had secured the rights to recruit exclusively in the northern Solomons and northeastern New Guinea for its plantations in New Guinea and Samoa, where mortality was particularly high.

Labour recruitment effected the historical changes in Melanesia which whaling had already brought about in Polynesia. It reversed Melanesia's fortunes once the sandalwood trade had collapsed. It exposed up to 100 000 Melanesians directly to European settlement life. And it introduced an unprecedented supply of manufactured goods, liquor and tobacco to Melanesians, who thereafter felt they could not live without these things. For the involved Europeans – mostly Britons and Germans – it meant the first rules of law in Melanesia, which then led to the formation of the High Commission for the Western Pacific as well as of the British and German governments of the Solomon Islands (see below).

Labour recruitment also formed new rhythms of village life in much of Melanesia. Destinations became more familiar.

Returning after three years' servitude with cash and goods, most labourers saw their community status greatly increased. Over the decades the voluntary exile became a pattern of Melanesian life, whereby even the traditional bride-price was expected to be earned through overseas experience.

One unexpected benefit of labour recruitment was the creation of common languages for the region. Solomon Islanders returned speaking Pijin, New Hebrideans Bislama and Papuans Tok Pisin. Now widely spoken in the region as a local *lingua franca* consisting of 80 to 90 per cent English with a mixture of local vocabularies, each is actually a separate indigenous language, formed on a foreign framework, which serves as a powerful emblem of the native franchise. Melanesians from disparate communities were now not only able to communicate with one another, but also to share an ethnic identity transcending traditional rivalries. In time, this ability would pilot Melanesians towards a concept of nationhood.

Many believe Melanesians would better have been spared the vices of sandalwood and labour recruitment, what with both's devastating repercussions. But the European incursion had been inevitable. Great wrongs were committed, certainly, but such things happened throughout Pacific Islands. The form of change which emerged in Melanesia left traditional lifestyles more intact than in Polynesia, as Melanesians generally escaped massive commercialization and colonization, and experienced a slower transition to a more Europeanized way of life. For outsiders, Melanesian settlement was a far more complex and hazardous undertaking than Polynesian settlement had ever been. Because of this, foreign settlers were few.

The French had early shown an interest in settling Melanesia. Its Society of Mary (Marist) missions there, first established in New Caledonia in 1843, then two years later in the Solomons, did not endure. Only Balade in New Caledonia survived, which eventually prompted France to annex New Caledonia in 1853 as a potential stage for mass settlement, in imitation of what Britain had done in New Zealand. The French government even instituted a generous policy of land grants there, greatly facilitated by simply ignoring traditional tenures of the 'Kanaks' or indigenous New Caledonians (from whaling-era pidgin and Hawaiian *kanaka* or 'person'). In the 1860s, gold was discovered in New Caledonia just as France decided to make the island a penal colony, again in imitation of what Britain had done over half a century earlier in New South Wales, Tasmania and Norfolk Island.

Whereupon a large number of both French and British settlers arrived on New Caledonia's Grande Terre. When Catholic and Protestant missions in the Loyalty Islands east of New Caledonia began squabbling with each other in 1864, New Caledonia's French Governor peremptorily annexed the entire group to France as well. Between 1864 and 1897 around 20 000 French convicts, sentenced to more than eight years' hard labour, arrived on the Grande Terre. From 1871 to 1879, these also included celebrated political prisoners from the Paris Commune, many of them cultured intellectuals. Convicts laboured mostly on public works and construction projects, but they were also hired out to work the land of free settlers.

New Caledonia was rich in other ores as well: nickel was discovered in 1864, copper in 1872 and cobalt in 1875. In 1876, the Société de Nickel was founded, whereupon New Caledonia became one of the world's leading suppliers of this ore. As a direct result, France accelerated its land seizures. Food became scarce as Kanak land rapidly disappeared. Because the Kanaks increasingly felt their world threatened, in 1878 chief Atai of La Foa united several central tribes and rose up against the French oppressors: 200 Frenchmen and 1200 Kanaks lost their lives in the subsequent fighting.

After this, France began placing the Kanaks in 'indigenous reservations' located on lands no one else wanted, then exploited most of the Grande Terre for mining and cattle. Clans who had lost traditional lands were forced to move elsewhere, infringing on other clans' lands and causing further conflict. Released convicts, siding with their government against the Kanaks, also took control of vast tracts as resident farmers. Their progeny then became the *caldoches*, New Caledonian-born Frenchmen and Frenchwomen. In this way, by the end of the 1800s France had seized title to two-thirds of the Grande Terre. A further quarter had been granted or sold to foreign settlers, leaving only 10 per cent – of unwanted hilly terrain – in Kanak ownership, whose titles were then often challenged. By then most tribes had been relocated to the 150 'reservations' policed by French gendarmes, their inhabitants imposed with a heavy poll tax forcing them to work for the settlers as day labourers in order to earn the cash to pay the tax. Within nine years alone, from 1878 to 1887, the Kanak population shrank by nearly a third.

At the same time as this was occurring, many settlers – most of them Britons – were establishing cotton and coconut plantations in the New Hebrides (now Vanuatu) northeast of New Caledonia. However, by the 1870s cotton prices had fallen and labour had become harder to acquire. By the 1880s, settlers were glad to sell and leave. Their plantations were being bought up by John Higginson, an Irishman with French citizenship, whose wish was to see the New Hebrides become a French colony. When France failed to respond to Higginson's overtures, however, Higginson founded his own company in 1882, which then commenced specifically buying up all the Britons' plantations to eliminate the British presence there. Local Presbyterian missionaries and their Australian benefactors did not relish the idea of yet another French annexation so close to Australia, especially once France was claiming, between 1882 and 1884, the New Hebrides as its protectorate. They eventually convinced Australian colonial governments to have the British government halt France's formal ratification of the protectorate. In 1887, Britain and France achieved a compromise agreement concerning the New Hebrides: neither would annex the group or create a protectorate there, but both would maintain a joint naval commission to oversee Europeans' interests in the islands.

Two years later, a group of Australians formed a rival company to Higginson's, which quickly prospered. By the mid-1890s both companies experienced financial straits and so re-organized themselves into two different legal entities: Higginson's French company became the Société Française des Nouvelles-Hébrides in 1894, subsidized by the French government; and the Australian company was taken over by Burns, Philp and Co. in 1897. Both prevented either country from mastery over the New Hebrides. European settlement and development grew steadily and peacefully in the group, albeit on a small scale because of isolation and climate.

In the 1870s, the natural dynamic of expanding colonial markets drove European entrepreneurs northward and westward: into the Solomons and New Guinea.

Missionization of the Solomons had earnestly commenced in the 1850s, with the arrival of Anglican Solomon Islander proselytes of New Zealand's Melanesian Mission (now the Church of Melanesia). By the 1860s, the several waves of traders in *bêche-de-mer*, mother-of-pearl, turtle shell and sandalwood had ceased. In the 1870s copra became a lucrative trade there. Many Solomon Islanders were also violently 'recruited' for Queensland's and Fiji's sugar-cane plantations at this time, which sparked a wave of anti-European reprisals, including the murder of several reputable traders and innocent missionaries. From 1870 to 1910, around 30 000 Solomon Islanders were recruited; 10 000 never came back.

Australia's alarm at Germany's sudden expansion into neighbouring New Guinea prompted Britain in 1884 to declare a protectorate over Papua, New Guinea's southeastern quarter. When in the early 1890s the Germans were forming plantations in their formal possessions Buka and Bougainville (North Solomons), the British in 1893 declared a protectorate over New Georgia, Guadalcanal, Makira and Malaita, where in truth only very few Europeans resided. Already in 1885 the British naturalist Charles Woodford had been dispatched by the British Museum to collect specimens in the Solomons. By 1896, he was Britain's resident commissioner there, with headquarters at Tulagi, a small island in the Florida Group. In 1898 and 1899 Woodford oversaw the incorporation of the Santa

Cruz group, Rennell and Bellona into the British Solomon Islands Protectorate. Finally, in 1900 Germany ceded to the British Crown the Shortlands, Choiseul, Santa Isabel and Ontong Java in return for Britain's promise not to prevent Germany's annexation of Samoa. Britain was now in full 'control' of the Solomons but, apart from major plantation establishments, life beyond the coastal strip changed little.

In the second half of the nineteenth century Pacific Islands' largest landmass, New Guinea, was the region's greatest magnet for traders, missionaries, prospectors and natural scientists from all over the globe. Its western half had been annexed by the Netherlands in 1828 and again in 1848, and was called Dutch New Guinea (now Irian Jaya). Britain had sent naval surveyors to Papua in the 1840s and 1850s. Missionaries had had little success there: a French Catholic mission was finally established on Woodlark Island in the southern Solomon Sea in 1847 but was abandoned eight years later. By the 1870s, the LMS and WMS had Polynesian and European missionaries on Papua's south coast and in the Bismarcks, whereupon a new generation of traders arrived with grandiose schemes for the region.

These were chiefly Germans who represented the firms Godeffroy und Sohn and Hernsheim und Co. By 1878 the manager of Godeffroy und Sohn had purchased substantial tracts of land, with harbours, in New Guinea and its offshore islands. However, gold had been discovered in Port Moresby's hinterland in 1877, which had also been attracting pro-spectors, mostly Australians and New Zealanders, to New Guinea's southern coast. Several colonizing associations were formed in the 1870s, chiefly in Australia, which manipulated public opinion to view New Guinea as a 'natural extension' of Australia's colonial destiny.

In 1878 Britain's High Commission for the Western Pacific announced that a Deputy Commissioner was to oversee all British subjects in New Guinea. By this time, so many Australians were prospecting in the Port Moresby area that Queensland dispatched a magistrate there. But in 1882, Queenland's labour recruiters began penetrating areas where German labour recruiters had been finding workers for Germany's Samoan plantations. The conflict that ensued greatly intensified when, in 1883, Queensland's premier independently declared his province's 'annexation' of Papua and its offshore islands.

The premier's move was a calculated attempt to prompt 'responsible' British intervention in order to secure New Guinea for Australian commercial development. Britain did respond, inviting Germany to negotiate a settlement. This resulted in the two countries partitioning New Guinea between each other in 1884, with the final boundaries of Britain's British New Guinea and Germany's Kaiser Wilhelms-Land (Northern Papua), Neu-Pommern (New Britain), Neu-Mecklenburg (New Ireland) and Buka and Bougainville in the Solomons agreed by both parties in 1886.

Despite the foreign settlement, most indigenous New Guineans in British New Guinea still lived in isolated communities and had no knowledge of their new international status, experiencing little or no contact with outsiders. In Deutsches Ost-Neuguinea, however, the two re-organized firms of the Deutsche Handels- und Plantagen-Gesellschaft (formerly Godeffroy und Sohn) and Robertson & Hernsheim (formerly Hernsheim und Co.) actively traded and recruited labour along the coasts, though inland penetration was still minimal. By 1900, many German trade settlements had been established there, paving the way for the colonization which was soon to follow.

Melanesia was now at the stage Polynesia had already reached around 1820. It was still generally isolated, hostile and awaiting exploitation – no longer by individual traders or shipmasters, but by the large companies which had usurped Pacific Islands' economies. Much had changed in Melanesia because of labour recruitment, population crashes, European settlement and local reliance on foreign manufactured goods. However, large parts of Melanesia, particularly in New Guinea, were not only untouched but unexplored, their inhabitants still unaware of the white trespassers and their dangerous gifts.

MICRONESIA

Though, like Melanesia, Micronesia was one of the first regions of Pacific Islands to be encountered by Europeans, it experienced continuous contact only late, in the 1850s. Of course, during most of the whaling era Kusaie (now Kosrae) and Ponape (Pohnpei) in the eastern Carolines were infamous for foreign vices of every breed. It was thus to these islands that the American Board of Commissioners for Foreign Missions – having been eminently successful in the Hawaiian Islands – sent its missionaries in 1852, assisted by native-Hawaiian proselytes. Their message and missions were much needed: both islands had abandoned time-honoured traditions for nothing of substance. Within a decade, they began recovering from the worst excesses of foreign contact, with most Islanders converting to Christianity.

This almost immediate acceptance of Christianity evidently fulfilled a deeply sensed need among Micronesians there. The Board also sent missionaries to the Marshall and Gilbert Islands in the late 1850s and these were similarly successful within a short period of time. Already by the 1870s – that is, within one generation – the new Christian churches and their own mission outreach programmes lay almost entirely in the hands of indigenous Micronesians. This had far-reaching repercussions for the general level of education, literacy and Europeanization or Americanization of the Micronesian people. Though a change in chieftancy intermittently saw 'heathen' movements challenging the Christian foothold, the missionaries and their faith were firm and most Micronesians were Christian by 1900 (in great contrast to many areas of Melanesia which have resisted conversion up to the present day).

Though political reforms were attempted by some missionaries and converted chiefs along Christian tenets – land tenure, more democratic representation and other initiatives – these seldom succeeded. Most missionaries simply concentrated on basics like belief, dress, sexual habits and general behaviour. The missionaries also greatly altered Micronesian settlement patterns by introducing the perceived Christian virtue of village life in individual households, concentrating populations around the missions. The work of the missionaries of course prepared the way for European and American traders (nearly all of whom, until then, had feared and avoided Micronesians).

For example, missionaries had also introduced to Micronesians many manufactured goods that the Islanders had soon grown to covet. This offered a ready market for traders, though traditional items such as firearms, alcohol and tobacco found little demand in these new mission communities. In exchange, Micronesians were encouraged to establish coconut tree plantations for copra which, by the 1870s, could then be marketed by large merchant companies with sufficient capital to invest, direct, distribute and cushion the trade. Small traders had never prospered in Micronesia, chiefly because of isolation, hostility and lack of local resources. But the international 'capitalization' of Pacific Islands in the 1870s allowed Micronesians at last to profit from Pacific commerce and Micronesia was opened up to global trade, providing a small share of the copra which eventually became Europe's and America's soap and candles.

Already in the 1860s Adolph Capelle had had a small fleet of schooners collecting copra in the Marshalls and eastern Carolines, and the Samoan vessels of the firm Godeffroy und Sohn were arriving then for copra, too. In the 1870s, these businesses were being challenged by Hernsheim und Co. from Germany and by Henderson and MacFarlane from New Zealand. However, copra yields in Micronesia were always small in comparison with those of the larger Polynesian islands, and international dealers, threatened by foreign competition in such small markets, sought the intervention of major powers to secure their fragile investments in the region. The navies of Britain, Germany and the USA conducted occasional patrols of Micronesia and also intervened on direct appeal from their nationals, on every occasion imposing unfair restrictions on local chiefs: this was because Micronesia lacked the large, hierarchical, centralized societies of Polynesia which usually obliged foreign powers to compromise. Each Micronesian island was considered 'fair game', with gun-boat diplomacy succeeding here as nowhere else on Earth at the time.

Micronesia also held insufficient numbers of foreigners to warrant the establishment of a Western-style state with a constitution (which might also have brought some form of legal protection to the Micronesians as well). Companies seeking political stability had to turn to their own countries for it. Godeffroy und Sohn, for example, were directly involving German naval officers and consuls in securing Company rights in the region. A similar treaty with Tonga had already been signed in 1876, whereupon two years later Captain von Werner reconnoitered German interests in the Western Pacific and purchased rights to several harbours in New Britain, as well as concluding a treaty with Jaluit's chief in the Marshalls. The Germans were the first, in 1878, to secure privileges for German nationals from their marionette 'king' of the Ralik group in the Marshall Islands. Similarly one-sided 'treaties' were concluded in the same year in the Gilberts. In essence, Micronesian chiefs lost all jurisdiction over Germans on their islands, any violation of German 'sanctity' to be met with swift German reprisal.

Only four years earlier than this, in 1874, Spain had declared its 'historical claim' to the Carolines, several islands of which Spanish explorers had first sighted in 1564 (see Chapter 3). As Europeans in both Europe and Micronesia were ever more vociferously calling for the annexation of entire groups in Micronesia, Spain reiterated its claim to the Carolines in the early 1880s. Yet, at the same time, Germany, which boasted the largest number of nationals in Micronesia (followed by Britain and the US), was actively undertaking the creation of protectorates there or trying to annex whole groups for the Kaiser.

In 1884, the German government was becoming formally involved in New Guinea, which Britain had until then largely ignored despite the precipitous 'annexation' of Papua (southeastern New Guinea) by Queensland's premier. Because Spain was protesting Germany's simultaneous machinations in 'Spain's Micronesia', a compromise agreement was signed in 1885: Spain 'allowed' Germany to annex the Marshalls, while Germany in turn 'allowed' Spain to annex the Carolines, so long as Spain conceded to Germany naval stations and trading rights there. When Britain had still been negotiating with Germany over the issue of New Guinea, Germany had declared New Guinea's northeastern quarter to be its protectorate. Britain had immediately retaliated by declaring New Guinea's southeastern quarter its protectorate, and shortly a border was agreed upon by both nations (see above). The ill feeling this had engendered between Germany and Britain led to the signing of a convention which spelt out exactly what belonged to which power in the region: Germany was allowed the Marshalls, Carolines, Palau and the northern Solomons (Buka, Bougainville, Choiseul and Santa Isabel), while Britain obtained the Gilbert Islands (now Kiribati) and Ellice Islands (Tuvalu).

With this international legitimization, Germany then proceeded to confirm its dominion over the entire region by establishing protectorates everywhere but the Carolines and Palau (bowing to the Spanish claims there). Whereupon Germany formed the Jaluit Company, which then incorporated all of Germany's businesses in the Marshalls and, in 1887, became the group's governing body. One year later, Germany annexed the island of Nauru as well.

Only the Gilbert and Ellice Islands lay outside foreign disposition, whose economy lay principally in British hands while Britain still abstained from making the islands its formal protectorates. But this had little meaning in a region which, by the 1880s, had lost as much as half of its population to disease and associated factors. By the end of the decade, Germany found that current treaties impacted badly on its labour recruitment in the Western Pacific, and complained to Britain for failing to control the illegal acts of its nationals in the region. Finally, in 1891, the Kaiser demanded of his aunt Queen Victoria that her government enforce Britain's laws there. Perhaps in response to the German insistence, Britain finally made the Gilbert and Ellice Islands its formal protectorates in 1892. One year later, Britain declared the southern Solomons its protectorate as well.

The conclusion of the nineteenth century brought a sudden rash of dispossessions. In 1898, the death of King Malietoa Laupepa of Samoa necessitated new international conferences on the 'Samoan Question' which produced no lasting solution. In 1899, Germany annexed Western Samoa, but in order to achieve this Germany had been forced to cede the German islands of the Solomons – but for Buka and Bougainville – to Britain. At the same time, Britain concluded a Treaty of Friendship with Tonga which all but created a British protectorate there. Germany then purchased from Spain the islands of the Marianas, Carolines and Palau in Micronesia, which it formally annexed. And the new Republican administration in the USA, as a result of its victory in the Spanish-American War of 1898, acquired Guam as it also endorsed the white revolutionaries of the 'Republic of Hawai'i', annexing all of the Hawaiian Islands to the USA; this was followed by the USA's acquisition of Eastern Samoa in 1899.

Like most of Polynesia, Micronesia had lost its traditions, its customs, even its people. What came in their place was neither understood nor fulfilling: a seeming vacuum which left Micronesians waiting for something of value that never arrived.

**

Though all of Pacific Islands had come under the authority of foreign states by 1900, this was neither political design nor 'racial' arrogance, as many historians earlier claimed, but rather the natural result of a long and bitterly contested historical dynamic. The foreign dispossession of Pacific Islands occurred – in most, but not all, instances – to contain the real or perceived confusion created by the frequently irrational and rapacious intercourse between trespassers and Islanders and between rival foreign powers. Each insular or archipelagic episode is merely a variant of this theme.

There was, then, no nineteenth-century European and American 'land-grab' in Pacific Islands. Britain, seemingly forever dedicated to the principle of insular indifference, found itself time and again drawn into political conflicts necessitating ever greater commitments which, in the end, saw Britain as the nation with the largest colonial encumbrance in the Pacific. France experienced separate Polynesian and Melanesian phases which, once its possessions were secured, at length simply wilted into administrative ennui. Germany's aggressive Pacific policy after national unification in the 1870s forced rivals to chase after what they otherwise might have ignored. This, in turn, drew in those final nations who shared the last slices of the 'Pacific pie'.

When trespass became invasion, all of Pacific Islands changed. Only superficially did each island or archipelago go its own way: underlying each episode of ineluctable assimilation were pan-Pacific constants, such as intertribal hatreds thwarting a united resistance, the Islanders' failure to establish lasting governments, and their increasing dependency on foreign masters' goods and customs. In contrast, Europeans and Americans always strengthened their hold in Pacific Islands, depressing the indigenous prerogative in order to replicate the foreign archetype. The trespassers brought disease, death and dependency to Pacific Islands. They also brought wealth, opportunity, productivity and a new dynamic which ultimately meant the Pacific's survival. The great tragedy of Pacific Islands in the nineteenth century is that potential compatriots in the end became opponents in different leagues. Only now, at the beginning of the twenty-first century, is the Pacific beginning to recover from the historical disparity.

The principle of indigenous self-government, which Britain early on had encouraged, was effectively dead by 1900; too much lay at stake for each colonial power to entrust their fate to the indigenous prerogative, as was universally believed by then. In some places, like New Zealand and Hawai'i, the subject was of course academic: there, non-Islanders already far outnumbered Islanders. For better or worse, a new people had taken over most of Pacific Islands, and there was no going back. The new institutions of the Pacific simply had to function, for there was no recourse elsewhere. Yet it was not so much that Pacific Islands was being absorbed by Europe and America, as it was that Europe's and America's emigrants and their ways were being absorbed, in barely perceptible fashion, by Pacific Islands. If, at first, of superficial European and American semblance, the altered societies of the Pacific were in fact transforming themselves into something altogether new, the likes of which the world had never seen.

5

. . . .

New Pacific Identities

COLONIAL REALITIES IN THE EARLY TWENTIETH CENTURY

Already by the First World War colonial patterns had been forged, for a variety of reasons, which would determine the nature of Pacific Islands' development for the next half century. Indigenous Pacific Islanders had had little part in this process. Indeed, theirs was a story of accelerating marginalization. The foreign trespassers, who first became settlers then the new lords of the Pacific, had usurped the right to create, for themselves and their own kind, the type of societies they wished to replace those traditional Pacific ones which had no value to them. Much was lost with this conveyance. But much was also gained.

With expanding administrations, social change accelerated, too, advanced by remarkable personalities who oversaw vast regions with unprecedented powers. The finest of these individuals even achieved a rare balance between exploitation and paternalism. However, the First World War essentially ended single-man rule and brought on, in most locales, two decades of bureaucratic ineptitude and indifference. Many indigenous Pacific Islanders served in the First World War, among them the French Polynesians and Kanaks of New Caledonia and the Loyalties, who suffered tremendous losses; the Māori of the

Māori Battalion (who were British citizens), whose losses were also disproportionately high; the Hawaiians (who were US citizens); and a non-combatant company of Fijian labourers.

The international peace negotiations which followed the First World War advanced the general consensus that all future relations between peoples should be founded on the principle of national self-determination: the era of competitive imperialism was over and the colonial possessions of defeated Germany and Turkey were to be nurtured to nationhood. To supervise this process, the League of Nations set up the Permanent Mandates Commission and selected various nations to administer for the Commission the respective former colonies. It was in this way that the Kaiser's colonies in Pacific Islands which had been occupied during the war by Japan, Australia and New Zealand were apportioned to these same occupying forces regardless of their contrasting abilities to govern them. Japan was entrusted with all of Micronesia north of the equator, Australia with New Guinea and Nauru, and New Zealand with German Samoa which now became Western Samoa.

As these were 'C-class' mandates – that is, colonies which would not experience independence until their economic and social situation was drastically improved – the Permanent Mandates Commission encharged the three custodial nations to develop them towards this end. The Commission also imposed restrictions: the mandates were not to be developed into military bastions (as the USA was doing in Guam and Hawai'i) and they were subject to annual assessment.

In principle, the League of Nations' plan was humanitarian, far-reaching and hopeful. In practice, it merely exchanged one colonial master – Germany – for three others – Japan, Australia and New Zealand – of varying competence. The new masters were pressed by more immediate issues: financing their mandate, raising colonial self-sufficiency to lessen their financial burden, and resolving local difficulties. The new colonial administrators found that under the Commission's edict, they were being forced to reconcile two seeming opposites: economic growth and indigenous welfare. Until then 'reconciliation' always lay in disadvantaged Islanders labouring for advantaged whites. During the interbellum years – that is, from 1918 to 1939 (December 1941 in the Pacific) – only white colonial masters still endorsed this fable while Islanders began exposing it.

Because new administrators no longer always supported the fable either, they were often hard pressed by the white elite for 'retarding economic growth' and by Islanders for 'ignoring their welfare'. As a result, the closing era of Pacific Islands colonialism was frequently a hodgepodge of vacillations which time and again saw the deferral of those solid schemes that might benefit everyone equitably.

NEW ZEALAND BECOMES A NATION

When Britain warred against the Afrikaner farmers of the Transvaal in the Boer War (1899–1902), New Zealand contributed more soldiers per capita than any other part of the British Empire. Then, New Zealanders – including all Māori – were still British citizens. However, things were changing. New Zealand took part in the negotiations for a centralized Australian administration which, on 1 January 1901, established the Commonwealth of Australia. But New Zealand rejected the proposal that it join politically with Australia (though Australia still retains today in its constitution a clause permitting New Zealand to join the Federation).

In 1907 Britain granted New Zealand sovereignty as an independent state. None the less, Britain maintained New Zealand's dominion status, which meant that Britain's ruling monarch still remained New Zealand's head of state. (Britain had done the same with Australia.) Because New Zealand had had a strong central government since the 1850s, it now experienced a smooth transition from colony to nation, with New Zealanders sensing no contradiction in being independent Kiwis unfailingly loyal to King Edward VII. New Zealand's Liberal Party, which governed from 1891 to 1912, introduced not only extensive social programmes, but also economic schemes which greatly expanded the country's dairy and meat-producing (sheep, cattle) industries. The country's railways and road system were also fully modernized.

It was the First World War that first awakened the perception of a separate New Zealand identity – though the appreciation came only much later as a public myth, and though the feeling of Britain as 'Home' lasted for many into the 1970s. When Britain entered the war in 1914, all its Pacific Islands' subjects enlisted in surprisingly high numbers, not as unaffected colonials but as convinced patriots. In New Zealand, around half of all eligible men left to fight for Britain on the other side of the globe. Casualties were disproportionately high: of the 100 000 New Zealanders who enlisted, 16 000 were killed and 45 000 were wounded. (Of all Allied forces, only the Australians suffered similar losses.) The war initially created a sense of 'Kiwiness' in that it set the New Zealanders apart as 'equal but different' British citizens. But it was primarily the Australian and New Zealand Army Corps (ANZAC) which awakened national pride, creating as it did the feeling of a shared Pacific uniqueness with other serving Pacific Islanders (Kanaks, Tahitians, Tongans, Samoans, Fijians) and with Australians in particular.

Central to incipient New Zealand perceptions of nationhood is Gallipoli. In 1915 an expeditionary force of mostly ANZACs landed in Turkey to force the Turks out of the war and to open up a sea route to Russia. But after nine months of mindless slaughter the campaign was abandoned as a failure. Because losses had been unusually high, public indignation – indeed, anger – was roused. Though the military and geopolitical explanations surrounding the Gallipoli campaign are complex, the rather simplistic public opinion about its ultimate outcome became a powerful myth: that is, Aussies and Kiwis bravely fought and died for Britain side by side, and their sacrifice created two new nations in the Pacific. Each 25 April is Anzac Day in Australia and New Zealand, where not only the public myth, but the dead of all wars are dutifully remembered – with Gallipoli commemorated as the symbolic crucible of nationhood.

From 1912 to 1930 New Zealand's Reform Party concentrated on agricultural legislation demanded by its farming constituency. In 1930 it achieved a coalition with the United Party, out of which emerged the new National Party whose principal opposition came from the Labour Party. The New Zealand parliamentary system contained no conservative faction: both the Labour Party and the opposing Liberals, Reformers and United members had believed government was responsible for national wellbeing; all had backed sweeping social reforms. While Labour represented miners, shearers and dockworkers, the three other parties supported manufacturers, merchants and farmers. A highly progressive society, New Zealand was never that concerned with constitutional autonomy; like the Australians, the New Zealanders did not have official citizenship until after the Second World War. (Though Britain's Statute of Westminster granted equal status to the self-governing dominions of the British Empire in 1931, extending these countries' sovereignty, New Zealand did not ratify the Statute of Westminster until 1949, whereupon all Kiwis became citizens of only New Zealand.)

New Zealand was dependent on export revenue from mutton, wool and agriculture, and so when international prices fell in the early 1930s, the country was greatly affected: unemployment rose to around 20 per cent (only Australia and Germany suffered worse). New Zealand had borrowed heavily in the 1920s to finance public works projects, providing industry and farming with a more modern infrastructure. When the loans were called in during the period of low international prices, it magnified the country's dilemma. There was no national unemployment scheme, private agencies were insufficiently prepared and financed, and, for the first time, New Zealand society split into extreme radicalism and extreme conservatism, polarizing the country.

This was when the Labour Party came to the fore, determined to protect New Zealanders from the worst excesses of international capitalism. Finally elected to govern in 1935, the Labour Party soon contained the chaos and began the long process of creating, just as in Australia, the welfare state, whose completion was interrupted by the Second World War.

THE INTEGRATION OF MELANESIA

Progress came slowly to Melanesia. This was because of isolation, enormous social and linguistic diversity, and difficult climate, all of which factors hindered and retarded the region's development. In divided New Guinea, for example, colonial administrations initiated two wholly different adminstrative styles to meet the complex challenges there.

British New Guinea (southeastern New Guinea) attracted hundreds of British and Australian planters because of its cheap labour and high returns. In 1906, Europeans cultivated 1500 acres there; by 1914, over 44 000; and by 1920, over 62 000. The territory's new British administration had adapted Arthur Gordon's Fijian scheme to suit local circumstances. It was not easy. Papuans lacked a tradition of hierarchical authority, were hardly or not at all acquainted with Europeans and their customs, and remained generally violent and suspicious of outsiders. Instrumental in bringing law and order to British New Guinea was Lieutenant-Governor William MacGregor who, in the last decade of the nineteenth century, working with a small staff achieved peace in most accessible areas, regulated Papuan life, eradicated most petty crimes and liaised productively with the London Missionary Society, Wesleyan Missionary Society, and Anglican and Catholic missionaries who helped him to effect a 'civilizing' change.

Subsequent Lieutenant-Governors there failed to sustain MacGregor's dynamic impetus. In 1906, British New Guinea became formally a part of the Australian Federation (Australia had attained sovereignty in 1901). The following year, Australian Hubert Murray became the new Lieutenant-Governor of Papua (as the territory was now officially renamed), who led the colony for the next 33 years. Murray was a humanitarian and paternalistic colonialist, a stance which irked resident British and Australian mine operators, planters and merchants who sought white supremacy in Papua. However, the British government had always fostered, and continued to foster, just such humanitarianism. Following Britain in this instance, the Australian government gave Murray *carte blanche* to administer Papua as he saw fit.

Murray's authority gradually subsumed an ever-larger domain. Easily accessible locales became more Europeanized, while isolated communities at least experienced a lessening of violence and an end to those traditional Papuan acts Britons and Australians considered repugnant. The prison at Port Moresby, Papua's capital, contained the spread of what was understood to be 'crime' as it also educated the Islanders in what their 'foreign masters' expected of them. Murray worked closely with the Christian missions generally to improve the Papuans' welfare, but overall maintained traditional regimens while suppressing only the most aberrant practices.

The result: most Papuan communities were re-established according to European concepts of hygiene; sorcery was outlawed; settlers were forbidden to use compulsory Papuan labour; Papuans were guaranteed their lands; Papuan women could not be indentured; warfare was banned and replaced with organized games, in particular rugby and cricket; and so forth. Many of these progressive ideas stemmed from F. E. Williams, the anthropologist Murray hired in 1922. Both Murray and Williams knew change was inevitable in Papua, but they appreciated that it would be less harmful for the Papuans if solutions were found which prioritized the Papuans' own traditional values, not those of the missionaries, settlers, merchants and administrators.

Most remarkably for Pacific Islands, Murray filled his staff with Papuans, which decreased the annual budget for salaries as it prepared a generation of Papuans in government and law. Murray also had Papuans trained as medical assistants: between 1932 and 1936, 40 Papuans experienced rudimentary medical training at the University of Sydney. (The project was then summarily cancelled after a furore caused by Australian white supremacists.) For his era, Murray was extraordinarily liberal, tolerant, pragmatic and successful, despite the contrary cries of unrealistic humanitarians and bigoted white settlers, and despite the woefully small budget alotted to Murray by a depression-wracked Australian government.

Such a modern stance had its price. Murray had begun his tenure encouraging development for the region according to Australia's greater economic scheme, but later had adopted the British model of paternalistic colonialism which prioritized the indigenous prerogative. This displeased Papua's Europeans, especially those from Australia. In addition, Australian legislation required that Papua's copra destined for Asia or Europe be shipped first to Sydney, a costly detour of over 2500 kilometres. Under Australian stewardship the Papuan economy eventually stagnated. After 1920, little additional area was turned to plantation; growth in general declined. Whereupon Papua became a Pacific backwater, similar to France's Polynesian territories.

Things were different in eastern New Guinea's northern half: Kaiser Wilhelms-Land, which Germany had secured in 1884. Unlike his aunt Queen Victoria of Great Britain, Kaiser Wilhelm had no interest in cultivating humanitarian colonies for eventual emancipation. Instead, he authorized the granting of a charter to a private company, the Neuguinea-Kompanie founded by Adolf von Hansemann in 1885, which was to rule the colony according to commercial needs. Two years later a further charter was granted to the Deutsche Handels- und Plantagen-Gesellschaft and to Robertson & Hernsheim, who together formed the Jaluit-Kompanie for the Marshall Islands. The scheme functioned profitably, though unsatisfactorily, in the Marshalls where a German Commissioner oversaw the colony's administration while the Jaluit-Kompanie concentrated on its balance sheets, financed the administration and left the issue of German settlement to the Commissioner. But in Kaiser Wilhelms-Land the Neuguinea-Kompanie was uniquely invested with full police and legislative powers; the Kompanie deemed the territory their private demesne, its occupants their vassals. The ill feeling this engendered among indigenous New Guineans soon turned into open hostility. When labourers refused to co-operate, the Kompanie punished them; when the labourers retaliated, the Kompanie brutally crushed them. Kompanie concerns took precedence over all humanitarian concerns. Of course, New Guinea's white settlers – few in number and plagued by financial straits and the unhealthy climate – invariably sided with the Kompanie.

When New Guineans finally refused to work for the Germans any longer, the Kompanie allowed its settlers to import labourers from other parts of Melanesia and from Asia. However, these imported labourers, too, suffered horrendously under the Kompanie's taskmasters. By the time the Kompanie's hegemony in New Guinea ended in 1899, when Kaiser Wilhelm's government, alarmed by the international protestations, assumed responsibility over all of the Kompanie's territories, as many as half of the imported Melanesian and Asian labourers had perished.

Kaiser Wilhelms-Land was occupied by Australian forces in the first year of the First World War. Seven years later, in 1921, it became a mandate of the League of Nations and was entrusted to Australia. The more liberal and humanitarian policies of the former Kaiser's colonial administration were continued, but now under a succession of Australian military officers who failed to appreciate the indigenous franchise and to receive clear leadership from their superiors in Canberra. The German plantations were confiscated and sold off to Australians who – like the French with the Kanaks in New Caledonia – regarded all New Guineans as their chattels.

As a result, northeastern New Guineans never attained that quality of public service which Hubert Murray had secured for the Papuans in the south. White Australian settlers were favoured by the colonial administration, which freely provided both New Guinean labour and land in order to develop plantations. However, the prosperity this scheme had promised its supporters failed to materialize, for a variety of reasons: indentured labour was basically inefficient, prices were depressed, markets were too distant, diseases and pests took their toll, and other problems.

Discovered on Mount Kaindi in 1926, gold alone seemed to be northeastern New Guinea's future – and its bane. Almost overnight, hundreds of Australian miners and prospectors were employing thousands of New Guineans in makeshift gold camps. However, the Australian administration was soon issuing permits to mining companies which then transformed the gold-rush into a gold industry which handsomely financed the territory throughout the 1930s, enabling a bureaucracy much better funded than Papua's. But the affluence had its human price. Miners and prospectors often encroached into regions beyond governmental control, setting up individual suzerainties employing large New Guinean work-forces. In their search for gold, the intruders would continue to discover hitherto unknown areas and peoples as late as the 1950s, the last places of Pacific Islands to experience the foreign trespass.

New Guinea was an extremely difficult place to administrate. (It remains so today.) The Australian military officers did little more than contain violence and regulate the planters' and miners' activities. They cared little about the welfare of the New Guineans, who were generally left to their own devices, to be exploited or neglected. Only the most rudimentary services were ever achieved, despite the enormous gold revenues: superficial administration, an incipient public service, the most basic medical services. New Guinea of the 1930s resembled Tahiti of the 1830s. Deprived of a Hubert Murray, the New Guineans experienced only severity or apathy. The Australian government in Canberra, pleased with the gold revenues, did not interfere in the territory's military administration. The incompetent stewardship of its huge mandate – the largest in Pacific Islands – left many open wounds which have still not completely healed.

New Guinea's offshore islands, though favoured with Christian missions and burgeoning trading settlements, had similarly suffered from German Kompanie excesses and governmental neglect. There had been many incidents of raiding and murder at the end of the nineteenth century. Indeed, the situation had become so grievous that the Kaiser's government had assumed full control in 1895, appointing Albert Hahl administrator of the Bismarck Islands (Neu-Pommern, Neu-Mecklenburg, the Admiralty Islands) and Bougainville the following year. Hahl was a brilliant colonial administrator. He implemented public works, encouraged peaceful commerce and settled land disputes together with local chiefs. Hahl ruled only indirectly, in that he appointed local leaders to act on his behalf; he also established an indigenous police force, which Hahl personally commanded. In 1902 Hahl became Governor of the Bismarcks, and thereafter administrated the region in a similarly fair and humane manner, maintaining a fine balance between humanitarian colonialism and commercial exploitation. In 1914 Germany lost the Bismarcks to Australia, which formally acquired the islands as a protectorate from the League of Nations in 1921.

Sharing those problems common to both Papua and New Guinea, the Solomon Islands additionally suffered from a dearth of economic opportunities: it lacked resources to finance its British colonial administration, one which Solomon Islanders resented and opposed. Unlike nearly everyone else in Pacific Islands, the Solomon Islanders had never experienced a community of European or American settlers in their chain. Britain's resident commissioner Charles Woodford (see Chapter 4) had attempted singlehandedly to generate an economy there by promising favourable concessions to potential copra planters.

As a result of Woodford's efforts, the first decade of the twentieth century witnessed the establishment by international companies of large coconut plantations in the Solomons. In 1901, the Pacific Islands Company obtained 200 000 acres on a 99-year lease. In 1905 this was conveyed to Lever Brothers on extremely favourable terms, as it was hoped this would be the foundation of the Solomons' future wealth. One year later

the Australian firm of Burns, Philp and Co. followed, and
Fairymead in 1909. With this influx of capital, Christian missions suddenly expanded throughout the Solomons, exercising
full control over the Islanders' education and providing medical services. The British administration on small Tulagi in the
Florida Group was almost invisible, seldom venturing beyond
the islands' coastal strip and appearing in villages for the sole
purpose of taxing or punishing.

In time, Lever Brothers did become the corporate king of
the Solomons, owning around half of all the plantations there.
Yet even the Lever acreage was relatively small, employing
only around a thousand Islanders, the production in part
funded by a sister firm. Because no substantial revenues were
forthcoming from the Solomons, the financially pressed
British administration oversaw only the basics there – law and
order and punishment – and left to the missionaries all
humanitarian services. Only in 1940 did British administration
finally extend throughout the archipelago, but on the larger
islands – Makira, Guadalcanal, Malaita, Santa Isabel, New
Georgia and Choiseul – its presence still remained weak.
Daily life in the Solomons had settled to a complacent compromise between the old and the new, with nothing disturbing
the peaceful isolation until the Japanese invaded in 1942.

Fiji saw the system of land tenure which Arthur Gordon
had established in the nineteenth century function well at the
beginning of the twentieth century. Any attempts to force
Fijians into autonomy were thwarted by the institutional-
ization of Gordon's scheme: both Fijians and European
plantation owners were clearly prospering. Moreover, the
Fijians profited from an administration which appeared to
provide equitable consultation, indigenous technical education, and a health service which trained indigenous personnel.
Few Fijians perceived a need for self-determination. Only
one fundamental weakness flawed the otherwise successful
colonial system: the Indian labourers in Fiji still lacked legal
and social protection both during and after their ten-year
indenture.

If only superficially, Fiji was to British what Samoa had been to German colonialism: apparent prosperity for 'everyone', a model land-tenure policy, educational and health services, and general orderliness. In the 1920s and 1930s, constitutional changes incorporated the native Fijian prerogative in a way which maintained the Fijian chiefs' respect for the British authority. Underlying this superficial success, however, lay incipient Fijian discontent and strong Indian resentment.

There were around 63 000 Indians in Fiji when the Indian indenture system ceased permanently in 1916 (there were c. 85 000 native Fijians). The Fijian Indians had suffered from a colonial policy which kept them apart, different and disenfranchised. Whereas native Fijians received mission assistances and educational services, the Indians received little or none of either. There were professional Fijians, but no professional Indians. Indians were further refused those civil and political rights all Europeans and Fijians enjoyed. And Indians could not own land: native Fijian land was inalienable and European-owned land unavailable. Yet, for half a century, the Indians had been the backbone of Fiji's economy.

The best that Indians could hope for was a 21-year lease of Fijian-owned land, and such leases were often not renewed. As a result, most Indians in Fiji were fated to grow sugar-cane on land the Colonial Sugar Refining Company either leased or subleased to them. Only in the late 1930s were leasing policies eased somewhat, but the harm had already been done to two full generations of Fijian-born Indians. It is an historical irony that the welfare of the native Fijians was financially secured by those among them whom they excluded from society's benefits. The inequity was of course a social timebomb.

THE USA IN THE PACIFIC

Pragmatism – not humanitarianism or imperialism – characterized the USA's Pacific policy at the beginning of the twentieth century. In contrast to German Samoa, American Samoa experienced a naval, not a civil, administration which had little to do with daily Samoan activities. The USA had annexed Tutuila and Aunu'u in 1900, and included the Manu'a group in 1904 when the Tu'i Manu'a, Eastern Samoa's highest-ranking chief, became the last to sign a cession agreement with the US government. (The act of annexation was not formally ratified by Congress until 1929.)

From the beginning, American Samoa was under the jurisdiction of the Navy Department, a situation which lasted until 1951. American administration transformed little in this part of Samoa. Unlike the robust incentives in German Samoa, incentives for development were few in American Samoa. Apart from the excesses of the Second World War, traditional lifestyles here remained fairly unaltered by white colonization or extensive commercialization until the 1960s.

The same obtains for Guam in Micronesia, which the USA had acquired in 1898 as booty from the Spanish-American War. In 1905 Guam became the central station of the Pacific cable network. Apra Harbor on the island's west coast became the US Navy's main fleet base in the Western Pacific. However, Guam remained isolated and undeveloped – its small economy focused on copra production – until the Japanese invaded in 1942.

The USA's involvement with Hawai'i in the first decades of the twentieth century was similar to Britain's involvement with New Zealand half a century earlier. Though officially a territory, Hawai'i was very much an American colony to be settled *en masse* by advantaged whites, displacing the resident Pacific Islanders whose population had been drastically reduced by pandemics, intermarriage, a low birth rate and other causes. Hawaiians lacked the close tribal affiliations of such Pacific Islanders as the Māori who had maintained traditional allegiances, and so the Hawaiians became more Westernized than most Pacific Islanders. They also intermarried more freely, not only with white settlers but in growing numbers with the imported labourers from Japan, Korea, the Philippines, China, Puerto Rico and Portugual. Already by the beginning of the twentieth century, a new breed was emerging in the Hawaiian Islands to represent a large segment of the population: half- and quarter-Islanders who, like the indigenous Hawaiians, were generally excluded from the islands' economic boom.

By the 1930s Hawai'i had become Pacific Islands' ultimate hierarchical society – but on the basis of Western-perceived race, not indigenous power and prestige. This ensured white supremacy, the mixed peoples condemned to permanent subordination and the few remaining 'pure' Hawaiians consigned to social and economic neglect. There were only few exceptions, such as those scions of Hawai'i's earliest missionaries who had married aristocratic Hawaiians and had acquired vast estates as a result. Five giant enterprises – the 'Big Five' – wielded all economic and political power in the Islands, exploiting the rigid caste system to ensure their hegemony. This was the true 'Hawaiian paradise' concealed by Washington and tourist agencies alike. The monopoly, and the lie, lasted until the 1950s.

TONGA AND WESTERN SAMOA

Tonga experienced little change and few difficulties in the first half of the twentieth century – certainly none of those problems encountered by other British-dominated islands. The British Consul supervised the daily running of the monarchy and held the right of veto over all governmental legislation by Tongans exercizing their constitutional authority. The European presence was minimal, because the Tongan government prohibited private ownership of land; this precluded the ethnic strife so common on other islands. Also, the Tongans' own rigid and centralized power base, a legacy of the society's traditional hierarchical structure, together with the absolutism of the British Consul, offered a dual control over the society which ensured civil rights and guaranteed positive development within the international marketplace. Tongans – not foreigners – held virtually all the copra plantations themselves, which meant that the Tongan government's books remained in the black, something nearly unparalleled in Pacific Islands. Much of this was due to Britain's paternalistic colonial policy, whose liberality was particularly evident in Tonga.

Western Samoa was quite different. The German flag first flew over Western Samoa on 1 March 1900. The Islands' two German governors, Wilhelm Solf (1900–10) and Erich Schultz (1912–14), avoided the excesses of New Guinea, believing Samoans were to be led, not pushed. Solf in particular resisted the white settlers' bigotry, supporting German enterprise but endorsing the indigenous Samoan prerogative. This polarized both communities, leaving Solf's main supporter the Deutsche Handels- und Plantagen-Gesellschaft (DHPG). Solf made a careful study of Samoan traditions in order to set one faction of Samoan opposition against the other to weaken their front, using the Samoans' own cultural concepts to achieve this. To deflate the white settlers, Solf refused to import further labourers or open up land sales, leaving the DHPG a virtual monopoly.

In 1909, one faction of Samoans rose up against Solf: he had them summarily deported to the Mariana Islands in Micronesia. Solf's deputy and successor, Erich Schultz, continued Solf's administrative policies and style. By then the Kaiser regarded Samoa as the brightest star in Germany's vast colonial galaxy, and with good reason: the humanitarian administration of Solf and Schultz skilfully protected the Samoans from colonial excesses while promoting commercial enterprise. Samoa had at last found a semblance of European harmony and affluence. Yet Germany's profits were only marginal: if the Kaiser had expected colonial riches, he failed to find them in his star colony.

Germany's colonial governors Albert Hahl of the Bismarck Islands and Wilhelm Solf of German Samoa managed to bridge the gap between the old and the new Pacific in an intelligent, humane and efficient fashion. However, both experienced empty triumphs: Germany's Pacific colonies failed to enrich the *Vaterland* and were then lost in the First World War. Still, in bringing humanitarian order to the chaos of transition the German governors showed the path that Pacific Islands had to take towards nationhood.

Governor Erich Schultz surrendered to the New Zealand Expeditionary Force on 29 August 1914. At once the highly productive German plantations – including those of the DHPG – were seized; these were later placed under direct control of the newly formed Samoa Land Corporation owned by the government (which still holds them today). This nationalization of erstwhile private plantations allowed Western Samoa to avoid surrending its wealth to foreign investors as it provided the new government with a strong economic foundation. At the same time, almost all of the 2000 southern Chinese labourers in Western Samoa were repatriated by the new New Zealand colonial administration. Western Samoa's production now lay almost entirely in Samoan hands, and this policy was continued by all subsequent New Zealand administrators.

From the onset, New Zealand's stewardship of Western Samoa was inept and, at times, even hazardous. The New Zealand military authorities allowed the SS *Talune* to dock at 'Apia in November 1918, despite the quarantine against the Spanish flu which was being strictly observed in American Samoa and Fiji: as a result, 8000 Samoans perished, more than one out of five of the total population. (New Zealand authorities had allowed the same to happen in New Zealand itself, where losses were equally high.) New Zealand militarily occupied Western Samoa until 1920, when a civilian government assumed authority. The New Zealand colonial administrators effected few changes in policy or law, but were not as efficient as their German predecessors. Most administrators, on fixed-term contracts, did not stay long enough to learn Samoan cultural values. Most held Samoans in low esteem and ruled with autocratic paternalism: though allowing the Samoans to hold the Fono of Faipule – the traditional Samoan assembly – they ignored its decisions and the elders' advice. In contrast, the few Europeans residing in Western Samoa were assimilating themselves into Samoan society by marriage and birth, becoming bicultural European-Samoans who prioritized indigenous interests.

Western Samoa was greatly affected by the arrival of a new administrator in 1923 – General George Richardson. At first Richardson appeared to acknowledge the Samoan privilege: he began learning the Samoan language, legally recognized the Fono of Faipule, and introduced a governing hierarchy in which the Fono of Faipule could actively assert itself with punitory authority. But then Richardson starting redesigning Samoan society along personal preferences, attempting to ban some traditions, regulate agriculture, individualize land tenure and other caprices. Dissent would be met with arbitrary punishment, frequently involving the public humiliation of a leading chief: for a titled Samoan a fate worse than death.

When in 1926 Richardson tried to interfere in the selection of *matai* or chiefly titles – insisting the *matai* choose their own successors and banning family selection – the Fono of Faipule itself protested. The organization 'O le Mau' was founded at this time, using as its motto Richardson's own slogan, '*Samoa mo Samoa*' (Samoa for Samoans). Richardson responded by banishing two leaders of the new organization. After this many Samoans began refusing to comply with governmental regulations and institutions. A Royal Commission appointed by New Zealand to hear the Samoans' grievances found in Richardson's favour that the Mau had been initiated by several '*afakasi* (English 'half-castes') and Europeans to challenge the New Zealand mandate. Richardson had these identified personalities deported, then arrested 400 further 'leaders' of the Mau – whereupon hundreds more turned up demanding to be gaoled with them! The Mau now voiced publicly that Western Samoa had to be governed by Samoans, not by New Zealanders.

By 1928, the year George Richardson was replaced by Stephen Allen, the Mau was actively fulfilling governmental roles. Of the 9300 adult Samoan men in the Islands, 8000 signed the Mau's petition to the League of Nations asking that its Mandates Commission hear Western Samoa's grievances against New Zealand; but the Commission declined. In 1929 Allen prohibited the Fono of Faipule, with one stroke crushing Samoa's only democratic assembly.

Several Mau chiefs and European followers hurriedly returned from exile, gathered all supporters and, on 28 December 1929, marched in protest through the streets of the capital 'Apia. The police tried to arrest some of the marchers 'for non-payment of taxes'. When, in the ensuing scuffle, one European policeman was killed, the remaining policemen began shooting their weapons. Machine-guns suddenly opened fire from a police station. On the day now known in Western Samoa as 'Black Saturday' several Samoans were killed, some of them high-ranking chiefs who had been trying to pacify the protestors when they were struck down by police bullets. Governor Allen blamed the Mau for the massacre and brought in New Zealand troops to ferret out Mau adherents. Many Samoans fled to the forests and hills as the New Zealanders scoured the villages.

Throughout the early 1930s the work of the outlawed Mau continued with the 'Women's Mau' led by the wives and widows of former Mau leaders. Travelling to all parts of Western Samoa they openly demonstrated and gathered support. At this time Stephen Allen exercized a stern authority with unusually harsh punishments which few believed could be excelled. But in 1933 Allen was replaced by another career officer who then arrested the returned O. F. Nelson, the half-Samoan leader of the Mau, who was subsequently sentenced to eight months' imprisonment in New Zealand and ten years' exile.

In 1936, New Zealand's new Labour government, which had been the first New Zealand political party to understand the Mau's true objectives, freed Nelson and recognized the Mau as a legitimate political entity. In Western Samoa, a new Fono of Faipule was elected which was comprised mostly of Mau leaders. More significantly, the new Fono of Faipule was then authorized by New Zealand's new colonial Governor of

Western Samoa to select members of the Legislative Council. This now allowed Western Samoans to participate in direct government for the first time.

New Zealand was the only colonial power in Pacific Islands which made the colonial state the chief proprietor of the productive assets of the colony. Having confiscated Germany's Samoan plantations, New Zealand did not sell them off to its nationals, as Australia had done in New Guinea, but kept them as Reparation Estates whose revenues then supported the local administration. This innovative scheme might have contributed positively to the Western Samoan economy and society, had the New Zealand administration itself not been so inept and unduly harsh towards its wards. Western Samoans gained nothing from New Zealand's innovative policy, which in the end merely replaced quality with mediocrity at best. Devoting little effort to developing Western Samoa, New Zealand was content simply to defray its administrative costs. As a result, everyone lost. Only in the second half of the 1930s was New Zealand able to correct the harm and set a new and more promising course for its victimized mandate.

FRANCE IN THE PACIFIC

France's colonial policy in Pacific Islands in the first half of the twentieth century featured benign neglect in Polynesia and rabid exploitation in New Caledonia. French Polynesia's succession of colonial administrators – aloof, dictatorial and heeding only Paris in all matters – performed, in effect, only two duties: collecting taxes and providing simple administration. Letting Polynesians conduct local village governance wherever possible, Paris's main involvement concerned the small white population in French Polynesia and their incessant demands for greater political influence.

By 1900 in Tahiti, capital of France's Polynesian territory, for example, though the days of cotton revenues had ceased there still remained a modest trade in vanilla, pearl-shell and copra. Substantial revenues also came from phosphate on Makatea in the Tuamotus, 200 kilometres northeast of Tahiti. Few Frenchmen were bothered by the fact that the 160 to 200 indigenous Makateans were summarily dispossessed and driven into exile when mining entrepreneurs descended; the entrepreneurs eventually consolidated themselves into the Compagnie française des phosphates de l'Océanie in 1908. As a result, phosphate investors made impressive profits, Paris earned sizeable revenues, Makateans lost their island, and no French Polynesians benefited at all because the Makatean enterprise used imported labour. (It was symptomatic of Pacific Islands' exploitation at the time, as similar wrongs were vexing Ocean Islanders (Banabans) and Nauruans in Micronesia.)

Actually, French Polynesia remained isolated, backward and humdrum, the goal of romantic adventurers or visionary artists like Paul Gauguin pursuing their own images of the South Pacific. Between 1880 and 1960 the most dramatic occurrence in the entire region was the arrival of the two German cruisers *Scharnhorst* and *Gneisenau*, which shelled Pape'ete and destroyed its marketplace on 22 September 1914. Immediately after this, a thousand Tahitian volunteers fought in the trenches for France – nearly one out of three becoming a casualty of the war.

Only in the late 1930s did administrators in Tahiti finally undertake substantial schemes for developing France's economic interests in Polynesia, but these schemes were soon halted by the outbreak of the Second World War. Tahiti itself was to remain a colonial territory until 1958, still part of the greater Établissements français de l'Océanie.

In New Caledonia, as its French Governor declared in 1914: 'The government has no native policy.' How true. By this time, the Kanaks were facing extinction and, wholly neglected by French authorities, found relief, organization and education only from the selfless missionaries there on the Grande Terre and neighbouring Loyalties. When the government finally impressed Kanaks into the French army in 1917, high chief Noel called on his fellow Kanaks to fight the French in New

Caledonia as valiantly as they were fighting the Germans in Europe, where ultimately c. 1000 Kanaks were killed. Armed conflicts against French police and *caldoches* (French settlers) ravaged the northern and northwestern Grande Terre for two months: 11 Europeans and 200 Kanaks died in the rebellion.

Otherwise, the First World War hardly affected New Caledonia. After the armistice, colonial administrators regularly came and went, all of them disinterested bureaucrats simply obeying Paris's directives. In 1925 a new governor, Georges Guyon, introduced a relatively liberal scheme to improve the lot of the Kanaks for the first time (there were only approximately 27 000 left). The French government finally offered educational and health services (until then domains of the Christian missions) whose costs were financed by the revenues from New Caledonia's metal ores. Guyon also implemented a scheme of road and wharf construction in order to upgrade the *caldoche* economy as well.

Georges Guyon was the most innovative and dynamic of 12 governors during this period, the majority of whom neglected Kanaks and *caldoches* alike. Typical of the New Caledonian administration – in great contrast to the Tahitian, which lacked large numbers of French settlers – was the prevalent sentiment that the Grande Terre was France's ethnic tenure. As one *caldoche* pithily asked in 1928: 'By what monstrous aberration do we continue to let the natives have more land than they can cultivate and than they need to live on?' The identical question was posed often by Europeans and Americans in the Pacific – pitting Western pragmatism against traditional birthright, with moneyed power the sole adjudicator. In New Caledonia, the end result was *cantonnement*: the confinement of Kanaks to reservations.

In 1932 the market collapsed. Ore revenues vanished, taking with them Guyon's liberal policy and tenure. The dire financial situation of the 1930s compelled successive Governors to confiscate more Kanak land. At the same time the world depression ruined a large number of small *caldoche* farmers as well, with the result that most of New Caledonia's land and wealth was conveyed to a small French elite (the situation which still obtains today). While the Kanaks' legal status improved somewhat at the end of the 1930s, general discrimination persisted. For the next half century dissatisfaction among the Kanaks grew, until violence superseded patience.

JAPAN'S MICRONESIAN COLONIES

Pacific residents for thousands of years, Japanese came relatively late to Pacific Islands. All but closed to the rest of the world until the US Navy forced open its harbours in the 1850s, within 20 years Japan was controlling Sakhalin and the Kuril Islands to its north, the Ryukyu Islands (most importantly Okinawa) to its south and the Bonin Islands (Ogasarawa) to the southeast. From the latter's harbours Japanese merchants would then sail in the last decades of the nineteenth century to Micronesia's Mariana and Caroline Islands to trade; many Japanese settled as well in New Guinea. In 1914, when the First World War broke out, Japan seized Germany's Pacific colonies north of the equator: Palau, the Marianas, Carolines and Marshalls. In 1919 Japan was awarded the Carolines as a mandate by the League of Nations; one year later it received Palau, the Marianas and Marshalls as additional mandates.

Japan handsomely subsidized its Micronesian administration. This made it financially more secure than either Australia's or New Zealand's at the time, whose colonial governments were outrageously underfinanced. Yet despite Japan's largesse, there was little of that entrenched effect which had characterized European colonialism in Polynesia, for example. Japan's presence in Micronesia was too recent and, as it turned out, too brief.

Just outside Japanese Micronesia's capital of Koror on Palau, the Japanese government built the Shinto shrine Kampei Taisha Nan'yo Jinja in 1940, which it then dedicated to the Japanese sun goddess who, Japanese believe, commenced the imperial line. Whereupon Palauan students were encouraged to pray there for Japan's soldiers who were then fighting in China. Smaller Shinto shrines had been erected on Chuuk, Saipan and Lamotrek Atoll. Japanese colonial officials took great pains in their attempt to familiarize Micronesians with Japanese rituals and ideals. However, it had little effect. Neither Buddhism nor Shintoism ever caught on with Micronesians, so deeply rooted were the teachings of the Christian missions by then.

Like most colonials in Pacific Islands, the Japanese were weakened by prejudice. They held Micronesians to be 'third-class' people, lower than Okinawans and Koreans. However, the Micronesian population remained almost static, no longer declining, while access to educational and health services greatly improved because of the Japanese government's liberal subsidies. Japan's purpose in this was certainly anything but altruistic: the conjunction of state and private enterprise was closer here than anywhere else in Pacific Islands, as Japan regarded Micronesia as a strategic asset.

The development of Japanese Micronesia was led by Matsue Haruji, who founded the Nan'yo Kohatsu, or South Seas Development Company. In the 1920s, the Kohatsu already had thousands of tenant farmers in Micronesia, most of them impoverished Okinawans, clearing land and planting sugar-cane. By the late 1930s, Matsue's sugar-cane plantations – with their mills, railways and distilleries – on Saipan and Taipan were producing nearly two-thirds the volume of Fiji's sugar production. Twenty years earlier, Chamorros and Caroline Islanders had made up two-thirds of the population there; Okinawan arrivals then reduced the representation of indigenous Micronesians to less than 10 per cent on both islands.

That Matsue was destined to be financially successful was obvious: he had no competition, his cheap Okinawan labourers knew the sugar-cane business, and he had the Japanese government offering him cheap land, planting subsidies and low taxes. By the mid-1930s, Japan's mining of Angaur's phosphate on Palau was even more profitable than the entire Micronesian copra trade. However, sugar remained king throughout the region. And the profits which Japanese Micronesia's sugar industry generated during the 1920s and 1930s was attributable primarily to the plentiful supply and industriousness of the imported Okinawan and Japanese labourers.

Japanese rule was similar to that of the British and Australians in the Solomons, Papua and New Guinea during this same period. That is, the Japanese appointed the village chief and the village headman, and then both did what the nearest Japanese police chief told them – mainly, to report offences, collect taxes and assist with census taking. A Japanese police chief customarily controlled each district. Unlike the British and Australian situations, however, not scores but hundreds of such Japanese officials existed. In fact, Micronesia was saturated with Japanese officialdom.

Japan's commitment to its Micronesian possession was also mirrored in the region's new educational system, no longer the sole franchise of Christian missionaries. Japan established a comprehensive network of public schools, with attendance being compulsory on the larger islands. By the 1930s in Palau, for example, the centre of Japanese administration in Micronesia, nearly all children were attending school. Throughout Micronesia at this time, more than half of all children of school age were at least exposed for two to three years to a daily curriculum which included reading and writing Japanese and lessons in loyalty to Japan, devotion to the Emperor and gratitude to the Japanese colonial officials. Nearly everywhere else in Pacific Islands at this time, schools, if they existed at all, were still run by Christian missions.

Until about 1930, Japan's colonial policy in Micronesia was uniquely characterized by a robust development programme. Land was alienable through the Japanese government alone, which made it readily available for viable commercial interests. After 1931 things changed, reflecting a sudden shift in Japan's foreign policy in general. With governmental approval, land was now obtainable directly from its Micronesian owner. Though Christian missions were still tolerated, official governmental schools, with their compulsory attendance, took precedence. Japan provided free health services (though areas of low population still went without). The level of an island's commercial development now determined its taxation.

Most striking in the 1930s were the enormous amounts of land taken from Micronesians and the huge numbers of Okinawans and Japanese who came to colonize the region – a situation very similar to the British suddenly arriving in New Zealand in the 1840s. Indeed, so great were their numbers that by 1937 Okinawans and Japanese already equalled the indigenous Micronesians. By then, the Micronesians retained only about one-fourth of their land, the remaining three-quarters having gone to Japanese sugar and copra plantations.

Despite Japan's extraordinary financial investment in Micronesia – certainly the most robust governmental scheme Pacific Islands had ever experienced – the Micronesians themselves scarcely profited from it. Their own financial opportunities seemed to dwindle as taxation soared. Of course, they enjoyed improved living conditions, better education and health. But Micronesian development, for all its promises, had turned into Micronesian dispossession. As this became evident to everyone with interests in the Pacific, Japan commenced, at the end of the 1930s, to construct military fortifications on its more strategic Micronesian islands. The act was symbolic of the end of old colonialism there, and of the beginning of an entirely new Micronesia – one which was to be born out of four years of bloodshed and terror.

THE COLONIAL LEGACY

Doubtless, the greatest effect of colonialism in Pacific Islands was the region's incorporation into the global economy. This was achieved by colonial powers who promoted and regulated trade and fostered those Pacific exports on which this trade depended. At the end of the 1930s most Pacific Islanders were still living from traditional village economies. However, a significant number of them were now living from an export economy, their villages supplying labour, cash crops or both to a larger, foreign market.

The colonial policy of all Pacific powers increasingly focused on how best to reconcile these two contrasting economies. Those Pacific Islanders who had little or nothing to offer colonial powers generally maintained their traditional lifestyles in relative peace; they also missed out on many of the real benefits of integration. Those who had both labour and cash crops to offer foreign powers gained in material wealth, education, health and general quality of life; the price they paid for this, however, was often the loss of identity and dignity, as they were almost universally elbowed to the margins of the white man's Pacific.

Wise colonial administrators – of whom there were too few – sought to achieve a balance between the protection of the Pacific identity and the development of local resources. Unhappily, this always remained an ideal, the victim of political necessity, economic reality and racial prejudice of every cast. For colonialism was not simply the imposition of a foreign nation's rule: it was the expansion of the capitalist economic order into the wide Pacific. In this way Pacific Islands became the playing field of the world's most competitive market contenders. This demanded human sacrifice.

Though Britain at least demonstrated a superficial belief in the Islander prerogative, each colonial power in Pacific Islands in the first half of the twentieth century, including Britain, was convinced of its own 'racial', cultural and political superiority. The policies of each were the expression of these biases (as well as of the inherent arrogance of any government towards the governed). That is, these 'enlightened' powers were convinced they had found primitive Islanders whom they had lifted up to the superior benefits of Western civilization.

One certainly cannot deny that the 'civilizing' influence of colonial powers in Pacific Islands halted most grievous acts of violence there, brought a Western concept of order to perceived chaos, regulated local and international trade, introduced hitherto unknown educational and health services, and inaugurated, in some regions, the first steps towards self-determination (particularly in British colonies). If injustices by virtue of race remained almost everywhere an unfortunate side-effect of colonialism at the end of the 1930s, this was principally, but not exclusively, because of the want of shared value systems and wealth, especially in Melanesia. Indeed, many non-Islanders deemed this inequity to be a social imperative, as it was thought to help 'civilize' the Pacific: that is, the socially advantaged helped to make the socially disadvantaged more like Europeans and Americans. Few voices yet uttered the word 'discrimination'; it was still not part of the political vocabulary. Other priorities fashioned popular attitudes. The age of the indigenous priority was still far off – in some cases, like with the USA and France in the Pacific, seemingly forever unattainable.

Commonly held, or superficially propagated, beliefs about Pacific Islanders' innate 'inferiority' – their childishness, slavishness, sexual perversity, aggressiveness and other ludicrous fables – revealed more about the white psyche than about the Islander character. Islanders did not always passively submit to this outrage. Islanders knew they had rights, and increasingly sensed it was time for these rights to be acknowledged by whites in the Pacific: not in token concessions, but in real conferrals. To attain these rights, Islanders would turn to strike action, to the boycotting of white businesses, or to the establishment of 'cargo cults'.

Strikes were rare. This was perhaps because of unfamiliarity with the effectiveness of strike action and because of a traditional lack of solidarity among Islander labourers who still prioritized tribal affiliations. A notable exception occurred in Rabaul, New Britain's administrative centre, in 1929, after which the horrified Australian officials there imposed severe sentences on the strike leaders and persecuted the indigenous police force and labour pool.

The second recourse for Islanders, the boycotting of white businesses, achieved a remarkable twist in Fiji, where just before the First World War the Fijian Apolosi Nawai founded what later came to be known as the Viti Company. Here, Fijians handled everything which until then white men had dealt with, including the hiring of white labourers at exploitative wages. The Viti Company grew in influence, acquiring nationalistic and religious implications for most Fijians, until Nawai was convicted of 'sedition' by the local British administration in 1917 and exiled to Rotuma where he spent nearly 20 years. The severe British response was meant to intimidate emulators.

'Cargo-cult' opposition, the Islanders' third recourse, was even more openly hostile towards whites, but in the end self-defeating for its irrelevance. Cargo-cults – the label deriving from the belief that European power resided in the wooden crates in which colonial officials received their goods – were common to New Guinea, the Solomons and other parts of Melanesia, and combined Christian and native belief. Beginning in the nineteenth century, growing in the 1930s and proliferating especially after the Second World War, they predicted the arrival of tribal gods or ancestors coming with goods on either ships or æroplanes to usher in a new age. In some places symbolic airstrips were even constructed in preparation for their arrival. By 1940 on Tanna in the New Hebrides, for example, the 'Jon Frum' movement (from English 'John from . . . '), building on predecessors, was endorsing the reversal of European and Tannese relationships, and the elimination of the concept of wealth as it heralded the coming of Jon Frum, a fictitious prophet. The lesson of the cargo-cults is that many Pacific Islanders wanted the Western world . . . but without the Westerner in it. Often the cargo-cults took on bizarre qualities. Though occasionally suppressed here and there by perplexed colonial officials, they would rise up repeatedly well into the second half of the twentieth century; in some places they are still popular today. This has cogent reasons. The cargo-cults, like a religious sect, gave their devotees hope amidst the confusion of all-too-rapid change. More importantly, however, they played, and continue to play, a significant role in the formation of proto-nationalisms (and micro-nationalisms) in Melanesia, principally through the establishment of unprecedented forms of unification behind ideologies of protest.

By the end of the 1930s, it was becoming evident to all concerned in Pacific Islands that colonialism in its traditional guise no longer functioned well there, and that something different would soon have to replace it. France began entertaining dynamic economic schemes for its Polynesian colonies which would include indigenous representation. In contrast, America was tightening its grip on Hawai'i and Guam, a move which took on strategic military significance. On the other end of the scale, Britain, still pursuing its long-time policy of what has been termed 'imperial benevolence', was seriously assessing the possibility of self-determination for many of its island colonies. Australia and New Zealand were superficially following Britain's lead, though the League of Nations took exception with how both countries administered their Pacific mandates. Chile, the Pacific's smallest colonial power, had annexed Rapanui (Easter Island) in 1888, and had kept its inhabitants confined to the island's single village after leasing the rest of the island to a Chilean-Scots sheep-farming company in 1893; neglecting Rapanui thereafter, it called the 3600-kilometre expanse of Pacific Ocean between it and Rapanui the 'Chilean Sea'. Ominously, Japan, the Pacific's third mandate power, had left the League of Nations altogether in 1934 but retained Micronesia – not as a mandate, but as a colonial territory. That historic changes in the Pacific were nigh was felt by everyone.

Each nation fostered its own idiosyncratic agenda in Pacific Islands, its island(s) and archipelago(s) in turn reflecting the foreign presence for better or worse in their distinctive fashion. Some Pacific Islands had been wholly transformed, like New Zealand and Hawai'i; others had hardly been touched: New Guinea, the Outliers and remote archipelagos like the Marquesas, Australs and Tuamotus.

The education of Islanders was initially not regarded as the responsibility of a colonial administration in the Pacific. The first decades of the twentieth century still saw missionaries alone offering this privilege nearly everywhere; indeed, missionaries ran all the schools in French Polynesia until well after the Second World War. However, a small number of colonial administrators soon initiated local schemes modelled on the schools in their home country. Whereas the priority of the missionary schools had been evangelizing, that of the colonial schools became loyalty to the respective power: village children thus now spent several hours of each day learning the catechism of King (Kaiser, Emperor) and Country. In truth, little of substance was learnt in Pacific Islands schools before the Second World War, apart from the training of Islander missionaries and pastors and the imparting of the basic ABCs to a handful of island children. In 1939, only New Zealand, American Samoa and Hawai'i had secular co-educational schools at which attendance was required by law (Palau's Japanese schools were not co-educational). Most colonial administrators did not even contemplate the notion of large-scale school systems until after the war. Of course, once this occurred it created the first generation of Islanders who could read and write ... and govern themselves.

The age of colonialism in Pacific Islands, like the preceding ages of early contact and settlement, comprised another step towards the region's international integration. Because no concept of 'statehood' had previously existed in Pacific Islands – only tribal bonds internally regulated by descent, rank, titles and achievements – colonialism crucially introduced the concept of self-determination. The colony supplanted (or attempted to supersede) the tribe, introducing Islanders to a different way of governing society which could encompass much larger groupings of peoples, including those of different ethnic backgrounds.

Colonial administrations, of themselves, were too weak, however, to realize those policies most non-Islanders hoped would lead the Islanders to emulate cosmopolitan ideals. The great number of Islander protests, abuses, initiatives and other distractions weakened even further the dynamic of development and modernization some colonial powers sporadically displayed.

Finally, colonialism utterly failed to introduce a cash economy, the basis of Western society, to the Pacific Islands village.

Nevertheless, colonialism forever changed the way Pacific Islanders viewed the world: personal social relations had yielded to impersonal market (labour) relations; kinship and rank status to education and knowledge status; group priority to individual priority; and superstition and sorcery to a fervent Island Christianity. Underlying all these important changes, however, was still the traditional Islander way, which continued to influence and mutate the Western borrowing, perpetuating millennia-old attitudes and customs in a wholly new Pacific.

In this way, colonialism created new Pacific identities with an unprecedented stratification – the new foreign atop the old indigenous – the immediate consequence of which was the emergence of the 'modern native' who was becoming the universally recognizable New Islander.

6

Pacific Islanders in Transit

WAR IN THE PACIFIC

Having signed the Axis Pact with Germany and Italy on 27 September 1940, Japan demanded from defeated France the bases in French Indo-China it required in order to win its three-year-old war against China. First securing its northern defences through a treaty of neutrality with the Soviet Union on 13 April 1941, Japan then occupied French Indo-China on 28 July and, from there, Thailand, with the consent of Thailand's dictator Pibul Songgram. With this, Japan was also hoping to create a base of operations against the British possessions in Malaya and Burma, which were tagged to become Japanese. On the same day that Japan militarily occupied Thailand – 7 December 1941 – Japan attacked the US Pacific Fleet at its home base of Pearl Harbor, Hawai'i, disabling the Americans and allowing Japan to advance swiftly into Southeast Asia and the Pacific.

By December's end, Japan had occupied Malaya, the Philippines, Borneo, Celebes, Guam, Wake Island and Hong Kong in rapid succession. In February 1942 the British surrendered Singapore, and in April the Americans surrendered Bataan on Luzón, the Philippines' main island. In May, symbolic Corregidor – American Manila's island fortress – fell as well. After this, Japan occupied Burma, Sumatra, Bali, Java, Timor and the Moluccas (the former Spice Islands), from where they bombed northern Australia with impunity.

Only three days after Pearl Harbor, intent on securing trans-Pacific communications – and before the USA or its allies Britain, Australia and New Zealand could respond militarily – Japanese forces had invaded Tarawa in Britain's Gilbert Islands, then gone on to take the USA's Ocean Island (Kure) in the Midways group west of Hawai'i and Australia's Nauru in Micronesia. Only one month later, Japan invaded New Guinea, where a sizable population of Japanese had been resident for decades: New Britain's Rabaul, administrative capital of Australia's Territory of New Guinea, fell to the Japanese on 23 January 1942. By month's end, Japanese forces had secured the southeastern tip of New Guinea, all the Bismarcks, Bougainville and were swiftly descending into the Solomons.

By the middle of 1942, Japan was dominating over 450 million people in Southeast Asia and the Pacific. Nevertheless, the Imperial command was to be short-lived.

This is because the response by the USA, though crippled by the attack on Pearl Harbor, had been equally swift. By March 1942, US forces had gathered along a line of islands and archipelagos to form a linked southern bulwark which stretched from New Caledonia in the west to Samoa in the east (eventually reaching even to Rapanui, at a longitude as far east as the US state of Arizona!). Whereupon the Americans then commenced massive construction: wharves, air-strips and military bases larger than Midwestern towns rapidly rose which would provide the infrastructure and supplies to wage war against the Japanese to the north and west. These bases – with their fleets of vehicles and heavy machinery, Quonset huts, aeroplanes, tens of thousands of both male and female personnel – within months transformed much of Pacific Islands into a transplanted USA, and altered indigenous perceptions there forever.

Guadalcanal in the Solomons was the turning point in the Pacific's land war. The Solomons, more than any other Pacific group, experienced the full savagery of war, leaving scars which have still not completely healed more than half a century later. On 3 May 1942, the Japanese forces – their road into the Pacific free after Singapore's fall in February – advanced to the Solomons' administrative capital since 1896, Tulagi, a small island in the Florida group. Already in 1939 Britain's colonial Governor there had established the Solomon Islands Defence Force (SIDF), but when the seven Europeans, two Chinese and 178 local policemen who comprised the SIDF in 1942 witnessed the thousands of Japanese landing they hurriedly fled. Whereupon a large Japanese invasion fleet then pushed on towards Port Moresby in Papua.

However, Japan's southern drive was halted at last when its invasion fleet was defeated on 7–8 May 1942 in the Battle of the Coral Sea, which raged half-way between the Solomons and Australia. One month later, on 4–6 June, Japan's eastward push into the North Pacific was arrested as well, by the defeat of Japan's second invasion fleet in the Battle of Midway west of Hawai'i, in which Japan lost four aircraft carriers. Both were major Allied victories which seriously impaired Japan's mobility in the Pacific. None the less, they did not stop Japan from landing on Guadalcanal, Tulagi's southern neighbour, on 7 July 1942, then hurriedly constructing an airfield there from which to attack Australia and defy the Americans' air base under construction on Espiritu Santo in the New Hebrides.

The combined US and Australian forces under US General Douglas MacArthur, Commander-in-Chief in the Pacific, now turned Japan's offence into a defence. The USA led the campaign, and there had been two opposing strategies for waging it: MacArthur had called for the incremental diminution of the Japanese beachheads, whereas US Admiral Chester Nimitz wanted to evade direct confrontation in the wide Pacific and to attack Japan directly. MacArthur's plan prevailed, bringing early victories but also enormous loss of human life. In this way, the watershed of the Pacific war became Guadalcanal.

On August 8 of 1942, 10 000 US Marines landed at Red Beach on Guadalcanal. Though they immediately captured

Japan's unfinished airfield, on the following day Japanese planes thwarted US supply ships' arrival and at night eight Japanese warships sank four Allied cruisers and two destroyers. One of the USA's worst naval defeats in history, it forced the Allied naval contingent to withdraw. This then exposed the Marines to probable annihilation by the superior Japanese forces. However, for six months the Marines held out on Guadalcanal, despite horrendous aerial bombardments, ground attacks and physical extremes. When American supplies and reinforcements finally arrived, the Japanese clandestinely moved their surviving troops back to New Georgia in February 1943. The Americans eventually followed in July, resulting in major confrontations at Rendova and Munda. Though several Japanese detachments held out on Choiseul and in the Shortland Islands until 1945, the Japanese had essentially lost the Solomons by the end of 1943.

Guadalcanal is well remembered in American history as the USA's first victory against Japan's land forces in the war. Approximately 25 000 Japanese and 5000 Americans were killed or wounded there. There is no official record of how many Solomon Islanders lost their lives in the fighting.

One year after Pearl Harbor, a joint Allied campaign retook Buna on New Guinea's eastern coast. After this, never again would Japan expand its Pacific front. But the fighting from village to village and from island to island which now followed – ever northwards and westwards, shrinking the arc of Japan's might – waxed long and terrible. It turned into a painfully protracted rout, with horrendous losses on both sides. Never in its 50 000-year history had Pacific Islands experienced carnage of such magnitude.

By November 1943 the front had reached Micronesia, where fighting remained ferocious. The US forces in the mid-Pacific under Admiral Nimitz, after having regained the Aleutian Islands (May to August 1943), first secured the Gilberts (November), and then the Marshalls (February 1944).

Japan's main Pacific base of Rabaul on New Britain in the Bismarcks was captured by the Allies after prolonged bombings and a massive landing in a campaign which lasted from December 1943 to March 1944. New Guinea's entire northern coast was finally rid of all Japanese troops by April 1944.

In the middle of 1944 Admiral Nimitz liberated Saipan and Guam in the Marianas, then joined up with General MacArthur's land forces to reconquer the Philippines. In November 1944 the USA commenced bombing raids on Japanese cities from the Marianas, then launched the successful invasion of Iwo Jima in the Volcano Islands north of the Marianas on 19 February 1945 and waged the extremely vicious Battle of Okinawa in the Ryukyu Islands just south of Japan from 26 March to 21 June 1945. Japan finally signed the document of capitulation – its unconditional surrender – on the battleship *Missouri* in Tokyo Harbour on 2 September 1945.

ISLANDERS IN UNIFORM

For over three years Pacific Islanders experienced heaven and hell. Nothing in the region would ever be the same again. While most of Melanesia and Micronesia suffered horribly, Polynesia enjoyed excitement, wealth and unparalleled growth. Often, occupied Islanders metamorphosed into Allied liberators, themselves taking brutal revenge for acts committed by their Japanese masters – especially in the last, frantic year and a half of the war when Japan had its back to the wall. Of course, there was a small number of native collaborators and traitors; better remembered, however, are the many thousands of Islander allies and heroes. Equally inspiring was that, for the first time in the history of Pacific Islands, white and brown bonded as brothers – full equals sharing supplies, blankets and danger. A new Pacific kinship was emerging out of the blood and sand, perhaps the ultimate achievement of Pacific Islands' 'finest generation'.

When Britain declared war on Germany in September 1939, Pacific peoples who were allied to Britain immediately rallied to the cause: just as they had done in the Boer War and the

First World War, thousands of Antipodeans left to fight on the other side of the globe. A quarter of all New Zealand males, for example, were drafted into the military and came to suffer a higher casualty rate than Australia's, already one of the Allies' highest. (Of the over 7700 Kiwis in the Crete campaign alone, half were killed, wounded or captured.) Deprived of its manpower, New Zealand still achieved the highest agricultural productivity of any combatant nation during the war; all the food it did not use itself it sent directly to Great Britain to lessen the burden there.

Three months after the fall of France on 22 June 1940, New Caledonia's Conseil Général voted unanimously to support the Free French government. As a result, the Governor, who was loyal to Marshal Pétain's pro-German government at Vichy, was forced into exile in French Indo-China. By March 1942, New Caledonia had become a strategic Allied base: indeed, the fleet which routed the Japanese in the Battle of the Coral Sea (May 1942), halting Japan's mobility in the southwest Pacific, was based at Noumea, New Caledonia's capital. American troops in their hundreds of thousands, and New Zealand troops in their tens of thousands, passed through New Caledonia on their way to the various Pacific theatres; of all Pacific ports, only San Francisco dispatched more wartime consignments than Noumea. New Caledonia's Kanaks experienced far better treatment from their American employers than they had ever received from their French and *caldoche* masters, and so came to realize for the first time the possibility of an egalitarian society.

The New Hebrideans northeast of New Caledonia, who had lived under the Anglo-French New Hebrides Condominium since formalization in 1914 and declaration in 1923, were the first French colony to recognize the Free French, on 20 July 1940. The Americans in early 1942 constructed and maintained on Espiritu Santo and Efate large military bases which they then used as staging areas for the Solomons campaign. The New Hebrideans never experienced front action; the US base at Espiritu Santo was only once bombed by the Japanese who, it was reported at the time, succeeded in killing only a cow. On the island of Tanna, the Americans' wealth, profligate when compared with local penury, revived the pre-war Jon Frum 'cargo-cult'. The American writer James A. Michener, then stationed at Espiritu Santo, was inspired by his view of Ambae on the horizon to create his imaginary 'Bali Ha'i' as there he wrote his first novel *Tales of the South Pacific*, later turned into a New York musical and Hollywood film (*South Pacific*) which did much to promote tourism and modern Pacific myths after the war.

Polynesia's isolated Ellice Islands (now Tuvalu), a British protectorate since 1892 and colony since 1916, were similarly inundated with Americans during the war, who built airfields at Funafuti, Nukufetau and Nanumea. Funafuti was particularly of importance, as here the US Seventh Air Force housed its B-24 Liberators which raided Japanese bases in the Marshalls and Gilberts. All planes flying from Wallis to the Gilberts refuelled in the Ellices as well. Though the islands were occasionally bombed by the Japanese, they were never invaded. Unfortunately, the USA covered Funafuti's most fertile land with airfield, which reduced the acreage planted in coconuts and swamp taro by a third, resulting in the latter's loss as a staple food on the island. Pits left behind when the Americans extracted coral for the airfields became stagnant lakes into which garbage has been dumped ever since, creating ideal breeding grounds for rats and mosquitoes. (The Ellices remained part of Britain's Gilbert and Ellice Islands Colony until 1975.)

Many more Pacific islands experienced Allied intrusion on a massive scale. In the Cooks, for example, the USA built air bases on Aitutaki and Penrhyn. And though Wallis and Futuna, a French protectorate since 1887 and colony since 1924, remained the only French colony in the Pacific to stay loyal to the pro-German Vichy government of France until after Pearl Harbor, both then supported the Free French, and Wallis, from 1942 to 1944, became a strategic US base housing up to 6000 troops.

The Établissements français de l'Océanie, created in 1880, declared its support for the Free French cause on 2 September 1940. In early 1942 the Americans arrived to establish on Bora Bora in the Society Islands one of their four major staging and supply bases in the Pacific. Until Japan's defeat in 1945, all of French Polynesia, including Tahiti, remained completely cut off from France – a particularly distressing state of affairs for the colony, as Paris had always overseen the most minute details of life there.

In December of 1942, Malaita in the Solomons became the home of a US Service Battalion comprising a couple of hundred Solomon Islanders trained to scout for the Marines. Dubbed the 'International Brigade', it also included Fijians, Britons and New Zealanders familiar with the Solomons; after Guadalcanal's liberation in 1943, the battalion was disbanded. Elsewhere in the Solomons, coast-watchers with radio transmitters reported on Japanese movements from behind enemy lines; many of these coast-watchers were resident British officials, planters, mission nurses, nuns and Solomon Islanders who daily risked their lives to send vital information and to rescue Allied personnel – such as the later US President John F. Kennedy.

The situation in wartime Fiji was both heroic and pathetic, indicative of the islands' continuing human dichotomy. Ten per cent of the indigenous Fijian population enlisted for war service, either as combatants or labourers. As in New Zealand, no coercion was necessary: like the Māori, Fijians had always been celebrated warriors and now harboured strong loyalties to the King and Union Jack. Fijians also raised private donations for the war effort; in this way, both the HMS *Fiji* was financed and the famous 'Sponsor a Spitfire' scheme benefited handsomely. During the war, Nadi was developed into an important Allied airfield with enthusiastic local support.

However, not all Fijians were enthusiastic. The Indians, who nearly to a man resented their treatment under Britain, generally refused to participate in the war effort; they even went on strike in 1943, while Indian merchants profited from the wartime economy. In August of 1943, 6371 Fijians were serving in the Fiji Military Forces, which included the Labour Corps, alongside 808 expatriate New Zealanders, but only 264 Indians. Though 2029 Fijians returned to Fiji from the Solomons campaign with their lives, 42 did not – and one of the fallen, Sefanaia Sukanaivalu, became the posthumous recipient of a Victoria Cross for heroism. It is understandable that there was great resentment among indigenous Fijians and resident Britons and New Zealanders, then, at the Indians' audacious reluctance to support the war effort, especially as Fiji's own existence was being threatened. 'Fijians are becoming increasingly resentful of the fact that Fijians are serving in large numbers in the war and Indians are not', stated a governmental report in 1943. 'Economic fear enters here also when Indians are seen to be trying to buy land with war profits or to lease land left vacant because the native owners are in uniform.' If anything, the war cemented the alliance between the Europeans and indigenous Fijians who wholeheartedly supported the Allied cause, appreciated to be a common cause. This divided Fijian society even more, as Indians were not part of this process. What might have been Fiji's historic opportunity for reconciliation and unification became the source of even greater bitterness, misunderstanding and division.

Unlike the Indians of Fiji, most Pacific Islanders did not hesitate to don uniform. Some 300 Polynesians and half-Polynesians volunteered in Tahiti to join the French Battalion of the Pacific, then fought valiantly in North Africa, Italy and Provence (Southern France) alongside compatriot New Caledonians. New Zealand's famous Māori Battalion distinguished itself in North Africa, Greece and Italy. Some 50 Tongans joined the Fiji Military Forces. As we have seen, over 2000 Fijians fought in the Solomon Islands campaign, where also 680 Solomon Islanders served in the SIDF. The Pacific Islands Regiment comprised more than 3500 Papuan and New Guinean combatants, with a further 3137 fighting police and 955 medical orderlies.

Other Islanders served without seeing action, such as the thousands in the Tongan Defence Force and the two American Samoan units of the Fitafita guard and First Samoan Battalion, Marine Corps Reserve.

Then there were the Micronesians in Japan's own colonies of Ponape and Palau, who served as non-combatants in Japan's volunteer units in New Guinea. When hostilities ceased, Palau's 104th Construction Detachment, for one, was simply abandoned there. It took them years to make it home again to Palau.

THE CHALLENGE OF PEACE

The principal consequence of the war in the Pacific – apart from halting, then crushing, Japan's campaign of acquisition – was the projection of US power throughout the region. It is a process which is still continuing today. Japan's attack on Pearl Harbor had thrust a reluctant and isolationist USA into the Second World War. By the time the war had ended, the USA was the world's dominant military and economic force. This of course forced a realignment of loyalties throughout the Pacific region.

The USA had become a Pacific colonial power at the end of the nineteenth century with its annexation of Hawai'i and acquisition of the Spanish colonies of the Philippines and Guam in 1898, followed by the acquisition of Eastern Samoa one year later. But two other colonial powers – Britain and Japan – had halted the USA's further expansion into the Pacific for nearly half a century. During this time, Japan had attempted to become Asia's dominant principal through the establishment of its 'Greater East-Asian Co-Prosperity Sphere'. This plan was thwarted after Japan's military occupation of French Indo-China in July 1941 when an embargo on iron from the USA and on oil from the Dutch East Indies forced Japan to choose one of the three recourses left to it: submit, withdraw or fight. Japan's dynamic expansion had been empowered by the doubling of its oil consumption between 1931 and 1937. Without oil and iron, Japan's military-industrial mill would grind to a halt. As much to stall the USA's defence of Allied interests in the Pacific as to save face, Japan chose to seize the offensive. It was a fateful decision, for half a million Japanese soldiers and civilians soon lost their lives in Micronesia and Melanesia. Their opponents during the conflict were mainly US troops concentrated in four major bases on New Caledonia's Grande Terre, Espiritu Santo in the New Hebrides (now Vanuatu), Guadalcanal in the Solomons, and Bora Bora in Polynesia's Society Islands. As the USA constructed large airfields throughout the South Pacific and dominated with its ships the southern supply routes from America to New Zealand and Australia, this created a new and powerful infrastructure which would not vanish once the war was over and the Japanese were gone.

War wreaked havoc on much of Melanesia and Micronesia – but perhaps its greatest victim of all was the very colonialism the Allies were so courageously defending. Years before Japan's defeat, politicians in London, Paris, Washington, Canberra and Wellington had already commenced designing a new Pacific. But because each power entertained different agendas, instead of creating one Pacific for all Pacific peoples – which wholly lay within their capability – each international authority after the war insinuated a separate, and contingent, identity in its sphere of influence. It was an imbalanced, inconsistent and, as ever, inequitable initiative which yielded the Pacific chessboard still wrestled over today.

In the Solomons, whose colonial capital Tulagi had been destroyed by the Japanese in 1942, the British established a new capital at Honiara on neighbouring Guadalcanal. This was because of the Americans' superior wartime infrastructure there. In fact, a great number of the Solomons' present roads and airfields are the legacy of the Americans. The British were not the only ones to profit from the American presence. When the thousands of Islanders on Malaita, for example, returned from the bush where they had been hiding to escape the carnage, they witnessed the American troops, their numbers, vehicles, culture and material wealth, and resolved to reconstitute their indigenous society on the basis of traditional custom and so founded the Ma'asina Ruru movement.

Alarmed by the movement's increasingly aggressive anti-colonial attitude after the war, the British administration in 1948 had their police crush the Ma'asina Ruru before the movement could spread any further. However, within a year over 2000 Solomon Islanders were in Honiara's prison for having 'refused to co-operate': Britain's crack-down had back-fired, only serving to politically unite the Malaitans for the first time. Realizing this, the British administration sought a compromise solution which would not prompt Islanders to further opposition, and in 1953 the Malaita Council was formed. Eminently successful, this proved to be the prototype of the system of local government still followed in the Solomon Islands today. A Legislative Council was established in 1960; four years later, elected members were included. By this time, local government councils were supervising all regional con-cerns in the Solomons.

In those regions not occupied by the Japanese – that is, the islands and archipelagos situated south and east of the Solomon Islands – the war had brought relatively little personal danger and great benefits: salaried employment, material goods, improved sanitation, electricity, medical assistance and many other perquisites of the American, Australian and New Zealand occupiers. Both Samoa and Fiji experienced the war in this way and, because both were advance staging areas, attained an affluence the Samoans and Fijians had never before known. A similar excitement, prosperity and cultural infusion occurred in the Cook Islands, Tonga and throughout much of French Polynesia, though to a lesser degree. Most Islanders at this time prioritized the learning of English, which language they now appreciated to be their passport to economic advantage.

The end of the war meant for most Pacific Islanders new challenges: the reconstruction and future development of the entire Pacific, of which greater body many now felt an integral part. (Before the war, the concept 'Pacific' meant nothing to isolated Islanders.) It heralded a break from the past, as this was sensed to be the time to redress the wrongs inherent in outdated colonialism. Reconstruction was two-pronged: first, the physical restoration of the devastated copra plantations of Melanesia and Micronesia which would take over a decade to replant and bear fruit; and second, the political establishment of new bodies to deal with pan-Pacific concerns in order to manage and promote Pacific economies within an immediate Pacific context – the beginning of decolonization.

There was already a history of such a reform. The League of Nations' concept of a 'Pacific stewardship' which had led to Japan's, Australia's and New Zealand's mandates had existed long before the First World War. In the 1920s and 1930s, international meetings and conferences had then addressed issues of health, marketing, administration, general welfare and other Pacific concerns. Even during the Second World War, Fiji set up a committee encharged with formulating post-war development; Britain passed an Act of Parliament promoting research and development in all its overseas colonies; and Australia and New Zealand frequently met to consider their Pacific agendas. This came from the perceived want of comprehensive information on Pacific peoples and resources, and the need to convert the general anthropological and scientific information that was there into policy-making relevance.

Australia assumed a particularly active role in this process. From 1942 to 1945 the Australian army took over the governing of all Papua and New Guinea and through its Directorate of Research and Civil Affairs came the training courses for administering the colony. Its School of Civil Affairs ultimately became the Australian School of Pacific Administration after the war, whose publications contributed towards the creation of an efficient and professional public sevice in Papua and New Guinea. Australia also founded the Australian National University in Canberra as a research institution, with its own school dedicated to policy-directed social research in the Pacific. Auckland University College (later the University of Auckland) modestly followed Australia's lead with a Professorship in Anthropology aimed at a more professional administration of New Zealand's several Pacific dependencies (Samoa, Niue, Cook Islands, Tokelau). For all this new impetus, the inertia of historical administration proved difficult to counteract. A willingness to change ideology was evident after the war, but the new ideology was a long time coming.

An initial result of post-war planning was the emergence of *regionalism* – the division of an area into administrative regions having partial autonomy. However, this occurred only circuitously. From Australia and New Zealand's frequent meetings came the idea of forming one all-encompassing body that might advise on South Pacific matters to constituent members. Out of this was born the South Pacific Commission (now named the Secretariat of the Pacific Community) in 1947, to which Britain, France, the Netherlands, the USA, Australia and New Zealand belonged. The Commission's public responsibility was to co-ordinate mutual enterprises, offer a forum promoting quality governing, conduct Pacific research and share the results with fellow members. Its not-so-public mission, on the other hand, was to perpetuate historical colonial realities through high-level co-ordination. Ironically, the conferences the Commission organized brought together for the first time leading Islander personalities who, in turn, accelerated regionalism's emergence – the opposite aim of the Commission's intention to maintain the colonial prerogative.

TOWARDS A FREER PACIFIC

New Zealand – Pacific Islands' only internal colonial power – was both acting and reacting during this sudden reshaping of the newer, superficially 'freer' Pacific. Its own most important change at this time involved its immigration policy. Before the

Second World War, New Zealand had practically excluded all migrants but those coming from Britain, which was still very much regarded as 'Home'. Despite significant numbers of Germans, Dalmatians, Italians and Scandinavians in New Zealand, legislation had been passed to discourage all non-British migrants to the country, especially Asians. However, in the late 1940s and throughout the 1950s this began to change. Fearing its economy would be seriously threatened by Asia's rapidly expanding economies, New Zealand, in concert with Australia, resolved to increase its population drastically through designed immigration. Both Australia and New Zealand financially assisted migrants with their passage by ship, and immediately after the war tens of thousands of mostly displaced persons – many of them non-English-speaking – entrusted their destinies to the Antipodes. This profoundly affected New Zealand's cultural identity, within one generation turning the country into a multi-ethnic society, which had the long-term effect of submerging its Māori heritage even more.

The war had also brought American culture to New Zealand, and on a grand scale. Dance, music, speech, tastes, commodities, even marriage ties – all these 'Yank' intrusions meant for most New Zealanders the first major break from the British motherland. The rapidly changing international situation of the 1940s forced New Zealand to reappraise its traditional loyalty to Britian, obliging the parliamentary acknowledgement of a separate national identity for the first time. For it was clear Britain could no longer maintain an influence east of Suez, whereas the USA exerted paramount influence throughout most of the Pacific. Both Australia and New Zealand were actively aligning their foreign relations more closely to those of the USA as well.

As a result, New Zealand's Parliament finally ratified in 1949 Britain's Statute of Westminster from 1931. Kiwis were now citizens only of an independent New Zealand, losing their British citizenship for good. And two years later, in 1951, Australia, New Zealand and the USA signed the ANZUS security pact – the first time either Australia or New Zealand had entered into an alliance which excluded Great Britain. Together with Australia, New Zealand also committed troops to the US-led United Nations' force in the Korean War (1950–53). It was the beginning of a major political and cultural realignment which was to accelerate in the last two decades of the twentieth century.

Despite New Zealand's vigorous growth – which would soon include its responsible piloting of Western Samoa into independence – the country failed to adequately address its Māori situation. New Zealand actually had no separate plan for its Māori – who were fully equal New Zealand citizens – apart from the one it had drafted in the 1930s and memorialized after the war in its Māori Social and Economic Advancement Act of 1945. This latter scheme endorsed the incorporation of all Māori into those aspects of New Zealand society they had been excluded from until then, on the principle that total assimilation would preclude social and legislative discrimination. (One must appreciate that this was very much the 'modern' view at the time, perceived as sensitive, liberal and right; it should not be judged by the greatly changed perceptions of two generations later.) As a result, the Māori could purchase alcohol the same as whites in 1948, and were bound to the same marriage laws as whites in 1951.

If the legislative emphasis had first been on economic and social equality of the Māori, throughout the rest of the 1950s this gradually developed into the establishment of legal equality for the Māori as well. The New Zealand Parliament passed the Māori Affairs Act to slim down the large amount of Māori legislation and to ease their direction, still pursuing the long-term goal of complete assimilation of the Māori people into New Zealand's white European society. However, at the same time, the question of what was a Māori came to the fore as an average of 16 per cent more Māori each year were moving to New Zealand's cities. And so many Māori had married European New Zealanders that, as in Hawai'i, two to three generations of mixed parentage were beginning to render the labels 'Māori' and 'European' irrelevant: all were simply New

Zealanders, citizens of one of the world's wealthiest, healthiest and most egalitarian countries in the 1950s.

In 1960, an inquiry into the Department of Māori Affairs made a case for a return to the earlier policy of 'positive discrimination' – favouring Māori over whites in civil legislation – so as to redress the Māori's increasing disadvantages following the massive urbanization of the late 1940s and 1950s. The inquiry also rejected assimilation, preferring *integration* instead: the Māori, it held, should preserve their cultural uniqueness and enjoy a socioeconomic distribution like the European New Zealanders. The call for integration, rather than assimilation, has grown in the decades since, often culminating in the rejection of European structures without their replacement with anything of value. The Māori's quality of life has greatly improved in the last half century. But because they are equal members of a multi-ethnic society – and not an intrinsic community like the Western Samoans living within the Samoan Islands – they have been compelled to compete with fellow citizens, as one finds in all egalitarian democracies. Many Māori feel this is unfair, and seek a special status in New Zealand for their people...who become increasingly difficult to distinguish as a separate 'race' with each new generation.

New Zealand's stewardship of Western Samoa after the war was exemplary. At the end of 1946, the new United Nations had made Western Samoa New Zealand's trusteeship (it was no longer a mandate). Immediately thereafter, Western Samoans petitioned the United Nations for self-governing status under New Zealand's guidance and protection. Though the UN Trusteeship Council considered the petition – it even dispatched a mission of inquiry to 'Apia – self-government was not granted. However, New Zealand was already of the view that Western Samoa had to be prepared, over several years, for the responsibilities of self-governance, and it actively incorporated native Samoans in the day-to-day process of government. Not all Samoans were pleased with the Western preconditions to independence, which to them appeared to disregard traditional Samoan ways. They also feared the changes these preconditions would effect in Samoa, perhaps making it more Western than Polynesian.

New Zealand was fully aware of the Samoans' reservations and, in turn, anticipated each. In 1947, New Zealand granted Western Samoa a Legislative Assembly, whereby some members were to be elected from among the *matai* (chiefs). A number of initiatives were started: the islands' agricultural potential was exploited through the Reparation Estates, Germany's erstwhile plantations; transport, electricity and water supply were modernized and expanded; and co-operatives – similar to Australia's in Papua New Guinea – were formed. Samoans' gradual integration into public service complemented small, regular modifications to the constitution in order to convey the ethnic responsibility. By 1959, the Western Samoans were wholly governing themselves, and one year later they adopted a constitution. In 1961 both the constitution and the question of independence were approved in a plebiscite by universal ballot. At last, on 1 January 1962, under the auspices of a Labour government in New Zealand, Western Samoa became the first Pacific Islands nation to re-establish its independence in the twentieth century.

Things progressed a bit more slowly in the Cook Islands. Legally still New Zealand soil, the Cooks were granted a Legislative Council in 1946. Eleven years later the Cook Islanders had their own Legislative Assembly with even greater powers of legislation, as New Zealand continued to train indigenous officials in self-government, with a view to granting independence within several years.

Similarly, New Zealand replaced Niue's appointed Island Council in 1959 with an elected Fono Ekepule (Legislative Assembly). The Tokelauans, on the other hand, who had been conveyed from British to New Zealand administration in 1925, became full citizens of New Zealand with the Tokelau Islands Act of 1948 when New Zealand assumed full sovereignty. Though New Zealand proposed that Tokelauans fuse with either the Cook Islands or Western Samoa, the Tokelauans themselves rejected this in 1964, preferring then, and since, to remain New Zealanders in order to maintain their preferential status and immediate benefits.

Fiji's situation was far more complex. Hoping like New Zealand to achieve a truly freer Pacific, Britain was similarly dedicated to the principal of self-determination for its old colony. Already in 1944, for example, it had allowed the Fijian chiefs to control their own administration to a degree unknown for nearly 30 years. Ratu Lala Sukuna, paramount chief of Lau, was instrumental in creating a separate administration for indigenous Fijians which would oversee all of the native land (which amounted to 83 per cent of Fiji's total). He also saw that villagers could still be obligated to grow food, construct houses and produce *tapa* for their chiefs according to tradition, rejecting the trends towards Western individualism. Until 1952, Suva still served as headquarters for the British Imperial Administration in the South Pacific. Fijians served Britain again as combatants from 1952 to 1956 suppressing Malaya's national liberation struggle. In 1954 Ratu Lala Sukuna established the Fijian Association, whose main purpose was seemingly to uphold the British Governor's campaign to thwart the Indians' initiatives to attain equal representation in Fijian society. Fiji's only indication of a change towards greater democratization was the foundation in 1960 of the National Federation Party to uphold the rights of Indian cane farmers. Independence lay a full decade away.

The new single Australian administration for both Papua and New Guinea prioritized the indigenous franchise, acknowledging that the pre-war injustices – particularly in New Guinea – were no longer to be practised. Any perceived wrongs were immediately to be redressed. Australia then backed this up by substantial increases in the colony's funding from Canberra. This new policy itself created a huge problem: those indigenous labourers forced to work during the war past the expiry date of their earlier indentures were discharged *en bloc* in October 1945 and paid all sums owing them as well as full compensation for any war losses. But with no banks and no goods to purchase, the labourers did not benefit from their new wealth. In addition, the region was immediately beset by a labour shortage. The well-funded Australian administration, now larger than before, was severely understaffed, and manufactured goods – so prevalent during the war – were difficult to procure well into the 1950s. The priorities of Australia's own labour, budgetary and material requirements actually left Papua and New Guinea – by this time called Papua New Guinea – far behind all good intentions. Despite the heavy critique this earned, Australia nevertheless achieved two important things in Papua New Guinea just after the war: the two territories' political amalgamation, formalized in 1949; and the establishment of co-operative societies, commercial enterprises owned and managed by and for the benefit of indigenous Papua-New Guinean workers and customers.

MYTH AND REALITY

The myth was that most victor nations believed that the war in the Pacific had been fought for democracy and, once won, should automatically lead to the region's self-determination – that is, to the end of old colonialism. The reality was that, one, the Pacific's development was too diverse to allow this to happen everywhere in the region, and, two, each colonial power had its own, usually quite different, agenda. Britain, Australia and New Zealand indeed believed in independence for their colonies, and eventually offered this alternative to their prepared Islanders. America either tightened its Pacific bonds – the erstwhile nation of Hawai'i was at last subsumed into the union of states – or promised eventual discussion of independence (Micronesia). France, Chile and Indonesia (which wrested Irian Jaya from the Netherlands in 1962, incorporating it the following year) remained nineteenth-century-style colonial masters, refusing any mention of independence.

Developing a highly diverse region like the Melanesian territories into a modern, homogeneous nation, as was actively envisaged and planned in the 1950s, was fraught with contradictions as well. To create an independent Western Samoa by 1960 was 'easy' in comparison, where one ethnicity speaking one Pacific Islands language lived in clearly defined islands enjoying decades of cultural contact with Westerners who had trained them in the Western art of modern civil administration. None of these features obtained in Melanesia. The creation of a modern 'state' there appeared to be more the myth of liberal democrats than the perpetual colonialism the reality seemingly demanded. Of greatest concern to the small number of Australians discussing Papua New Guinea's future in the 1950s was the disconcerting disparity between the territorial tribes: those civilized through the Western contact of over a century differed drastically from those discovered in the Highlands only in the 1950s. One could well soon create an independent nation with only those Melanesians of Western tutelage, but at the cost of disadvantaging the others; or Australia could postpone independence altogether, waiting to develop the neolithic tribes of the Highlands first, disadvantaging thereby all the relatively sophisticated coastal Melanesians.

Australia's Minister for Territories from 1951 to 1963, Paul Hasluck, took a position squarely between the two camps – those who endorsed rapid independence for Papua New Guinea and those who argued for gradual development leading eventually to independence. Though Hasluck personally favoured rapid progress, too hasty a development, he realized, would merely profit the 'expats' (particularly the Australian investors). Hasluck also argued for a policy of uniform development within one territory, in order to avoid Westernized Melanesians taking unfair advantage of non-Westernized Melanesians.

However, this moderate policy frustrated the new elite among the Melanesians, who clearly saw the advantages to them of accelerated development and who resented the postponement of their perceived destiny. It was at this time that the Melanesian 'cargo-cults' (see Chapter 5) experienced their greatest proliferation, as the numerous economic development programmes the colonial officials were encouraging the Melanesians to implement had brought few immediate returns. This compelled many to seek in one of the hundreds of 'cargo-cults' more immediate gratification, couched in traditional ritual.

The 'cargo-cult' mentality of the 1950s (and even later) revealed, above all, two things: the Melanesians' perceived need for radical economic change, and their inability to implement this change without outside assistance. Europeans hoped to understand the Melanesian mindset through academic research, the results of which could then profit colonial officials in piloting Melanesians towards modern governing. But how to achieve this was a never-ending debate. Some felt Melanesians had to learn the modern world in a modern workplace performing menial labour. Others believed elaborate educational programmes could best prepare the Melanesians in the essentials of twentieth-century life in the Pacific. For the time being there was no definitive answer, however, and events continued to move forward despite the lack of a resolution.

At the other extreme, American Samoa, the USA's only territory south of the equator, was administered as a 'military colony' by the US Department of the Navy until 1951. Its declassification thereafter came not as a result of any decolonization policy by Washington, but by the fact that military technology had simply rendered American Samoa's strategic significance obsolete. Since the early 1950s control of American Samoa has lain with civilian colonial administrators who, over the next half century, created here a small welfare state in the Pacific. American Samoa has remained an 'unincorporated' territory of the USA, in that the US constitution and other mainland laws do not apply here. In this way, traditional titles and tenures remain untouched and continental entrepreneurs are restricted access, precluding foreign exploitation. Still today, American Samoans resist all talk of independence, as they benefit handsomely from US subsidies and as most American Samoans live permanently in the continental USA. American Samoans represent Pacific Islands' most advantaged indigenous population, enjoying a quality of life better than that of most of New Zealand's Māori.

Guam, like American Samoa a territory of the USA since the end of the nineteenth century, saw its approximately 60 000 Chamorros given free access to the USA in 1950 when the 'Organic Act' granted them full US citizenship and introduced a US system of education. Shortly afterwards many Chamorros moved to the USA in search of employment and even better education, whereupon Palauans started moving to Guam in a 'migrant drag-chain' to take advantage of the better employment possibilities for them there. Guam has always remained a territory of the USA, its strategic importance for the USA having greatly increased since the closure of the USA's bases in the Philippines in the 1990s. The question of indigenous autonomy or independence being non-existent, Guam and its Chamorro people are coupled with the USA in perpetuity, it seems. Everyone in Guam benefits from governmental subsidies designed to maintain and protect the status quo. A third of Guam's 549 square kilometres is devoted to US military installations.

America also had acquired most of Micronesia after the Second World War, which had swept away the old League of Nations with its mandates forbidding militarization. The new United Nations introduced 'trusteeships' which were subject to no standard restrictions, having given up the old class distinctions for mandates (A, B, C) and having resolved that it would conclude individual agreements with each territory's trustee. The trusteeships were wholly voluntary; all that prevented a trustee from annexing its entrusted territory was perceived international censure. Though trustees were obliged to guarantee human rights and social development, in practice each trustee governed its trusteeship as if it were its own sovereign soil. Australia still administered New Guinea and Nauru, while New Zealand still held Western Samoa. But because Japan had lost the war, most of Micronesia – but for Guam, Nauru and the Gilberts – now had no legally invested colonial master.

The Trust Territory of the Pacific Islands, comprising Japan's pre-war colonial territories, was therefore created by the United Nations shortly after the end of the war. At first the UN offered the Trust Territory to its military occupier, the USA, on terms similar to those of a League of Nations mandate – that is, forbidding militarization. Refusing, the USA declared it would simply annex its Micronesian islands – the USA holding Japan's former colonies 'by right of conquest' – if the UN's trustee terms were not phrased as the USA dictated. Whereupon the UN formalized the trusteeship on America's terms in 1947. In this manner, the Caroline Islands, the Northern Marianas, Palau and the Marshall Islands came under the jurisdiction of the USA, which, for its part, pledged to 'promote development ... toward self-government or independence as may be appropriate'. In return for this pledge to the UN, the USA was granted the right to establish new military bases within the Trust Territory. (Discussions with Micronesians on the possibility of self-government would not actually begin until 1969.)

Washington then subsidized local economies on a grand scale – turning many Micronesian populations into life-long beneficiaries – while concentrating on its real priority: military development of the region (see Chapter 7). The dictate of national security survived unchallenged until the 1970s.

Though this policy later earned harsh critique internationally, one must understand the era's constraint. As a result of the traumatic Japanese invasion, the USA was justifiably convinced that its strategic defence lay vested in its comprehensive defence of Micronesia. It was for this reason that the USA had insisted on, and received, a separate category of trusteeship from the UN which no other nation had been granted: a 'strategic trust'. This uniquely permitted the USA to seal off all, or any part, of Micronesia for 'reasons of security', as defined by Washington and the Pentagon, and to fortify Micronesia as the USA saw fit. This historically understandable act of self-protection by the Pacific's greatest power, the consequence of the era's military disposition, was unfortunately to lead to great injustices towards the Micronesian peoples themselves, however, for whom no largesse could replace health and homeland.

The USA's post-war policy towards the former Polynesian kingdom of Hawai'i was even more conclusive. Already before the Second World War, the USA had turned its Territory of Hawai'i into the greatest fortress in the Pacific, with Pearl Harbor the headquarters of the US Pacific Fleet. After the war, the military prerogative dominated the Hawaiian Islands. All of Kaho'olawe Island, for example, became a target range for the US Navy, whose artillery also bombed rural Hawaiian valleys. The military was allowed to declare martial law at will there, to forcibly evict families from homes and to conscript all Hawaiians, including those who rejected US citizenship.

The question of statehood for Hawai'i, long sought by commercial interests and white Americans of nationalistic sentiment, was finally voted on in 1959 in a simple 'yes-no' plebicite. Only two choices were offered – statehood or status quo (independence was not an alternative) – to voters who had to be 'American citizens residing in Hawai'i'. American Hawaiians voted for statehood; Hawaiians who did not consider themselves to be Americans simply did not vote. Though Hawai'i's official international status as a 'non-self-governing territory' had obliged the USA since 1946 to report annually to the UN, the overwhelming yes-vote now meant the full assimilation of Hawai'i into an independent state of the USA – and thus relieved the USA of any further accountability towards the UN in its regard. Indeed, the UN's General Assembly accepted that the 'Hawaiians' had, through their yes-vote, freely exercized the right to self-determination. With this, Hawai'i's national identity ceased to exist. It was an 'independence' of unprecedented quality in the history of Pacific Islands.

Chile similarly abused the Polynesian franchise. Since 1893, Chile had leased almost all of Rapanui (Easter Island) to a Chilean-Scots wool firm which controlled the island as a 'company estate' until the lease expired in 1953 and was not renewed. Thereafter, the Chilean Navy assumed full control of the island. However, little changed but the harsh militarization of Earth's second-remotest inhabited island. Though they finally had a public school beginning in 1938, the Rapanui people could still not venture beyond the limits of the island's only village without written permission. Chile's nineteenth-century-style repressive colonialism continued well into the 1960s, with the Rapanui people unable to lodge a formal complaint, vote or represent themselves in any democratic fashion because Chilean citizenship was denied them.

After the war, France, too, abused its Pacific obligation, though this was not at all its initial policy. After victory in the Second World War, France at first wholeheartedly embraced the universal dynamic towards self-determination for all Islanders. The 1946 French constitution even included wording which acknowledged colonial peoples' right to develop their society and control their own affairs. French citizenship and the right to found political parties were granted to all overseas colonials. In New Caledonia, anticipating the effects of the war's liberal employment schemes for the Kanaks France's post-war government adopted a much more progressive attitude, similar to that of Britain, Australia and New Zealand. Partly prompted by an acute labour shortage in New Caledonia's all-important nickel industry, already in 1946 France conveyed full citizenship to the Kanaks, too, and repealed the regulations which had forbidden Kanaks from leaving their reservations on the Grande Terre without police permission. When, five years later, the French Parliament granted suffrage to a large number of native peoples in the French Union, Maurice Lenormand, leader of New Caledonia's multiracial Union Calédonienne, was elected to the French National Assembly in Paris. Lenormand's subsequent lobbying eventually achieved for New Caledonia the right to hold an elected Territorial Assembly, one empowered to enact local laws. When New Caledonia became a Territoire d'Outre-Mer (Overseas Territory) in 1957, the world was confident that, like Western Samoa, New Caledonia was soon to achieve full independence.

Whereupon disgruntled *caldoches* – the French settlers of New Caledonia – orchestrated an armed revolt on 18 June

1958, three weeks after the ultra-conservative Charles de Gaulle had come to power in France. De Gaulle dissolved New Caledonia's Territorial Assembly and appointed a repressive Governor to encourage the *caldoches'* continued loyalty to Paris. Instead of fostering independence, the new colonial regime in 1963 gaoled Lenormand for one year and deprived him of civil liberties in consequence of a political frame-up concerning the bombing of New Caledonia's Territorial Assembly. Also in 1963, France divested New Caledonia of its limited autonomy and reconstituted full colonial power in its Governor.

A similar situation obtained in French Polynesia. After annexation of French Polynesia was complete in 1880, the Établissements français de l'Océanie – France's Society, Marquesas, Tuamotu, Gambier and Austral groups – languished in a colonial backwater, both undercolonized and unprofitable. One year after the Second World War, French Polynesia was made a Territoire d'Outre-Mer and granted its own elected Territorial Assembly, situated in Pape'ete, Tahiti. In addition, French Polynesia was given representation in the French Parliament for the first time. Throughout the 1950s French Polynesians won increasing autonomy. Like New Zealand's stewardship of Western Samoa, it seemed that France was similarly preparing the entire vast region for independence. The prospect's climax was the Deffere Law of 1957 granting all of French Polynesia partial autonomy, whereby the Territorial Assembly acquired new economic powers, among other improvements.

All these promising reforms in French Polynesia had found a parallel in the emerging Tahitian nationalist movement, led by the remarkable Pouvana'a a 'O'opa of Huahine in the Society Islands. A First World War hero, in 1942 Pouvana'a had been exiled by the French back to Huahine for having petitioned for political reform in Pape'ete; whereupon he had sailed in an open canoe to the US naval base at Bora Bora to send a 'Polynesian petition' to General Charles de Gaulle of the Free French, whom Pouvana'a supported. Displeased that he had turned to the Americans for help, the French colonial administration detained Pouvana'a yet again, and then a third time for a further transgression. In 1949 Pouvana'a became the first Polynesian elected to the French Chamber of Deputies after his newly founded Rassemblement Démocratique des Populations Tahitiennes (RDPT) won an election aimed at the political and social reform of Tahiti. Pouvana'a and his party were not seeking independence from France, but rather political autonomy in close association with France. The party's popularity, especially among poorer rural Tahitians, guaranteed electoral victories throughout the 1950s.

In 1953 Pouvana'a's RDPT assumed control of the Territorial Assembly, and four years later Pouvana'a himself became Vice-President of French Polynesia's newly established Government Council. When, in the following year, Pouvana'a pushed for complete independence from France in a territorial referendum, Pouvana'a's world – and French Polynesia's opportunity for self-determination – collapsed.

This was because the RDPT had introduced a new income-tax bill to the Territorial Assembly in April 1958, which pro-government supporters had used as a pretext for stoning Pape'ete's Territorial Assembly building while Governor Bailly's police force looked on in silence. Whereupon Bailly collaborated with the opposition Union Tahitienne Démocratique to suppress the income-tax bill. Pouvana'a's RDPT boycotted the vote as a protest of the illegal governmental interference.

France's Fourth Republic collapsed one month later, General Charles de Gaulle assuming political control on 29 May 1958. De Gaulle summarily reversed France's Pacific policies after a cleverly worded referendum gave him the mandate to thwart any further moves towards autonomy or independence. By this time, Pouvana'a had been campaigning for complete independence from France, but had failed to secure a majority as he was denied the radio access only 'loyal' politicians enjoyed, among other injustices. After the referendum, Governor Bailly dissolved the Territorial Assembly and only days later arrested Pouvana'a and many of his supporters on trumped-up charges of 'arson'.

The prisoners waited a year in prison before their trial, whereupon Pouvana'a was sentenced to eight years' gaol and 15 years' exile in France. (Pouvana'a would not be free until 1968.) As Governor Bailly declared, 'those who remain on the road to discord would have no more right either to pardon or to pity'.

Whereupon the era of Tahiti's 'poisoned reign' began. The Territorial Assembly dutifully 'requested' a reduction in those powers it had won only one year earlier. Paris 'consented' and added further restrictions which now accommodated De Gaulle's new military plans for the region (see Chapter 7). Paris also seemingly redefined the position of Governor as dictator and inspector general in one, answerable to Paris in even the smallest matters. It heralded a return to nineteenth-century colonialism at its worst.

***

It was not long after the Second World War that the USA and France had created in Micronesia and French Polynesia their own Pacific Islands which were far removed from the independent, self-governing and autonomous bodies fostered, and then realized, elsewhere by Britain, Australia and New Zealand. This is because, for the USA and France, the region represented merely a means to an end: the creation not of a freer Pacific, but of a *nuclear* Pacific.

7

Reinventing Pacific Islands

THE NUCLEAR PACIFIC

The Pacific was 'reinvented' after 1945 as colonial powers acted primarily for themselves and only secondarily for Islanders. The historically most challenging symbol of this posture: the two atomic bombs which exploded over Hiroshima and Nagasaki in August of that year, which may have ended the Second World War but which also began an arms race that turned the region into a nuclear arena. Though the Russians tested their nuclear weapons within the Soviet Union (but not in Russia itself), the USA, Britain and France tested in the Pacific because of sparse and ethnically different populations. Over exactly half a century – between 1946 and 1996 – more than 250 nuclear devices were detonated at Bikini, Enewetak, Johnston Atoll, Christmas Island, Malden, Moruroa and Fangataufa. Once the signing of the Partial Nuclear Test Ban Treaty with the Soviet Union compelled the USA and Britain to conclude their testing in the Pacific in 1963 (the last test had taken place there in 1962), three years later France commenced its testing of nuclear weapons in the Tuamotus and, ignoring wave after wave of international protest, continued detonations there until 1996.

The consequencies of Pacific nuclear testing were devastating. The USA destroyed whole islands and their societies, especially in Micronesia's Marshall Islands, still the issue of sensitive litigation. A minor participant, Britain none the less contaminated land and exposed many to radioactive fall-out. France ruined Moruroa and Fangataufa in the Tuamotus, then subsequently blocked independent monitoring of the damage (recent reports claim significant contamination); as in the Marshalls, the economic dependence of the testing programme greatly crippled French Polynesia's political development.

The tragedy began in 1946 and 1947 when the USA evacuated the Micronesians of Bikini and Enewetak, among the world's largest atolls and possibly Remote Oceania's most ancient communities (Bikini), then pulverized their villages, fauna, flora and fishlife with incredibly powerful atmospheric explosions. Exposed to fall-out, the people of neighbouring Rongelap and Utrik were removed only several days after the infamous 1954 Bravo test which comprised atmospheric testing of a thermonuclear weapon: the hydrogen bomb. When the Marshallese demanded an immediate halt to testing in their islands, the Trusteeship Council of the United Nations responded with platitudes and assurances. Subsequently, a petition, civil suit and more vehement protests by Micronesians similarly fell on deaf ears, as the USA invariably invoked the catholicon 'national security'. In one year, 1958, as many nuclear devices were detonated over Bikini and Enewetak as in all previous tests in the Pacific. Fall-out from these tests contaminated neighbouring islands.

The end finally came in November 1962 when President John F. Kennedy publicly announced the USA's halting of all nuclear tests in the Pacific, concealing his secret agreement with Premier Nikita Khrushchev of the Soviet Union in consequence of the Cuban missile crisis of October 1962. Whereupon in 1963 the USA, Britain and the Soviet Union signed the Partial Test Ban Treaty, halting all nuclear tests in the atmosphere. (Though invited, France chose not to sign.) This formally ended the USA's and Britain's test programme in the Pacific; tests were never carried out there again by either nation and all their sites were decommissioned. In one of history's tragic ironies, however, 1963 was also the year that President Charles de Gaulle announced he was shifting France's nuclear test programme from Algeria to the Tuamotus.

Preoccupied with Cold War priorities, Washington bureaucrats had had little time for Pacific lives. Yet, by the 1960s, the Marshallese had already been displaying incontrovertible signs of radioactive injury as well as increased risk of malignant disease. Finally, in 1986, the USA established a trust fund to be distributed in the Marshalls through a nuclear claims tribunal. Though the people of Rongelap and Utrik had been able to return home three years after the 1954 Bravo test, those of Enewetak returned only in 1980 – and then to only three of the atoll's islands, the other 37 being too radioactive. Over 100 Bikinians returned to their atoll in the 1970s, but left again in 1978. In 1985 the people of Rongelap also fled their atoll, similarly fearing radioactivity; the US Congress pledged funds to enable their return one day. Congress also authorized a more thorough decontamination of Bikini, which commenced in 1988.

The USA has subsequently paid hundreds of millions of dollars for the decontamination, food aid, compensation and resettlement of the affected Micronesian islands and their people. Still, these Islanders are in many ways worse off than before: reliant on the USA's white flour, white rice, canned fish, doughnuts and pancakes, these 'nuclear dependents' live crowded lives within exile communities on alien islands, knowing only the existence of state beneficiaries. Their former world is gone, perhaps forever.

Britain had grabbed the nuclear promise as it had offered Britain an opportunity to demonstrate that it still wielded global power after the war. But the USA was reluctant to co-operate with its former wartime ally in this new enterprise, seemingly an American monopoly: when Britain wanted to use Enewetak Atoll for British nuclear testing in the early 1950s, the USA declined. So Britain first tested its atomic weapons in Australia, then its hydrogen weapons on two islands in Britain's Gilbert and Ellice Islands Colony. Though Britain's testing programme contributed only 4 per cent of the total amount of global fall-out up to 1980 – Britain last atmospherically tested in 1958 and ceased entirely in 1962 just before the Partial Test Ban Treaty – it, too, is guilty of gross irresponsibility towards Pacific Islanders in this regard.

In 1957 and 1958, Britain detonated hydrogen weapons over Christmas Island (now Kiritimati) in the Line Islands half-way between Hawai'i and the Societies; in 1958, it also tested over Malden c. 750 kilometres to the southeast. Christmas is the largest purely coral island in the world; today, it comprises more than half of the Kiribati nation's total land area. At the time, there were several hundred Gilbertese working on Christmas's copra plantations, some of whom were hired by the British for construction work at the nuclear project. During the detonations the labourers were removed to offshore vessels. In 1962, Britain permitted the USA to conduct its last atmospheric tests on Christmas, when locals were similarly evacuated. Nearly all the tests here were high atmospheric detonations with 'minimal' fall-out. Nevertheless, the danger of vestigial radioactive contamination on both islands is real.

France's Pacific nuclear testing programme was different, but equally irresponsible. The history of French Polynesia since 1962 has essentially been that of France's nuclear campaign: it alone determined economics and politics there, and greatly affected all of society in the region and beyond. During the 30 years – 1966 to 1996 – of actual nuclear detonations in the Tuamotus, French military spending made all of French Polynesia a 'nuclear vassal'. Most Islanders did not support their nationalist leaders, who were seeking independence during these years, because most jobs, services and property conveyances, funded directly from Paris, came in exchange for political votes endorsing the nuclear mandate. In the mid-1960s a building boom transformed Tahiti as thousands of French military personnel descended to begin construction of the nuclear administration there. The region's umbilical cord was re-attached to Paris, the colony's life blood – military patronage – coursed through every vein of Tahitian society. Only two governmental bodies effectively 'ruled' French Polynesia during this time: the Commission d'Energie Atomique (CEA) and the Centre Expérimentation du Pacifique (CEP).

The CEA, founded in 1954, had located two sites for France's nuclear testing programme – Algeria's Sahara and French Polynesia's Tuamotus. Between 1960 and 1962 France conducted four atmospheric and 13 underground tests in Algeria. But Algeria became independent in July 1962, and so France – which found the idea of testing in France abhorrent – created the CEP in the same month and, without consultation with any French Polynesian territorial representatives, resolved to relocate the Algerian testing facilities to Moruroa Atoll in the Tuamotus, over 1200 kilometres southeast of Tahiti. Construction commenced in 1963.

The nationalist parties in Pape'ete strongly protested this military 'invasion', despite its promise of greater wealth for Tahiti. Whereupon President Charles de Gaulle banned all political parties in the territory.

The first atmospheric detonation took place over Moruroa on 2 July 1966. Monitors in both Peru and New Zealand registered contamination from the blast. The international protests against French testing forced France to test only underground as of 1974. These then continued until 1996.

Polynesian opposition continued throughout this period. Though Pouvana'a a 'O'opa was still imprisoned when testing began, his two party successors, John Teariki and Francis Sanford, continued the struggle for Polynesian independence, which now included vociferous opposition to France's nuclear testing programme. In 1968 Pouvana'a won a presidential release and was welcomed back to Tahiti as a national hero. In 1971 he secured the French Polynesian seat in the French Senate, and in 1972 he became President of the Territorial Assembly in Pape'ete.

On 23 June 1973, the World Court urged France to halt its testing programme in the Pacific because of the danger of contaminating neighbours. France's response was to announce that the World Court was incompetent in such matters. Whereupon New Zealand's Prime Minister Norman Kirk ordered the NZ frigate *Otago* to enter Moruroa's exclusion zone, and Peru broke off diplomatic relations with France. A month later, French commandos violently boarded the protest vessels *Fri* and *Greenpeace*, arresting their crews. The following year, France's President Valéry Giscard d'Estaing limited the programme to underground testing only.

In Tahiti, Pouvana'a occupied his powerful offices until his death in 1977 at 77 years of age. (His statue now fronts Pape'ete's Territorial Assembly.) In the same year, French Polynesia was granted a new statute which permitted partial autonomy for the region, and Francis Sanford was elected premier. Five years after Pouvana'a's death the Tahoera'a Huira'atira (Popular Union), made up of supporters of De Gaulle and the Governor, defeated the nationalists in the territorial elections, making Gaston Flosse, a local mayor who supported nuclear testing and opposed independence, the leader of local government in Tahiti. An astute politician, Flosse recognized the historical dynamic of the independence movement and, to retard its momentum, negotiated incremental autonomy for the territory. In 1984, the French Parliament passed a new statute of local government which granted Islanders a number of concessions.

Docked at Auckland, New Zealand, in preparation for a protest voyage to Moruroa, the Greenpeace vessel *Rainbow Warrior* was sunk on 10 July 1985 by French secret service agents, killing a Greenpeace photographer. That same year, nearly every Pacific nation signed the protocols of the South Pacific Nuclear-Free Zone Treaty. However, the USA, Britain and France refused to sign, explaining that the Treaty was counterproductive to their respective national securities. Though the USA and Britain had halted their testing programmes in the Pacific 23 years earlier, they still fully supported, and shared information from, France's continued testing there.

At the same time, such powerful personalities as Oscar Temaru, founder in 1978 of the Tavini Huira'atira (Polynesian

Liberation Front), continued to press for French Polynesia's full independence from France. Temaru's cause was greatly enhanced in the mid-1990s by France's incomprehensible return to massive nuclear testing in the Pacific.

This new episode began in 1991, when the Russians at last halted their nuclear test programme. In April 1992, having assessed this remarkable development and grasped the true significance of the world's near-unanimous condemnation of France's own nuclear tests, President François Mitterand, a liberal socialist, announced the 'suspension' of France's testing in the Pacific. However, the Tuamotuan test sites were fully maintained after this announcement, and no downsizing of the CEA or CEP at Pape'ete occurred. That same October, the Americans discontinued their nuclear testing in the Nevada desert.

In June 1995 the ultra-conservative Jacques Chirac was elected France's President who, again without consultation with French Polynesian territorial representatives, summarily ordered the resumption of underground testing in the Tuamotus. The first detonation of the new series was to take place on 5 September 1995. Aware of its media impact, Greenpeace sailed the *Rainbow Warrior II* into the exclusion zone around Moruroa on 10 July 1995, ten years to the day since the French secret service agents had sunk its namesake and killed the photographer. As the first test approached, parliamentarians from Australia, New Zealand, Japan and Europe (the USA, which had facilitated matériel transport for the test series, was not represented) marched with Polynesians in protest through Pape'ete's streets. In the exclusion zone, the *Rainbow Warrior II* launched six Zodiacs, whereupon the vessel was boarded by military commandos firing tear-gas and destroying generators, computers, even the vessel's engine. The *Greenpeace*, waiting in international waters, was boarded and seized as well. Both vessels were impounded and their crews deported.

On 5 September 1995, France detonated the first of a planned series of eight nuclear bombs under Moruroa. The very next morning, civil insurrection – virtually unknown in modern Polynesia – erupted in Pape'ete. At first, non-violent demonstrators, convinced Gaston Flosse was escaping to France, merely blocked the runway at the international airport. When French gendarmes violently charged them, the demonstrators turned upon the airport building, pelting it with iron bars and bricks and damaging it with a bulldozer. Whereupon the gendarmes responded with tear-gas and stun grenades, at which point the demonstrators became rioters who swept into Pape'ete, overturning cars, looting shops and setting buildings alight. Independence leader Oscar Temaru succeeded in calming the rioters, after which France flew in riot police from overseas to guard a Pape'ete under military curfew.

When Jacques Chirac resumed nuclear testing one month later, the entire world was outraged. The South Pacific Forum immediately suspended France as a 'dialogue partner'. Stunned by the severity of the international censure, Chirac announced he was reducing France's test series to six, and in January 1996 France detonated its last nuclear weapon, under Fangataufa. The two Tuamotuan test sites were then decommissioned.

In March of the same year, the USA, Britain and France at last signed the protocols of the South Pacific Nuclear-Free Zone Treaty of 1985. Also in 1996, clearly to weaken the momentum towards independence, the French Parliament granted additional, but still limited, powers to French Polynesia. With the conclusion of the nuclear testing programme in French Polynesia, 1000 workers lost their jobs, the substantial tax revenues on military imports disappeared, positions in government and service industries vanished. As compensation, France signed a 'Pacte de Progrès' subsidizing the territory with US $200 million per year until 2005.

But in 2001, French Polynesia remains as French as Eastern Samoa is American. Even more so: the constitution of the Republic of France is French Polynesia's supreme law. All laws enacted by the Territorial Assembly in Pape'ete can be overturned by either the French Parliament or the Constitutional Commission. All administrative decisions passed down by territorial officials can be overruled by French judges. Even so, the Moruroa testing facilities in the Tuamotus have been dismantled, and it appears no further nuclear testing, by any foreign power, will ever disgrace the Pacific again. Fangataufa now lies abandoned, and 30 French Foreign Legionnaires guard Moruroa's airstrip, wharf and concrete bunkers against those wishing to test the island's vestigial radioactivity.

Pacific Islands' colonies had been powerless to halt the international powers' nuclear tests, but the independent nations of the Pacific which were emerging as a result of the protracted decolonization process in the 1960s and 1970s rallied, with Australia and New Zealand, behind the common cause of a 'nuclear-free Pacific'. Indeed, it became a modern crusade, uniting Pacific peoples in unprecedented numbers for the first time and contributing further to the creation of a shared Pacific identity.

The first Conference for a Nuclear-Free Pacific was held in Fiji in 1975, and the nascent movement in subsequent years embraced a number of protests against abuses, as well as the vision of an independent Pacific. Also in 1975, the South Pacific Forum adopted in principle New Zealand's concept of a South Pacific Nuclear-Free Zone. Eight years later Australia formally proposed its adoption at the South Pacific Forum – more to support US strategic interests (long-range missile testing and visits by nuclear ships) by channelling and curtailing Pacific Islanders' protests – and two years later the protocols of the South Pacific Nuclear-Free Zone Treaty were signed, moderate in tone and directed foremost at France's testing programme. As a US Congressional report pithily summarized in 1989, 'the Treaty has no adverse impact on the interests of the United States, since we are not precluded from doing anything we had been doing or were planning to do'. (The USA still continues to test its long-range missiles in the region, particularly from Kwajalein in the central Ralik Chain of the Marshall Islands.)

By 1996, 12 of the 16 member countries of the South Pacific Forum had signed the Treaty. Its protocols had been presented to the world's nuclear powers as well, and China and the former Soviet Union had signed; but the USA, Britain and France had refused. Only after France finally bowed to international pressure and ceased its abuse of Pacific Islands and Islanders by halting its nuclear testing there did France finally sign the Treaty, as did the USA and Britain. None the less, the 'nuclear Pacific' is not a finished story. Its legacy will continue to haunt all of Pacific Islands and its peoples...

For tens of thousands of years.

INDEPENDENCE AND BEYOND

In 1960 the United Nations issued the 'Declaration of Granting of Independence to Colonial Countries and Peoples' which called for the active promotion of self-governance throughout the world. It was the expression of a global sentiment which, in the 1960s and 1970s, saw most of Africa and seven Pacific Islands colonies under British, Australian and New Zealand colonial administration gain their independence: Western Samoa, Fiji, Tonga, Papua New Guinea, Solomon Islands, Vanuatu (formerly the New Hebrides), and Kiribati and Tuvalu (both formerly the Gilbert and Ellice Islands Colony). In 1971, newly independent states of the Pacific united to establish the South Pacific Forum, a regional body dedicated to addressing both political and social concerns in the South Pacific. Papua New Guinea, the Solomons and Vanuatu subsequently formed their own Melanesian Spearhead Group in 1988, to which Fiji attached itself in 1996. Independence and regional consolidation characterized most of the British Commonwealth's Pacific Islands in the last quarter of the twentieth century.

However, much of Pacific Islands has not gone this route. Tiny Pitcairn remains a British colony. Cook Islanders and Niueans enjoy their independence only in free association with New Zealand; Tokelauans still prefer New Zealand citizenship over independence. American Samoa is fully USA, as is Guam where the Chamorro people, however, are beginning to re-awaken to their Pacific Islands identity and to question the American presence. Hawai'i is a state of the union, an inseparable part of the USA. All French territories in Pacific Islands – New Caledonia, Wallis and Futuna, and French Polynesia – possess internal autonomy under local French officials not answerable to the respective Territorial Assemblies; it is here that Pacific Islands' most active independence movements foment. Rapanui remains a colony of Chile. And Irian Jaya (Western New Guinea) still suffers under Indonesia's harsh administration.

By and large, decolonization in Pacific Islands has been a peaceful process, because it came from the top down. That is, the colonial powers Britain, Australia and New Zealand found it in their own best interest to decolonize and the Islanders did not resist, as this is what they also wished. Where colonial powers have rejected the Islanders' aspirations – as in New Caledonia, French Polynesia and Irian Jaya – it has led to a violence otherwise unknown in the region. The USA has largely avoided this problem because the majority of its 'Islanders' choose to remain American citizens; as a result, they generally enjoy Pacific Islands' highest standard of living.

Fiji's situation was unique. Its Indians, who had been outnumbering indigenous Fijians since before the Second World War, co-operated neither with the Fijians nor with the British colonial administration because of perceived grievances against both. Fiji has always been a country divided, lacking a national identity and a shared goal. In 1961 Fiji's Governor introduced minor reforms which anticipated a protracted conveyance of power from Britain to all the peoples of Fiji. Both Fijians and Europeans protested, anxious about the Indian representation this would entail, but the administration continued along these lines, expanding the numbers in, and authority of, the Fijian legislature.

In 1964, the British administration in Fiji formed a committee to elaborate a scheme for constitutional reform – a precursor to independence talks. Fijians resisted the notion of a Western-style democracy, but the Indians pressed for just this, aware of their numerical advantage in a democracy; the few Europeans in Fiji wanted equal representation for themselves and so, like the Fijians, resisted democratic initiatives. The negotiations and debate continued for years, with few compromises achieved.

The celebrated concept of the 'Pacific Way' was introduced in a speech by Fiji's first Prime Minister, Ratu Sir Kamisese Mara, on the occasion of Fiji's independence from Britain in October 1970. In its essence, the 'Pacific Way' meant regarding the value of co-operation and consensus as part of the traditional Pacific Islands approach to problem-solving. Fiji had used this to achieve a workable scheme for independence on which all three parties could at last fundamentally agree. But Fiji's original problem remained: that is, the racial divide initially set up by Sir Arthur Gordon in the 1870s.

The voting system of a common electoral role which the Indians had demanded was now, after independence, ignored in favour of a communal role which sought to avoid the racial divide in elections. This encouraged cross-voting (with four separate votes for each voter) which diminished the danger of racial politics and increased the development of multiracial political parties. Already in the year of independence, the Alliance, a new multiracial party, grouped about it a substantial percentage of voters representing associations of all three ethnic communities. However, the real winners in the new Fijian constitution were the indigenous Fijians: they retained their old land rights and this could not be changed unless 75 per cent of both the House and Senate approved. But the Fijian Senate held an indigenous bias – eight senators were to be appointed by the Prime Minister, seven by the opposition leader, and another eight by the Great Council of Chiefs. Fiji's 'Pacific Way' may have appealed to co-operation and consensus in theory, but in practice it strained Indian patience and remained a formula for future strife.

Fiji has had a troubled history since Alliance Party leader Ratu Sir Kamisese Mara won the first post-independence elections in 1972. The April 1987 elections saw a coalition of

Labour and the Indians' National Federation Party (NFP) securing a majority of the seats in the House, mostly as a result of support for Labour from urban Fijians and part-Fijians. The new, progressive, multi-ethnic government incensed conservative Fijians, however, and in May 1987 Lt Col Sitiveni Rabuka staged a bloodless *coup d'état*. After new elections and a new constitution were discussed in July and August, in September, just hours before a transitional government of national unity leading to new elections was to be announced, Rabuka staged a second coup, annulling Fiji's 1970 constitution and declaring himself to be 'head of state'. In October 1987, Rabuka declared Fiji to be a republic. Fiji was then immediately expelled from the British Commonwealth.

The economy plunged, and inflation skyrocketed. In the ten years between 1986 and 1996 nearly 60 000 Fijian Indians emigrated to Australia, New Zealand, Canada and the USA, seriously depleting Fiji's human resources and economy and tipping the ethnic balance forever. Ratu Mara and his Alliance Party took over governing and years of political wrangling ensued between opposing Fijian factions. The constitutional impasse was finally resolved when all factions agreed to a power-sharing formula, enshrined in the Constitution Amendment Bill signed into law by President Ratu Mara on 25 July 1997. Fiji was welcomed back into the British Commonwealth in October of the same year.

In the 1999 election, Labour leader Mahendra Chaudhry became Fiji's first Indian prime minister. However, the in-fighting between indigenous Fijian factions continued. This only superficially manifested itself as a protest against the Indian prime minister, as the underlying causes lay with competing Fijian power brokers. In 2000 the former Fijian businessman George Speight and heavily armed supporters took Prime Minister Chaudhry and the government hostage for eight weeks. The insurrectionists eventually surrendered to the Fijian army which, though its leaders had clandestinely supported the rebels, resolved in the end to remain loyal to the constitution. The case has now become the most serious criminal investigation in Fiji's history. It has left Fiji again in turmoil, with unsustainable losses in tourism, the sugar industry and clothes manufacture. Nearly all Indians who remain in Fiji plan to emigrate soon. Fiji's future is more uncertain than ever.

In comparison, Tonga seems a bastion of peace and prosperity. Though Tonga had always remained 'independent', since 1905 the British consul had wielded colonial-like powers there, allowing Britain to intervene directly in local government. Public service lay almost entirely in Tongan hands and legislation was enacted by the Tongan Parliament and the monarch, first Tupou I's grandson King George Tupou II (ruled 1893–1918), then the remarkable Queen Salote Tupou III (1918–1965), and finally the imposing King Tāufa'āhau Tupou IV (1965 to present), the first Tongan to earn a university degree (University of Sydney). By the 1960s, nearly all senior governmental positions were held by university-trained Tongans. Britain relinquished the powers of its consul in 1970 when, as the Tongan government phrased it, Tonga 're-entered the comity of nations'. In this way, Tonga was recognized internationally as a fully independent monarchy – the status both it and Hawai'i' had enjoyed in the nineteenth century. Tonga's 'rise' to unencumbered independence was characterized foremost by its seeming uneventfulness, the result of a long tradition of nationhood and, with little foreign settlement, a shared identity with a strong and clearly defined hierarchical structure. The present monarch is dearly loved by his subjects, but Tonga's missionary-inspired constitution is now sensed by many politicians to be an anachronism: constitutional reform and a fully elected parliament comprise the peaceful kingdom's most pressing tasks at the beginning of the twenty-first century.

Papua New Guinea's passage to independence was troubled. In 1962 a report of the United Nations' Visiting Mission to Australia's Trust Territory of New Guinea highly criticized Australia's procrastination in developing its territory towards self-governance as pledged. Australia responded immediately by commissioning the World Bank to provide an economic survey and policy recommendation; by planning a university for Papua New Guinea; and by forming an elected House of Representatives there. Australia's subsidies to the territory were also increased, facilitating the creation of an expanded public service. Development schemes were implemented. A new and vibrant political scene then emerged, with the creation of several political parties, most of them either small interest groups or Australian proxies.

But in 1967, the Pangu – Papua New Guinea Unity – Pati stood out for its radical advocacy of rapid self-governance leading to full independence from Australia. Its highly educated and charismatic leader, journalist Michael Somare from the Sepik River, saw Pangu being the single most successful party in the House elections of 1968. But most seats were won by independents, who then vigorously opposed Somare and his plans for independence. Somare rejected the offer of a ministerial position at this time, refusing to compromise his platform. His calculated reticence worked in his favour – in the elections of 1972 his was a household name. The new, wealthier and university-educated elite of Papua New Guinea embraced Somare, his message of full independence and the new world it represented, a far cry from the Trust Territory the UN mission had decried only ten years earlier. The development schemes of the 1960s had created an infrastructure which now guaranteed for the territory those foreign revenues which were essential for an independent future.

By the elections of 1972, Papua New Guinean politics had so fragmented that no political party – not even Somare's Pangu Pati – won a clear majority. Whereupon Somare seized the historic moment, formed a coalition with like-minded pro-independence groups, and had himself appointed Chief Minister. Fortuitously, later in 1972 Australians voted the Labour Party into power, which supported early independence for Papua New Guinea. Within one year, Australia had helped the territory to self-governance. And in 1975 Papua New Guineans achieved their full independence from Australia, despite great opposition from the large white-settler community who feared the loss of wealth and status and resented the indigenous franchise.

Since independence, the active dynamics of the various political parties have shaped the country's daily progress, almost to the same frenetic extent as in Fiji and New Zealand. Michael Somare and his Pangu-dominated coalition won the first independent elections of 1977, but three years later Somare lost a vote of no-confidence and was replaced by his former coalition partner Julius Chan. Somare returned to power later, but then lost yet another vote of no-confidence, as did his successor. Papua New Guinean politics has involved fragile coalitions of multiple parties each vying for popular support among rival tribes. Until now the constitution, and the peoples' wish to maintain democratic principles, have generally prevented those abuses many had feared before the territory's independence.

At the same time as Papua New Guinea was moving towards independence, a secessionist movement emerged in its territory of Bougainville, largest of the North Solomon Islands but historically part of Papua New Guinea. Here lies the Con-Zinc Rio Tinto mine at Panguna, one of the world's largest open-cast copper mines and earner of a large part of Papua New Guinea's export revenues. Secessionist passions flared in 1989 when environmental reports revealed the mine's pollution and local landowners were brusquely denied compensation. Sabotage halted all mining, and a group declaring itself to be the Bougainville Revolutionary Army (BRA) challenged the government in Port Moresby for control of the island. In the years of armed conflict which followed, as many as 6000 people may have died. The Papua New Guinea army regained control of much of Bougainville by 1994, but the mine still remained in the hands of the BRA. A final peace package now lies before the Papua New Guinea cabinet allowing Bougainville an Australian-style statehood within Papua New Guinea, with its own police, courts and taxation powers; the Papua New Guinea army is to be virtually excluded from the province. If this peace package is approved, it will mean internal autonomy at last for the troubled island.

The Cook Islands had not been a Trusteeship Territory but, since 1901, part of New Zealand itself. A strong trade union movement after the Second World War eventually yielded the Cooks Islands Party, led by Albert Henry, whose ultimate goal was self-governance for the Cooks. However, because the Cooks were so small and poor, dependent on its exports of bananas and citrus fruit to New Zealand for nearly all of its revenues, New Zealand did not favourably view independence for the Cooks, fearing for the Islands' economic viability. But a compromise solution was reached in 1965, when the Cooks became self-governing while leaving defence and foreign affairs to New Zealand. At the same time, Cook Islanders remained New Zealand citizens and continued to receive New Zealand aid. The Cook Islanders were free to declare full independence whenever they wished, but have never done so. This scheme of 'associated independence' – offering the pride of nationhood without the perils of full independence – worked so well that Niue adopted it also in 1974, becoming internally self-governing in free association with New Zealand.

The Cook Islands had set a precedent for the demonstrable viability of a small Pacific Islands nation. Others soon followed as well, like Nauru, under official Australian administration since 1919, a mandate of the League of Nations as of 1920 and a United Nations Trusteeship under joint Australian, New Zealand and British administration following the Second World War. The island having been made all but uninhabitable by the British Phosphate Commissioners' mining operations for many decades, Australia had several times offered to resettle the Nauruans elsewhere. (Just as the Banabans had been resettled by Britain to Rabi in Fiji in 1945.) But the Nauruans always refused. Not without difficulty, the Nauruans finally achieved their full independence in 1968 and, with it, all rights over their phosphate deposits.

By the 1970s Britain had only two remaining territories to pilot into independence: the Solomon Islands Protectorate and the Gilbert and Ellice Islands Colony (tiny Pitcairn Island would remain British). Solomon Islanders accepted the idea of independence readily when first proposed by Britain in the early 1970s. Political parties formed according to factional priorities, but without the extremes seen elsewhere in Pacific Islands at the time. The Legislative Council, created in 1960, became a full Legislative Assembly in 1974, with almost entirely elected members. Two years later the Solomons were internally self-governing, and full independence was granted by Britain on 7 July 1978.

The Solomons joined Papua New Guinea and Vanuatu in 1988 to form the Melanesian Spearhead Group in order to further New Caledonia's struggle for independence. Four years later Papua New Guinea Defence Force troops intruded into the Solomons in pursuit of Bougainville freedom fighters. In 1993 the Solomons government sent police into the Short- land Islands when Papua New Guinean forces landed on Mono Island; shots were exchanged. In 1998 it was revealed that the Solomons' new prime minister had clandestinely received US military equipment worth several millions, some of which was allegedly for the Bougainville freedom fighters. Australia, for one, strongly criticized the US-backed desta- bilization of this particularly sensitive part of Pacific Islands.

Far more ominous for the Solomons' political future, at the end of 1998 Malaitans – natives of the archipelago's third- largest island – violently resisted their attempted expulsion from Guadalcanal, to where they had migrated after the Second World War to assume key jobs and eventually control the economy. Over the following 18 months of armed struggle, more than 50 Islanders died or disappeared and 20 000 fled their homes. In June 2000, Malaitan rebels seized control of the nation's capital Honiara, taking the prime minister hostage as they declared their wish to re-instate law and order, while around 1000 members of the two rival ethnic groups of Malaitans and Guadalcanal Islanders clashed outside the capital.

The Gilbert and Ellice Islands Colony is yet another unique story. There had never been a demand for outright independence by the Gilbertese and Ellice Islanders, who had sought only more local control. Both island groups actually lacked the natural resources necessary to finance an independent nation. Only Ocean Island (Banaba), part of the Gilberts since 1901, generated substantial revenues from its phosphate mining, but its reserves were nearly exhausted by the end of the 1960s. Once Britain intimated future independence for the Colony, in a 1974 referendum the Ellice Islanders, who are Polynesians, vehemently protested to any union with the Micronesian Gilbertese whom they saw as the foreign invaders (in prehistory the Gilbertese had resettled the Ellice island of Nui). Ellice Islanders further resented and feared the Gilbertese's numerical superiority (48 000 to their mere 8000). For their part, the Gilbertese resented the Ellice Islanders' over-representation in the Colony's public service and their sharing the Gilbertese revenues from Ocean Island's phosphate mining.

Britain agreed with the decision of the Ellice Islanders in 1975, and the Ellices became internally self-governing in April 1978 and only five months later, on 1 October 1978, fully independent under the traditional name of Tuvalu or 'Cluster of Eight (Islands)'. Political independence has brought Tuvalu more international attention and economic aid (Tuvalu Trust Fund) than surely would have been the case had it remained an appendage of the greater Gilbert Islands. Fishing rights and collectors' postage stamps earn substantial revenues. Its telecommunications excess provides 10 per cent of the country's entire budget through telephone sex routed through New Zealand. Tuvaluan passports and 'ambassadorships' are also a lucrative trade.

The Gilbert Islands achieved independence from Britain in July 1979, at which time the new nation assumed the legal name Kiribati (pronounced KEE-REE-BASS), the Gilbertese name for the group, from English 'Gilberts'. With Tuvalu and Kiribati, the UN Committee on Decolonization noted with surprise how both had expressed regret at Britain's decision to grant them independence, as both had been content with their experience of British colonialism. Such regret had been unprecedented in modern Pacific Islands history.

Britain also wished to withdraw from the New Hebrides south of the Solomons, but France, its partner in the Anglo-French Condominium since 1906, opposed decolonization, fearing its spread to mineral-rich French New Caledonia. In the late 1960s, the New Hebrideans, taking advantage of the lack of a unified Anglo-French policy, formed a very small nationalist movement based on the issue of land. The subsequent New Hebrides National Party, founded in the early 1970s by Walter Lini, an Anglican priest, enjoyed great popular support, inspiring rival parties which represented either New Hebrideans or French-centred settlers. Measuring the popular mood, the Anglo-French Condominium created a Representative Assembly in 1975, but this was dissolved two years later once the Vanua'aku Party, the reconstituted National Party, began demanding the elimination of government-appointed Assembly members and immediate independence.

In 1978, Walter Lini declared the People's Provisional Government, but continued to negotiate with Britain and France, enjoying the support of Pacific Islands independent nations and the consideration of the United Nations. One year later, a constitution was agreed upon by all parties; foreign owners of New Hebridean land were dispossessed, receiving compensation from their own governments; new elections saw the Vanua'aku Party and Walter Lini winning 62 per cent of the popular vote; and a date was set for full independence from Britain and France.

France was not pleased. Two serious rebellions erupted on Tanna and Espiritu Santo – captured documents revealed France's direct involvement; it appeared France wanted Espiritu Santo to become a separate French colony – but Chief Minister Lini nevertheless announced he would unilaterally declare New Hebrides' independence if Britain and France now reneged.

On the agreed date of 31 July 1980, Walter Lini formally proclaimed independence for the new nation, which was renamed Vanuatu or 'Land Eternal'. Whereupon French officials – not

British – tore out telephones, air-conditioners and all equipment and furnishings from administrative offices so as to burden the new public service and its budget. Vanuatu was alone in Pacific Islands in attaining independence at the perceived cost of defeating a more powerful, and openly antagonistic, adversary. Had it not been for Britain, independence would still have been a dream today in Vanuatu.

Vanuatu's sullied decolonization left Islanders there with bitter feelings and a profound distrust of foreign intrusion of any sort. Yet though the new government spoke out against colonialism and a nuclear presence in the Pacific, it none the less still followed the capitalistic policies of the old Condominium. Port Vila was the centre of power and development, where Vanuatuan politicians forged deals with wealthy foreigners. In 1983, the government passed legislation making Vanuatu the first nuclear-free nation in the Pacific, a move which earned the new indigenous government great international respect. By the early 1990s, Walter Lini had lost re-election because of the more consultative leadership style of opponent Donald Kalpokas, the former foreign minister. Lini then formed his own National United Party, dividing the Vanua'aku Party and encouraging a succession of new coalitions which brought growing political unrest: this ultimately led to the president's hostage-taking in a mini-coup in 1996. Rioting broke out in Port Vila in 1998 when top government officials were linked to corruption, and a four-week state of emergency followed. Donald Kalpokas, free of scandal, enacted months later a Leadership Code to prevent further abuse of power. Political turmoil continues to burden Vanuatu as rival factions in the ruling coalition struggle for pre-eminence.

NEOCOLONIALISM AND VESTIGIAL COLONIALISM

So long as the USA required the Trust Territory of the Pacific Islands as its nuclear arena in the interest of national security, any discussion of self-determination with the Micronesians, as initially pledged, held low priority. Cold War exigencies prevailed. None the less, the USA was sensitive to the exact wording of its UN trusteeship and to the international opinion on its stewardship there. Concessions were made. As early as the late 1950s, Micronesian leaders were integrated into informal talks about the region's long-term future. By 1965 these talks had produced the Congress of Micronesia, a representative body assembled from all districts which also provided intensive political training to indigenous leaders. The Congress of Micronesia also established a commission to advise on matters concerning constitutional development, but negotiations in this regard commenced only in 1969 and were protracted over 15 years as new concerns arose and Micronesian factions were played one against the other to win the USA more time.

The truth was that, since the signing of the Partial Nuclear Test Ban Treaty in 1963 which finally closed the USA's and Britian's nuclear testing programmes in the Pacific (tests had halted in 1962), the USA still had no intention of weakening national security by demilitarizing the region. President John F. Kennedy at this time had commissioned what later came to be known as the 'Solomon Report' which elaborated a calculated strategy designed to ensure that any altered political status for the Trust Territory of the Pacific Islands would coincide with US national security goals. This report underpinned all subsequent US policy in the region. The Congress of Micronesia's seeming sluggishness in making headway lay in the USA's desire to publicly champion devolution – the transfer of authority from a central government to regional governments – while privately hindering it. The USA's Micronesian policy seemingly differed from France's Pacific policy only in that France wore no mask.

The protracted negotiations with the US government thus brought inversely proportional returns for the Micronesians. If the first negotiations in 1969 commenced with the seeming status of free association for the Islanders, as if they were Niueans consulting with New Zealanders, within four years

the USA had broken down negotiations into respective archipelagic compartments, fragmenting the Congress of Micronesia's united front. By 1976, the Mariana Islands had become
a commonwealth of the USA, thereby relinquishing any future
claim to independence. The remaining Trust Territory of the
Pacific Islands was then divided into three parts, renamed the
Federated States of Micronesia (formerly the Caroline Islands,
including Yap, Chuuk, Pohnpei and Kosrae), the Republic of
the Marshall Islands and the Republic of Belau (formerly
Palau).

In the early 1980s the Federated States of Micronesia and
the Republic of the Marshall Islands negotiated a scheme for
free association with the USA which was then approved by
popular plebiscite. The US Congress delayed the scheme's
implementation until 1987, imposing its conditions of free
association: in matters of foreign affairs and defence, the USA
would continue to enjoy considerable authority. For these
concessions both states would receive, however, extremely
generous subsidies from Washington, as well as special trade
considerations for 15 years. The Islanders agreed with the
USA's terms and in 1990 both achieved their respective
independence under these neocolonial conditions.

The Republic of Belau balked at this, however, as the
defence provisions of the USA's offered free-association compact violated Belau's new constitution which ensured Belau
would remain nuclear-free. Several plebiscites confirmed the
Belauans' desire to achieve independence in free association
with the USA, but the constitutional ban on nuclear materials
thwarted further progress and the USA would not move from
its position on the issue of defence priorities. A 75 per cent
yes-vote by the Belauan population was needed, but never
attained. The debate became acrimonious: a president was
shot in 1985, his successor committed suicide three years
later, the father of an anti-nuclear activist was gunned down.
A 1992 referendum to amend the constitution finally put paid
to the 75 per cent hurdle, as a simple majority would now
suffice. In 1993 the Belauans voted for free association on

the USA's terms, including military jurisdiction in times of 'crisis or hostilities', and independence was declared in Belau on 1 October 1994.

Micronesia's nominal 'independence' is a new incarnation of colonialism in that the independence has been conditional: the Micronesian nations are allowed to be what their former trustee the USA wants them to be. In such a guise, they remain in part divorced from both the wholly independent and the freely associated nations of other parts of Pacific Islands. They also remain generally excluded from the dynamic of integration and unification engaging the free peoples of Pacific Islands, as this still conflicts with strategic US interests. However, the radically shifting geopolitical fulcrum which characterizes the beginning of the twenty-first century suggests a possible slackening of the US harness, intimating Micronesia's closer association with Pacific Islands neighbours in the near future.

With regard to Polynesia, the USA and the United Nations are currently negotiating to delist American Samoa as a colony. In contrast to many Micronesians' aspirations of full independence, American Samoans are now arguing that since American Samoa is not a colony, but a territory in free association with the USA, there is no longer any need for the United Nations' supervision. Governor Tauese Sunia himself has formally appealed to the United Nations to remove American Samoa from the UN's list of colonies. Removing the UN's supervision will of course tie the territory even closer to the USA, creating a territorial legitimacy only one step removed from statehood.

A state of the US union since 1959, Hawai'i experienced a reassessment of its ethnic identity in the 1960s with the African-American struggle for equality and the beginnings of the Native American movement. At the same time, Hawaiian culture was rediscovered and rejuvenated. In the 1970s this led to questions of traditional land rights, self-determination and even sovereignty, with Ceded Lands (see Chapter 4) now being interpreted as stolen property. The State Constitutional

Convention of 1978 created the Office of Hawaiian Affairs whose mission, some believed, lay in securing an apology and reparations from the US government for what it had done to the erstwhile Hawaiian kingdom. During Democratic President Jimmy Carter's liberal administration, the US Congress established the Native Hawaiians Study Commission, defining 'Hawaiian' as any person with an aboriginal ancestor, regardless of ethnic dilution.

But before the Commission could commence its task of redressing past and present grievances, the conservative Republicans were voted into power and remained there for 12 years. The Carter appointees (six Hawaiians and three mainlanders) on the Commission were dismissed by President Ronald Reagan and replaced (six mainlanders and three Hawaiians). Their draft report of 1982 outraged native Hawaiians, because it absolved the USA of any guilt or responsibility for the overthrow of the monarchy and esssentially concluded that the USA owed the Hawaiians nothing. The final report was issued in 1983 in two volumes: the six mainlanders' case and the three Hawaiians' rebuttal. Thereafter, the Office of Hawaiian Affairs struggled to survive, its budget financed by state agencies hesitant to pay, and its existence dependent on the colonial constitution of Hawai'i. Under this, the question of Hawaiian sovereignty can only be expressed in terms of a 'tribal nation' similar to that of mainland Native Americans (Apache, Cherokee, Lakota and so forth), not legal citizens of a formerly recognized kingdom.

The 1993 centenary of Queen Lili'uokalani's overthrow was marked by weeks of demonstrations, re-enactments and public debate on what truly happened and its significance for Hawai'i's future. In a dramatic gesture, Governor Waihe'e ordered the US flag lowered and the Hawaiian state flag, that of the old monarchy, to fly alone over all state buildings. Both houses of the state legislature issued a joint resolution on the occasion, declaring they believed 'the United States military committed the first overt act to overthrow the independent nation of Hawai'i', which was 'an overt act of military aggression against a peaceful and independent nation', concluding: 'BE IT RESOLVED...that the Legislature encourages the promotion of debate revolving around the future of Hawai'i as a Pacific Island society, within or without the United States of America'. In November of that same year, the new Democratic President of the USA, Bill Clinton, signed a joint resolution of both houses of the US Congress which formally apologized to the native Hawaiians for the complicity of the US government in the overthrow of the Hawaiian nation.

Those who claim Hawaiian ancestry comprise nearly 20 per cent of the state's 1.2 million inhabitants. Though they differ on what form self-governance should take, dozens of political factions concur on this: Hawaiians should control Hawaiian land. In a special 1996 referendum, 73 per cent of these native Hawaiians approved the election of delegates to propose an indigenous government. Some school children refuse to pledge alliance to the USA. Many adults deny the jurisdiction of US courts and refuse to file US tax returns. Hawai'i still plays a vital and sensitive role in the USA's national security strategy, though its importance has greatly diminished since the collapse of the former Soviet Union. There is a new vision of a restored, but different Hawaiian nation emerging, one in which not race but perhaps acculturation will determine one's place in the new, multi-ethnic Pacific Islands society there.

With the end of the Cold War, the USA downgraded its interests in Pacific Islands. In 1995 Washington closed the regional office of the Agency for International Development; one year later the US Information Agency in the region shut its doors. Similarly, the Washington-funded Asia Foundation has closed and the USA is frequently defaulting on its dues to regional organizations. Because the Philippines has closed its US military bases, Guam has assumed a new strategic significance in the region, while Hawai'i is suffering from its decline in military importance and from associated funding cutbacks affecting all aspects of life in the Islands. If current geopolitical trends continue, the USA will rate Pacific Islands low in priority, opening the possibility of some autonomy for

American Samoans and Hawaiians (not for Guam's Chamorros). However, whether the democratic majority of these 'American Islanders' will desire autonomy is another question altogether.

France's post-war conduct in Pacific Islands has been more openly colonialistic, as noted above with French Polynesia and the nuclear testing programme. France has always held that New Caledonia's mineral wealth was not to be forfeited, regardless of world opinion or indigenous demands. Already in 1944 various political parties had formed in New Caledonia which represented a spectrum of opinion. Both the *caldoches* (white-settler families) and the Kanaks (indigenous New Caledonians) desired more local power from Paris – though only for themselves, not to be shared with the other faction. Agitation to attain this power alternated with modest reforms aimed not at long-term equity but short-term appeasement, until 1958 when the new President of France Charles de Gaulle held a referendum in each of France's overseas territories to decide their future. A majority of New Caledonians voted for continued French association, with Maurice Lenormand, leader of the pro-Melanesian party, abstaining from calling for independence.

In the 1960s, as in Tahiti many of New Caledonia's hard-won reforms were abrogated. Lenormand was gaoled for a year on trumped-up charges, the French National Assembly revoked New Caledonia's limited autonomy, and all effective power was reinvested in the Governor. Different from French Polynesia, full independence from France was never the expressed goal of the New Caledonian reformists; these sought racial equality and social justice. Lenormand's successor, Roch Pidjot, Kanak chief of the La Conception tribe near Noumea, represented the Union Calédonienne in the French National Assembly for two decades, during which time both autonomy and racial injustice became central issues. Kanaks were by then a minority in New Caledonia, having seen over 90 per cent of their land taken with no social compensation.

In December 1984, a gang of *caldoches* hunted down and murdered ten unarmed Kanak nationalists. The immediate consequence of this tragedy was a call for greater autonomy and reforms. The Socialist President François Mitterand of France negotiated an agreement between the Kanaks and the *caldoches*, dividing New Caledonia into provinces and promising to hold a referendum on independence. However, little was done, and the ultra-conservative Jacques Chirac soon became prime minister in France, who adopted a hard, anti-independence policy similar to that of De Gaulle nearly 30 years earlier. Funds were redirected away from the regional councils. Development aid to Kanaks halted and the agency responsible was abolished. Lands purchased by Mitterand's Socialist government for redistribution to Kanak tribes were sold by the Gaullists to *caldoches* instead. Whereupon Paris stationed special troops in mobile camps next to Kanak villages – just as France had done in Algeria and Chad to intimidate potential opponents.

This was all too much for the South Pacific Forum. At its August 1986 meeting, it voted unanimously to request that the UN reinscribe New Caledonia on its list of 'non-self-governing territories'. In September 1986 the seven self-confessed murderers of the ten Kanaks were released by a French magistrate, but then an appeal court ruled they had to stand trial. In December the UN General Assembly did reinscribe New Caledonia on the decolonization list, signalling a major diplomatic defeat for France, but in October 1987 the seven self-confessed murderers were acquitted all the same.

This prompted general riots in New Caledonia during the 1988 French elections. On West 'Uvea in the Loyalties, Kanak nationalists killed four French *gendarmes* then took 16 further *gendarmes* hostage. Three days before the French elections Jacques Chirac ordered the military to intervene. Nineteen Kanaks were massacred; their leader, Alphonse Dianou, a former student priest, was bludgeoned to death by French troops as he lay wounded on a stretcher. When six further Kanaks surrendered, they were shot in cold blood. Thirty-three Kanaks were deported to France. No one was ever brought to justice for these atrocities. And Jacques Chirac was re-elected prime minister.

One year after the massacre, in 1989, at a commemorative service on West 'Uvea, the two leading moderate Kanak leaders were slain. In subsequent provincial elections in 1989 and 1995 the Kanak nationalist party gained majorities in the north and the Loyalty Islands, while the *caldoches* party won in the south, the centre of industry, wealth and whites. In the 1990s the French government invested more than a billion US dollars in improving New Caledonia's infrastructure, administration and schools, clearly intending to bind it even closer to France. The new jobs the scheme created went almost entirely to newly arrived Frenchmen. In May 1998 representatives of the Kanak party, *caldoches* party and the French government signed the Noumea Accords agreeing to a protracted devolution of French authority over 15 to 20 years. In November of the same year, the 'consensual solution' was approved in a referendum by 72 per cent of New Caledonia's voters. This means that in about 2018 yet another generation will be deciding on New Caledonia's relationship to France. Until then, France will remain in full control of all New Caledonians... and their mineral riches.

The twentieth-century wave of independence for the Western Pacific Islands halted abruptly at New Caledonia's shore. France's stewardship of New Caledonia has been one of the most insensitive in the more recent history of Pacific Islands. It is possible, however, that the new international geopolitical realignment will excuse the French from the region within the next generation. Independence for France's Pacific Islands colonies has never really been an issue for Paris, which sees them not as colonies but 'overseas territories': part of France, in other words, but different. The concessions which France's Pacific territories won after the Second World War – citizenship, Territorial Assemblies, seats in the French Parliament – far exceeded what other colonial powers were granting at the same time. However, when the independence movement swept through the Pacific in the 1960s and 1970s, France's 'concessions' were recognized to be merely the accessories of colonial domination. Since the débâcle of its final nuclear test series in the Tuamotus, France has attempted to improve its image in Pacific Islands by offering economic aid to the region's newly independent states and by granting more autonomy to its territories there. Once France becomes wholly integrated into the new united Europe, it is possible that France's will and capability to maintain distant colonies in the Pacific will wane. That would then leave only the USA, Chile and Indonesia as Pacific Islands' last colonial powers.

Rapanui, or Easter Island, is locked in the time-warp of vestigial colonialism. Only following the local protests of 1964–65 did the moderate Christian Democratic government of Chile, the Pacific's smallest colonial power, permit Easter Islanders to elect a local mayor and council. Chilean citizenship was at last granted to the Rapanui people in 1966. However, General Augusto Pinochet's military coup in Chile in 1973 ended elected offices on Rapanui and the autocratic rule which followed lasted until 1990. Since then, Rapanui has become an incorporated part of the Fifth Region of Chile, with Valparaíso as capital. The Chilean-appointed Governor administrates for Chile on the island, while the elected mayor and local council wield little actual power. The island is heavily subsidized by Chile, which maintains a military and official presence amounting to about one-third of the island's current population of c. 3500. While the Rapanui people speak of self-determination and possible independence, the Chilean government is contemplating the construction of a naval base at this western periphery of its self-styled 'Sea of Chile' to signal Chilean sovereignty there. Chile is also increasing its police presence to cope with growing civil unrest and skyrocketing tourism (a 500 per cent increase from 1991 to 2001). Though Rapanui's cultural integration into the new Pacific has already occurred, its political integration seems improbable in the foreseeable future.

New Guinea's western half, known earlier as Dutch New Guinea, became the beneficiary of an ambitious development project by the Netherlands following the Second World War. However, the Dutch were forced to cede all sovereignty over their share of New Guinea to Indonesia in 1962, which then imposed a rigorous military administration in what became, one year later, the separate Indonesian province of Irian Jaya, Bahasa Indonesia for 'Victorious Hot Land'. Since then, Indonesia has ruled the Melanesian province in a style reminiscent of early colonial barbarism. In the 1970s and 1980s the Indonesian Army crushed an incipient independence movement; thousands of locals died. In July 2001 at Manokwari on northwest Bird's Head Peninsula, protesters rose up against the Indonesian presence, killing five policemen. In consequence, as many as 60 insurrectionists were taken into custody, all but five of them denied legal help; hundreds more fled to the mountains in fear of military reprisal. Indonesia steadfastly refuses to accept any critique of its stewardship there. Political dissent in Irian Jaya is a criminal activity. All talk of Pacific integration or independence is futile with the government of a nation which itself now seems to be self-destructing. Irian Jaya, Pacific Islands' portal to island Southeast Asia, will always remain of strategic importance to the region. Perhaps one day, following Indonesia's possible fragmentation, a free or incorporated 'Western New Guinea' will be allowed, in peace, to play a more active role in the comity of Pacific Islands.

***

Pacific Islands' independence, for those islands and archipelagos fortunate enough to have experienced this, has not been like African nations' independence – that is, not racked by the corruption and tribal warfare which keeps much of Africa from attaining its merited majority. In general, peace, unity and modest progress have prevailed, with only wealth eluding most new nations in the region. Amiable with their neighbours, Pacific Islands' free peoples now harbour aspirations of federalism. For, at the beginning of the twenty-first century, Pacific Islands remains a geographical, ethnic and cultural, but not a political label, though the region's 'reinvention' after the Second World War, in many guises, has clearly brought it closer than ever before to a shared identity.

The 'Pacific Way' first voiced by Fiji's Ratu Sir Kamisese Mara – that is, the value of traditional co-operation and consensus – will indeed work wonders, especially when parties share the same goal from the onset. It will not work, however, when colonial powers place self-interest above the indigenous franchise. Britain, Australia and New Zealand reinvented an independent and rapidly consolidating Pacific Islands. The USA, France, Chile and Indonesia reinvented new forms of colonialism: full assimilation, dependent independence, partial autonomy or brutal domination. While half of Pacific Islands is now free to choose its destiny, half still remains powerless or handicapped. The 'reinvention' of Pacific Islands after the Second World War was a story with two endings but only one moral:

The disempowered can make history, but only the empowered shape history.

8

The 'New Pacific'

THE DIASPORA

The brown, indigenous, uni-insular Pacific Islander is an anachronism. Demographic heterogeneity now characterizes much of Pacific Islands, with multiple ethnicities defying traditional categorizations. Far more Europeans and/or Asians than Polynesians reside in New Zealand and Hawai'i, for example, many of these boasting Islander ancestors. There are more Chamorros, Niueans and Tokelauans living abroad than on their ancestral isles, many of them with children of mixed heritage. The islands are currently uniting all indigenous (and acculturated) Islanders in a way not seen in the Pacific since the great voyaging spheres of the Middle Ages. Indeed, the phenomenon is so widespread it has been labelled 'contemporary voyaging'.

Many Islanders who had traditionally been linked by intermarriage and trade but had suffered separation through nineteenth-century colonialism – such as the Rotumans in Kosrae, I-Kiribati in the Marshall Islands, and Tongans in Fiji, to name but three – have now followed modern migration routes to more lucrative jobs and higher education in Pacific Rim countries and beyond. It is Polynesians and Micronesians – the heirs of the Austronesian voyagers – who migrate internationally; in the main, Melanesians migrate internally (this is because nearly all of them are restricted free entry elsewhere). French Islanders chiefly migrate within France's overseas territories in the Pacific, almost exclusively to New Caledonia and Tahiti; very few migrate to France. In contrast, American, New Zealand and Chilean Islanders enjoy free access to their respective metropolises and make abundant use of the right.

Numerically, the first destination of Pacific Islanders is New Zealand, where they make up 4.9 per cent of the nation's total population (11 per cent if one includes the indigenous Māori). Their numbers are steadily increasing. Auckland is now the Polynesian capital of the world, hosting the largest concentration and most diverse population of Polynesians anywhere. Though Samoans dominate numerically among New Zealand's Pacific immigrants, other expatriate communities reside there with a higher percentage in New Zealand than at home: the Cook Islands (69 per cent), Tokelau (70) and Niue (85). Family reunion programmes have allowed a large number of Tongans – whose government is not in free association with New Zealand – to live there as well (c. 30 000 in 2001).

Islanders' second destination is the USA which, in the 1990 census, counted 154 010 Pacific Islanders in residence, almost half of them, however, having been born in the USA; native Hawaiians (that is, those choosing to identify themselves as predominately ethnic Hawaiians, despite mixed heritage) numbered an additional 211 014. The USA's average population growth rate since 1980 had been 9.8 per cent; Islanders, in contrast, had averaged 41.5 per cent. As in New Zealand, Samoans comprised the largest Pacific immigrant population (but, in the USA, Eastern, not Western Samoans as in New Zealand). More Chamorros, now a minority in their native Guam, live in the USA than at home, almost 50 000 of them. However, some of the preceding figures may be misleading, in that as a result of the recent resurgence of ethnic pride they might reflect a shift in ethnic re-identification rather than 'true' ethnicity (now a questionable classification nearly everywhere in the Pacific).

Australia appears to be Islanders' third destination, though details here are sketchy: Australia does not particularize 'ethnicity' on its census forms. Some 40 per cent of Australia's Islanders in 1986 were NZ Māori (26 000) who enjoy free access as a result of the Trans-Tasman Agreement between Australia and New Zealand; other Islanders have also entered Australia on the same terms, through New Zealand, leading to sizeable communities there of especially Western Samoans and Cook Islanders. In addition, Fijians, Tongans, Nauruans and Papua New Guineans have recently emigrated to Australia in significant numbers. Tens of thousands of Fijian Indians arrived after Fiji's two coups of 1987.

As in prehistory, the hub of Polynesian migrations is the Samoan archipelago, with the ultimate destination either New Zealand or the USA depending on the fluctuating economic situation. In the 1960s thousands of Islanders flocked to Auckland via Samoa, but by the 1970s New Zealand's recession had redirected this flow of human resources towards American Samoa and the USA (Hawai'i, and then the mainland). New Zealand's sudden economic boom of the 1980s saw Islanders again migrating to Auckland, but the New Zealand crash of 1988 then saw the trend reversed once again. As a consequence of these continued, if punctuated, migrations, nearly half of Western Samoa's and American Samoa's populations now live abroad.

Recent Micronesian migration has been mainly determined by the respective relationship to the USA. When Chamorros were given free entry to the USA, many moved there for education and employment; in turn, thousands of Palauans moved to Guam, taking over the Chamorros' jobs there. In the 1960s, the Trust Territory of the Pacific Islands transferred its administrative centre to Saipan in the southern central Marianas north of Guam, hiring diverse Micronesians but mainly Palauans, who then developed a new Micronesian melting pot there which was financed and formed by its US employer. Many other Micronesians received stipends to study in the USA, and in 1990 (1994 for Palauans) Micronesians from the Federated

States of Micronesia and the Republic of the Marshall Islands, like those of the Commonwealth of the Northern Mariana Islands, were given free entry to the USA, too. Many then moved immediately to Guam – 1600 in 1990, over 6000 in 1991, most of these from Chuuk, the Federated States' most densely populated state; others headed for Saipan. In present-day Micronesia, a multi-ethnic society of indigenous Micronesians, Filipinos and other Asians provides professional, skilled, semi-skilled and unskilled service and labour, having replaced the erstwhile indigenous population with an international pot-pourri similar to that now emerging in Polynesia. Such mixed populations invariably transcend both insular and archipelagic boundaries.

Melanesian migration is foremost characterized by increasing internal urbanization, causing cultural congestions similar to those brought about by Polynesian and Micronesian external migrations, which result in escalating insular urbanization. Melanesian towns have always been European, thus colonial, and traditional restrictions still prevail. The tribal and social divide is most visually manifest in the many squatter villages abutting Melanesia's major cities and towns. Though land titles in such communities have usually not been conveyed, some of the neighbourhoods have evolved from corrugated iron dumps into substantial cement settlements whose residents – mostly insecure labourers – are elaborating with local landowners kinship and exchange systems permitting possible permanence.

Only a fraction of Islander migrants join the local elite. Nearly always occupying the new society's lowest socio-economic rung, the vast majority of first-generation intruders never ascend the social ladder. All the same, they generally, but not invariably, enjoy better lives than their kinfolk back home. Most never return. Their children – who begin life biculturally and bilingually – eventually assume the new home-land's identity completely, better enabling social ascension.

Heavy emigration, without commensurate replacement, can of course devastate smaller island societies. Nearly one-third of the men of Tuvalu and Kiribati work abroad as seamen in national, regional and European shipping, reminiscent of those Hawaiians, Māori and other Polynesians on early nineteenth-century sealers and whalers; the trade has caused a serious depletion of males in these islands, boding ill for local population growth rates. In 1996, only 18 904 Cook Islanders were living in the Cooks while around 40 000 people calling themselves Cook Islanders were living permanently in New Zealand and another 20 000 in Australia. When Niue achieved internal self-government and free association with New Zealand in 1974, the majority of the then 4000 Niueans left for New Zealand. In 2001 only around 1480 Niueans were left on the island, whereas some 15 000 New Zealanders are claiming to be Niueans – most of them second- and third-generation Niueans who have never seen Niue, now the world's smallest independent state.

In such a drastic situation as Niue, of course the question of what constitutes a legal constituency arises. And faced with possible abandonment altogether – like the Pacific's erstwhile 'Mystery Islands' (see Chapter 2) – the Niuean government is presently struggling with the preservation of an entire nation. Only development projects employing substantial numbers of unskilled and semi-skilled labourers, such as has replaced or supplemented the emigration-depleted populations of Palau, Kwajalein, American Samoa and other places, will alter these dramatic trends. Increasingly, Asians are being imported for construction projects in the Western Pacific, a development which might see a return of the Asian incursion of the late nineteenth and early twentieth centuries.

Not only the smaller and poorer nations of Pacific Islands can experience an ominous emigration: larger, more developed nations are also becoming justifiably concerned. Boasting an otherwise robust population, Tonga (1996: 97 446) has experienced acute emigration of late, particularly to New Zealand where over 30 000 Tongans now live permanently. Every year, around 3000 Tongans are leaving the country for good, which has reduced the growth rate of Tonga's population to 0.5 per cent and has caused a critical shortage of agricultural labourers. Similarly, the drift of New Zealanders to Australia increased dramatically in the 1970s and 1980s and became a veritable flood by the end of the 1990s; for the first time in history, New Zealand's population is not only falling, but simultaneously ageing.

At the start of the twenty-first century Pacific Islands is home to nearly 14 million people, of whom 81 per cent live in Papua New Guinea (4.5 million), New Zealand (3.6), Irian Jaya (2) and Hawai'i (1.2). Pacific populations show an annual growth rate of around 2.3 per cent, the higher rates being in Melanesia and Micronesia. If this growth continues, Pacific Islands' population will be around 25 million by 2020. Through improved diet and hygiene because of nationally monitored social services and better economic conditions, Pacific Islanders are overall experiencing higher birth and infant survival rates, and longer longevity with lower death rates. In 1950, Papua New Guineans had an average life expectancy of 35; now it is 50. In all of Pacific Islands it is about 60, a significant increase. However, an ever-larger proportion of the Islander population is under 20, placing a new burden on strained educational budgets and social services as children are being prepared for jobs which are not there.

As detailed in previous chapters, the history of Pacific Islands has been one of countless discrete migrations. But the introduction of modern transportation to the region has led to a continuous migration of unprecedented magnitude. In particular, the Pacific's growing commercial and administrative centres – Port Moresby, Noumea, Suva, Auckland, Honolulu, Tahiti, Saipan and others – have drawn Islanders like a magnet for their jobs, schools, hospitals and other benefits and services not found on small, isolated islands or in rural mountainous provinces. Many young Pacific Islanders migrate to flee the often stifling constraints of village life; others seek the glamour and excitement seen in Western videos or related by returnees. Various communities have long fostered circular migration whereby young male wage-earners, whose island parents and siblings survive on the remittances from Pago Pago, Sydney or Suva, have pledged to eventually return to wed and start a family. However, as mentioned above, large cities like Auckland or Port Moresby include tens of thousands of second- and third-generation migrants who have never seen 'Home'. And this trend is increasing.

The urban growth which has characterized particularly the past generation in Pacific Islands defies many fledgling nations to provide the necessary infrastructure and social services. Authorities who then conscientiously address and resolve problems of water supplies, waste disposal, health, employment and rising crime as more and more shanty towns spring up alongside the Pacific's expanding coastal metropolises, experience that the resulting improved quality of urban life there only draws even more migrants, further depopulating rural countrysides and entire islands. Rural labour forces shrink, agricultural production declines and the national economy suffers: more food needs to be imported, straining near-empty coffers. The key to breaking this vicious cycle lies in implementing policies which retard rural drift through development, while ensuring satisfactory urban living standards.

Not all of Pacific Islands struggles with urbanization. Around 70 per cent of Polynesians are still rural dwellers. In Papua New Guinea, more than 80 per cent live rurally. In Irian Jaya, Vanuatu and the Solomons, the figure is as high as 85 per cent.

Still, emigration beckons millions in the region. If one excludes all New Guineans, more than one in nine Pacific Islanders now lives abroad, nearly all of these migrants choosing another Pacific Islands nation or territory, or a country of the Pacific Rim, as their new home. On small, crowded islands – Ebeye, an islet in the Kwajalein atoll of the Marshall Islands, houses c. 7000 people on only 33 hectares (81.5 acres) – emigration can of course relieve unmanageable social pressures. It also solves the nearly ubiquitous unemployment problem. The remittances migrants send home maintain families and create investment resources, so that more jobs can be created locally. However, the remittances and material gifts then fuel an increased demand for imported goods: cars, motorcycles, tele-visions, videos, computers, stereos, microwave ovens, refriger-ators and more. Ironically, this can put an even greater strain on the island economy in the end, resulting in accelerated emigration.

CHANGING ECONOMIES

The traditional Pacific Islands village economy (see Chapter 2) remains important today. Nevertheless, local agriculture has declined in most places as labourers migrate and more and more foodstuffs are being imported. A cash economy has gen-erally replaced the barter economy and self-sufficiency which once characterized the region. In addition, Pacific Islands almost entirely exports cheap raw materials and imports expensive manufactured goods: so exports and imports rarely balance. This means a trade deficit, and it puts nearly all of Pacific Islands in a particularly vulnerable position on the global stage.

Until recently, plantation (copra, sugar) and cash crops dominated Pacific Islands' economies, providing the region's major source of income. To be sure, Papua New Guinea still relies on its exports of coffee, tea and cocoa. Fiji's main indus-try is still sugar, vital to the national economy – almost half a million metric tonnes are sold annually to Malaysia, Japan, Britain and other nations. Meat, dairy products and wool remain New Zealand's major source of income. And many smaller nations of Pacific Islands still rely on their exports of passion fruit, papaya, pineapples, bananas, vanilla, citrus fruit and sweet potatoes, though this increasingly puts them at the mercy of fluctuating and highly competitive world mar-kets beyond their control. However, agriculture no longer leads Pacific Islands' national planning. (Agriculture in New Caledonia, for example, accounts for only 4.9 per cent of the gross domestic product.) There are now more lucrative and secure sources of revenue for most islands and archipelagos.

Melanesia, for example, has more recently turned to timber, with Japan buying up most of its tropical hardwoods. Extensive logging has negatively impacted on vast swathes of forest in Papua New Guinea, the Solomons, New Caledonia, Vanuatu, Fiji and Western Samoa because the current high value of their quality timber forces these cash-strapped nations to court multinational corporations to the detriment of fragile ecosystems.

By far the greatest export revenues in Pacific Islands are generated not by timber, but by minerals. Minerals now account for some 46 per cent of Pacific Islands' total annual income. However, mineral reserves are concentrated unevenly in the region. Melanesia – with New Guinea's enormous land mass – clearly promises untold wealth from mineral deposits for centuries to come. Large reserves of gold and copper await exploitation in both Irian Jaya and Papua New Guinea, and there are indications of vast stores of natural gas there as well. Nauru still profits from its phosphate mines, benefiting the local population with relative prosperity at the price of environmental ruin and imminent depletion. Bougainville in the Solomons has vast reserves of copper. And New Caledonia is the world's third largest producer of nickel.

Both logging and mining have compelled Pacific Islands nations to prioritize sustainable development – that is, ensuring financial returns while using forest and mineral resources in such a way as to preserve natural environments and guarantee regeneration of timber resources. Unhappily, the demands of huge multinational corporations seldom coincide with the national priorities of tiny insular societies. Many necessary compromises have perpetuated grievous abuses. A new political economy – 'neo-tribal capitalism' – has even emerged which frequently sees tribal bodies exploiting both the environment and themselves beyond the limits of sustainable development for the immediate foreign exchange needed to postpone imminent insolvency.

But what is 'sustainable development'? The term is merely a statement of principle, one lacking the theoretical and methodological specificity to be measured and the clarity of policy to be implemented. Many experts have tried to elucidate the nebulous concept of sustainable development through the suggestion of new approaches. One such suggestion, for example, has been the 'inside-out approach': that is, Pacific Islanders are invited to become active players who re-contextualize, using local beliefs, the alien elements within their economies; these societies are then 'island laboratories' in which globalization is played out in unique and diverse settings. However, local environmental ethics and institutions are no panacea for solving the ills of contemporary Pacific Islands development. In fact, local tenure models require just the right resource-use strategy, and management initiatives will always require top-down monitoring. National governments and regional organizations will always have to play a vital role in the process of sustainable development, however this may be defined.

In addition to agriculture, timber and minerals, the sale of fishing rights also generates handsome foreign revenues, as many island states hold economic rights over immense tracts of ocean. According to international law, islands enjoy a 322-kilometre (200-mile) Exclusive Economic Zone. Nine Pacific Islands nations boast Zones comprising more than one million square kilometres each. Marine revenues of all kinds are crucial for those Pacific Islands, like Tuvalu and Kiribati, lacking onshore development and resources. Fisheries and seafoods are second only to mining as Pacific Islands' biggest export earner, chief among the catches being tuna fished by large commercial fleets operating mainly out of Japan, the USA, Korea and Taiwan. Though all island states are, through licensing agreements, entitled to income from foreign trawlers fishing in their Zone, smaller states negotiating independently have encountered difficulties in establishing proper fees. Because of this, the South Pacific Forum founded the Forum Fisheries Agency to better bargain regional licensing agreements, specifically with Japan and the USA. Policing of the respective Zones remains a difficult matter, however, and overfishing by enormous fleets of foreign trawlers using giant purse-seine nets now threatens entire archipelagic reserves.

Inshore fisheries must also be preserved, in order to ensure local food needs and to stimulate indigenous development. Commercial canneries generate profits and employ thousands in New Zealand, Fiji, the Solomons, American Samoa and Hawai'i. However, most Pacific catches are processed elsewhere, then exported back into the Pacific at inflated prices.

Another realm still wholly untouched underlies the marine resources of Pacific Islands. Vast stores of metal-rich nodules – minable clumps in a matrix of different rock material – lie within the Zones of several island nations, like Kiribati and the Cooks. And oil reserves mottle certain Pacific regions as well, such as offshore from New Zealand. International agreement is still pending on the distribution of benefits from resources outside a respective Zone, and in most cases the cost of extraction still remains prohibitive, at least to the extent that poorer Pacific Islands nations could not participate in or substantially profit from the enterprise. But increasing world demand, particularly for oil as other reserves are becoming depleted, might change this to benefit Pacific Islands in ways that are still unknown.

Manufacturing in Pacific Islands – apart from New Zealand and Hawai'i – has failed to achieve extensive development principally because of the restrictive costs of importing materials, the small volume of local markets, and the difficulties of transport. All the same, ever-resourceful Tonga has diversified into small industries, producing a variety of commodities from woolen ware to luxury yachts. And Fiji's gross national product now relies on the local garment industry which employs 15 000 and exports chiefly to Australia and New Zealand; favourable entry to these two lucrative markets was provided by the South Pacific Regional Trade and Economic Cooperation Arrangement (SPARTECA), allowing partial duty- and quota-free entry of goods with at least 50 per cent local content. However, SPARTECA prohibits manufacturers from importing quality fabrics from outside the region, and so

Fijian garments satisfy only the bottom demands of the market. Unhappily, Asian competition and growing free trade make both this scheme and similar agreements in the Pacific vulnerable and exploitable.

Where natural resources are wanting and manufacturing is impracticable, Pacific Islands nations have turned to service industries. Offshore banking was first introduced to Pacific Islands by the New Hebrides Condominium (now Vanuatu), followed by the Cook Islands, Nauru, Tonga and Western Samoa. Flags of convenience for foreign ships are also sold by Nauru, Tonga and Western Samoa. Many Pacific nations live beyond their means – Cook Islands, for example, imports 11 times the amount it exports – and so, to compensate, robust revenue-generating schemes must be elaborated. The Cook Islands Philatelic Bureau generates revenues of 1.4 million dollars a year from the sale of collectors' postage stamps, and Tuvalu has introduced a similar scheme. Resourceful Tonga has set up Tongasat and sent two satellites into orbit from Kazakhstan for telecommunications; Tongasat and the Tongan government have earned tens of millions of dollars in foreign revenue from the enterprise.

Pacific Islands' newest money-making scheme is the world's fifth-largest online casino, Casinos of the South Pacific, based in the Cook Islands since 1997 and offering blackjack, draw poker, roulette and slots. Some islands now offer for sale international internet codes – like Tonga's '.to' – for use in registering catchy domain names already occupied under '.com'. A disturbing new development in Pacific Islands is the money-laundering which has occurred in the Cook Islands, the Marshalls, Nauru, Niue, Western Samoa and Vanuatu whereby 'empty shells', international commercial companies existing only on paper (many alleged to be East Asian and Russian mafia and Latin American drug cartels) pay large annual registration fees which help to sustain struggling island budgets.

Tourism, the world's largest and fastest-growing industry and the only one allowing a net flow of wealth from richer to poorer countries, is one of the few reliable recourses in Pacific

Islands' current economic straits, providing resource-poor island states with the immediate foreign exchange required to pay for massive imports. There is certainly no difficulty in enticing Pacific Rim peoples and distant Europeans to the region. New Zealand, Fiji, the Cooks, Hawai'i, Tahiti and Tonga all have large, established tourist industries, and smaller islands such as Niue and Rapanui are vigorously promoting tourism as their major source of revenue apart from aid.

Some touristic figures for the region are staggering. Annual visitors to Guam outnumber locals by four to one, to Rapanui by seven to one, and to the Northern Marianas by nine to one. In all, over ten million tourists visit Pacific Islands each year, and their numbers are rapidly increasing. New Zealand alone receives over 1.3 million visitors. However, with over seven million annual tourists Hawai'i surpasses the rest of Pacific Islands by far, as it networks with Japan and the USA. Tourism is the leading industry in French Polynesia, Hawai'i, Tonga, Western Samoa, the Cooks, Vanuatu and Fiji. Peripheral earnings from handicrafts, transport, tour guiding, food and entertainment help to sustain many island families who otherwise would have an insufficient or no income. In Vanuatu, which receives more cruise-ship passengers than any other Pacific Islands country, tourism accounts for around 20 per cent of wage employment. Tourism in Fiji earns more than the sugar and gold industries combined.

However, tourism, too, is hardly Pacific Islands' panacea. Only around 40 per cent of the net earnings from tourism remains in the host country, the other 60 per cent is lost to foreign wages, repatriated profits, commissions, imported goods and other things. The maintenance of the infrastructure which modern competitive tourism demands burdens host governments. And the environmental and social effects of tourism generally impact negatively on small island nations: traditional landscapes are insensitively 'Bali Ha'i-ed' and indigenous lifestyles are stereotyped, commercialized and eroded. Yet though it is true that the traditional significance of Pacific dance and song is lost when endlessly paraded before incomprehending though appreciative tourists, on the other hand these tourists have provided both the stimulus and financial resources which revived Pacific traditions in the twentieth century. Recent calls have come from all parties for a more environmentally and culturally sensitive tourism in Pacific Islands. But, at least for the time being, bulk tourism will continue to have priority because of its immediate rewards.

Another major source of income for Pacific Islands is aid from richer cosmopolitan donors. Despite the many revenues mentioned above, most nations of the region rely on aid from foreign governments and other international bodies to compensate for daunting budgetary shortfalls. Africa and Pacific Islands receive the highest per capita payments of foreign aid in the world, and there is no end in sight for either's need. As might be expected, the greatest benefactors are those Islanders living in free association and/or under neo-colonialism – those in the USA's former Trust Territory, in New Zealand's former colonies and in France's overseas territories. Without New Zealand's annual aid of about 5.5 million dollars (NZ 12 million), for example, the Cook Islands would be bankrupt. Australia generously assists its former colony Papua New Guinea, as well as other Pacific Islands. And both Japan and Britain charitably support several Pacific economies.

As mentioned above with migration, remittances – the monies Islanders living and working abroad send back home – also contribute significantly to island economies. Even robust economies like Tonga's rely heavily on remittances, in this case primarily from Tongans living and working in New Zealand and Australia: in the 1980s, for example, these remittances accounted for over a third of Tonga's foreign exchange earnings, more than the country's exports and tourism combined.

WOMEN IN THE PACIFIC

Too infrequently figuring in a history of the region, women are Pacific Islands' greatest forgotten resource. As described much earlier (see 'Gender Roles' in Chapter 2), women's position in prehistoric Pacific Islands societies varied greatly, depending on island and status: Melanesia's matrilineal societies highly valued their women, its patrilineal societies little valued them; and Polynesians held women to be either sacred or inferior, depending on island and circumstance. With Western contact, the Christian notion of the subordinate woman who is universally marginalized to an inferior position in society tended to reinforce and validate the generally practised supremacy of Pacific Islands' males, weakening time-honoured female privileges. Today's educated Melanesian women criticize *kastom* – the perceived traditional ways of a tribe – as a modern male tool invented to subordinate the Melanesian female. Similarly, contemporary Māori women are disputing whether the prohibition against women speaking on the *marae*, the tribal meeting place, is truly 'traditional', suspecting the negative influence of early nineteenth-century missionaries here, too.

In certain areas of Pacific Islands – such as in New Zealand, Hawai'i and the USA's former Trust Territories in Micronesia – women have been granted greater legal and civil rights, and in most of the islands girls now enjoy the same benefits of education earlier reserved only for boys. Nearly everywhere women can now occupy high public office, where they frequently display that remarkable political leadership which characterized such historical personalities as Tahiti's Queen Pomare Vahine IV, Hawai'i's Queen Lili'ukalani and Tonga's Queen Salote Tupou III. Be that as it may, women in Pacific Islands still have neither achieved the social equity of Western women nor regained the special privileges they once enjoyed in many precontact Pacific societies.

The role of Western education in altering women's perceptions of their place in society should not be undervalued. For the first time, because of literacy and general education, Islander women have begun to question both their Christian and pseudo-traditional obligation of subordination. With the great influx of Western tourists, and with many Islander women working Western hours as wage earners, new ideas about the relationship between the sexes have, in general, rendered most, but not all, inherited gender roles obsolete. Many Pacific Islands families are now beginning to resemble their Western counterparts, a trend already completed in Hawai'i, nearly completed in New Zealand and rapidly spreading elsewhere. (Rural Melanesia, especially New Guinea, shows the greatest resistance to such change.) Throughout most of Pacific Islands, mainly as a consequence of successful family planning programmes, women are having smaller families, remaining at their jobs longer, accumulating more personal wealth and, as a result of their raised socioeconomic standing, publicly demanding complete social equality. At the forefront of this latter-day 'emancipation' – actually, a return to precontact privilege, though in wholly changed parametres – stand the women of Polynesia, closely followed by their Micronesian sisters from the USA's former Trust Territory.

Nevertheless, men continue to dominate public life throughout all of the Pacific. Many cultural barriers still hinder women's access to education and employment. More girls than boys leave school early. As in the West in the 1950s and 1960s, career-minded Islander girls are mainly steered towards nursing and secretarial work. Where industry is present, as in Fiji, Tahiti, Western Samoa and American Samoa, women and young girls often work for below-market wages and in poor conditions. Domestic violence also haunts much of Pacific Islands, but its level varies greatly throughout the region. For example, more Indian Fijian men find it acceptable to beat their wives than do indigenous Fijian men: in Vanua Levu's Macuata Province the suicide rate for women is seven times higher than the world average, most of the victims being Indian. In addition, relationships between the women themselves often display the level of violence characteristic elsewhere in relationships between women and men.

Throughout Polynesia and Micronesia, women's extensive economic associations now provide networks through which women can train, find employment, acquire knowledge, become politically active and secure their resources and interests. One can confidently generalize that the Pacific Islands woman of 2001 has, in fact, very little in common with the Pacific Islands woman of 1901, though change in this regard is coming only slowly to most of Melanesia.

PACIFIC SPORT

Similarly too infrequently appreciated in regional histories, sport plays a crucial part in modern Pacific Islands societies, acquiring a unifying significance its Western prototype – now largely commercial – lost long ago. Pacific Islands has always known many types of sport. The region's surfing, canoe racing and bungee-jumping have gone on to inspire the world. But also kite-flying, spear- and dart-throwing, sledding, archery, wrestling, footracing, sham battles and many more organized activities enthused Pacific societies for millennia. It is said missionaries first introduced cricket to the Trobriand Islanders of eastern Papua New Guinea in the nineteenth century to discourage endemic inter-village battles and sexual festivals at harvest time. Initially, most Islanders merely watched the games of colonial officials and naval officers in amazed hilarity; whereupon many then copied what they saw, often replacing their indigenous sports altogether with these introductions. When Hubert Murray, Australia's Lieutenant-Governor of Papua from 1907 to 1940, banned warfare there, he introduced organized, frequent Western games, in particular rugby and cricket, as intentional replacements; the scheme functioned eminently.

In New Zealand, Fiji, Tonga, Western Samoa and the Cook Islands, rugby is the national passion. New Zealand's All Blacks, one of the world's most celebrated teams, have long held a high percentage of Islander team members, especially Māori and New Zealand-resident Western Samoans. In most British Commonwealth islands of the Pacific rugby remains the major men's sport, with matches keenly contested every weekend of the season at every level of the game.

As of the 1980s, New Zealand women – many of them Māori and resident Islanders – have developed netball into the entire region's most popular women's sport. Tennis and volleyball are played in rural villages throughout the Pacific. Lawn bowling is enthusiastically practised in Western Samoa and other islands of British, Australian and New Zealand influence, with Islanders frequently jetting to international bowls competitions, including to Europe.

Traditional French sports – but also borrowed rugby of excellent quality – are found throughout France's Pacific territories. Just as in southern France, pétanque is played in nearly every village. Tahiti's 'Heiva i Tahiti' festival leading up to the annual Bastille Day celebrations of 14 July includes competitive pétanque, archery, cycling and canoe racing. Tahiti is also a centre of Pacific soccer.

In the Micronesian nations of the USA's former Trust Territory, baseball is the most popular sport, with competitions held between neighbouring islands and nations.

In the Trobriand Islands, cricket has taken on a new dimension since its nineteenth-century introduction: as many as 60 Trobriand men dress, paint and accoutre themselves as if for traditional dance before stepping out on to the pitch, while dancing and chanting accompany the matches which are more like tournaments in that they can last up to several weeks. Perhaps even more popular than rugby, cricket and baseball, the martial arts and body-building are today's pan-Pacific passions: clubs and associations promoting both can be found on even the smallest and remotest islands.

Regional sports competitions are now regularly held, the most important of these being the quadrennial South Pacific Games. Between the Games are the Mini Games, for which event itself elaborate facilities are constructed: for Vanuatu's Mini Games, for example, a completely new national sports complex, the Municipal Stadium, was built in Port Vila, the South Pacific's most beautiful capital city. Both Games feature Western sports – athletics, soccer, baseball, tennis, table-tennis, boxing, golf and women's netball – as well as traditional Pacific Islands sports: canoe racing, coconut-tree climbing, underwater spearfishing and other events. Though the largest teams come from the financially more secure French territories, Fiji and Papua New Guinea, the Olympic Sporting Solidarity Movement provides funding to the smaller Pacific states to enable their attendance and encourage regional sporting co-operation.

Because of television on even the remotest islands, and because of increasingly mobile populations who live for years overseas or regularly visit there, sporting influences are becoming even more complex in the Pacific. What was once the *marae* or traditional ceremonial centre is now the rugby field, cricket pitch or volleyball court – the centre of community activity. More importantly for the future, Pacific sports now link islands, nations and entire regions in ways which were quite inconceivable only two generations ago. Local competitions are a focus of community pride, while international competitions bring prominence to many a fledgling island state. The ethnic interaction is of particular significance, with Islanders pitted against ancestrally related Islanders for the first time in centuries – tellingly not in war, but in the constructive environment of healthy sport.

There is a further, often overlooked dimension as well. Such 'superstars' of international sport as Western Samoans Jonah Lomu (rugby) and David Tua (boxing), both residents of New Zealand, inspire young Islanders to emulation as they awaken ethnic pride, heralding at the same time Pacific Islanders' prowess far beyond the South Pacific.

MODERN PACIFIC IDENTITIES

Already by the end of the eighteenth century, with increasing foreign intrusion, the Pacific was emerging as a new entity. Over 200 years later, mixed heritage and unprecedented international mobility justify the critical question: what is a Pacific Islander? For identity in the region seems to be more one of acculturation than 'race'. The indigenous populations' relations with traders and visiting sailors; intermarriage with settlers, colonists and imported workers; and, above all, the influx of tens of thousands of non-Islanders and the prolificacy of their mixed descendants have produced a remarkably heterogeneous people who share one fundamental quality: the perception of the Pacific as 'Home'. Official censuses have rarely reflected this heterogeneity in the past, with the region's multiple ethnicities forever eluding convenient categorization. But this, too, is now changing, as the indigenous and non-indigenous Islander, and the mixture of both, are being recognized as New Islanders – an emergent label embracing the region's resultant variety and mobility.

An extraordinary expression of this new, integrated Pacific is the quadrennial Festival of Pacific Arts, the region's major cultural gathering. Representatives from all Pacific Islands nations, territories, colonies and provinces, including Aborigines from Australia, come together to share their diverse cultures as one united people of the Pacific in performance, demonstration and display. First held in 1972 under the auspices of the South Pacific Commission, each Festival has been co-ordinated at a different venue by the Commission's Council of Pacific Arts: Suva, Fiji (1972); Rotorua, New Zealand (1976); Port Moresby, Papua New Guinea (1980); Pape'ete, Tahiti (1985); Townsville, Australia (1988); Avarua, Rarotonga, Cook Islands (1992); 'Apia, Western Samoa (1996); and Noumea, New Caledonia (2000). Its magnificent array of cultural resources overwhelms participants and attendees alike of every ethnic background: traditional voyaging canoes arrive from distant islands as thousands of Islanders in colourful costumes share in story-telling, music and dance; watch carving and canoe-making; engage in tapa quilt-making, basketry, earth-oven cooking and tattooing; thrill at fire-walking; and admire countless other Pacific arts and crafts. Participation in the Festival has become a badge of honour in many island societies, now the Pacific equivalent of a pilgrimage to Mecca. Not only can small insular societies here take pride in sharing their customarily isolated culture with similar and like-minded Islanders, but the Festival has foremost demonstrated the concordant unity of all Pacific peoples of every hue and heritage.

However, it is not without irony that, with greater ethnic integration, has also come a reverse discrimination, as many Islanders cling to a recently created 'traditionalism' in order to retard integration and exalt a perceived uniqueness. Many Tahitians, Hawaiians and Māori, above all, are at present denying their European or other non-Polynesian ancestry, in many ways re-enacting a modern Polynesian farce of Rousseau's 'return to nature' (see Chapter 3), which similarly had little to do with historical fact. In New Zealand, for example, some Māori are now labelling their perceived predicament 'post-colonial trauma disorder' as they struggle to adapt to accelerating change. The rigorous analytic study of Māori language, literature and culture as practised primarily by scholars of European heritage is currently being restricted by many Māori who now occupy leading academic positions in favour of the learning of the language for practical purposes only. Each Pacific island and archipelago is presently wrestling with its historical baggage, each possesses its own arsenal of chauvinism, each is elaborating its own solutions, most of these beneficial, others provocative and even potentially dangerous.

Yet this new Pacific is Home, too. It houses a new family – not Papuans, Austronesians, Europeans, Americans or Asians, but a mixture of all these – who increasingly view themselves as intrinsically possessing a greater identity. In the twentieth century, the concept of the insular tribe inflated to include the 'national tribe', a revolutionary notion for the Pacific. Now, in the twenty-first century, in tandem with similar movements in Europe, Africa, the Americas and Asia, all peoples of the Pacific are beginning to recognize the viability of the 'regional tribe' while a number of international organizations and their agencies are committed to making this inspiration a reality (see below).

It will then no longer matter, for example, that Samoa – Western Samoa and American Samoa – is split in two, not when, at a higher level, all Samoans will in fact be one again: as equal citizens of a larger federation.

TOWARDS A 'UNION OF PACIFIC ISLANDS'

Regionalism has characterized the economic planning of most Pacific Islands governments for some time now. This has led to ever-more frequent co-operation between responsible governmental agencies, calling forth a host of new bodies. Two major organizations have dominated Pacific Islands for a number of decades: the cosmopolitan South Pacific Commission, founded in 1947 and renamed the Secretariat of the Pacific Community in 1997; and the indigenous South Pacific Forum, established in 1971.

Based in Noumea, New Caledonia, the Secretariat of the Pacific Community, originally founded to promote regional economic and social development (see Chapter 6, under 'South Pacific Commission'), now comprises 22 Pacific states and territories and the vested nations of Australia, New Zealand, Britain, France and the USA. (The Netherlands withdrew in 1962 after losing Dutch New Guinea to Indonesia.) Since 1950, delegates have met annually to address the Commission's/Secretariat's programme and budget, financed to around 90 per cent by its four wealthiest members. Ongoing programmes address rural development, fisheries, agriculture, health, education, women's and family development, training, statistical services and environmental management. (Because of France, in the main, such issues as nuclear testing never appeared on the old Commission's agenda.) Dissatisfaction with the Commission's political steerage by its non-Pacific members eventually led to the foundation of the wholly separate South Pacific Forum in 1971, which organization then, one year later, established in turn the South Pacific Bureau for Economic Co-operation to serve as its executive body. (In 1988 the Bureau was renamed the Forum Secretariat.)

Based in Suva, Fiji, the South Pacific Forum is smaller and does not include Britain, France and the USA among its 16 self-governing members. Founded in opposition to colonialism and neo-colonialism, it is led by Australia and New Zealand, who also provide two-thirds of the annual budget. The Forum focuses on regional trade, investment, sustainable development and international affairs. Its annual meetings consist of the respective heads of each member country coming together to informally discuss topical issues of mutual concern. In 1994 the Forum was granted observer status at the United Nations. One year later it began holding a parallel forum at each annual meeting; this consists of non-governmental organizations addressing social and environmental matters.

The Forum has set up its own regional shipping line – Pacific Forum Line – as a joint venture among ten island members. The Forum Fisheries Agency, based in Honiara, Solomon Islands, manages and co-ordinates the fisheries policies of Forum members, including licensing agreements, scientific and commercial studies, surveillance and enforcement, and other pursuits. It is chiefly the Forum Secretariat, however, which oversees and promotes Pacific Islands co-operative projects, such as its recent involvement in the region's telecommunications development.

In 1982, the Commission, Forum and United Nations established the South Pacific Regional Environment Programme, based in 'Apia, Western Samoa (this became autonomous in 1993 with 26 member states). Dedicated to promoting sustainable development, the Programme undertakes initiatives in species conservation, nature reserves, environmental and pollution management, and actively oversees international co-ordination and educational initiatives in this regard.

The growing importance and political weight of the South Pacific Forum, in particular, resulted in mounting tension between it and the then South Pacific Commission, which was still dominated by Britain, France and the USA. So many inter-governmental agencies, created by both organizations, had led to redundancy, friction and confusion. To resolve this, and to cope with the sudden proliferation of regional bodies in the 1980s, the South Pacific Organizations Co-ordinating Committee was founded in 1988.

Elsewhere in the world, organizations like the South Pacific Forum are often nascent federations, in that they unite, regulate and protect a given region sharing like identities and goals. In 2001 the Forum Secretariat began investigating a possible Free Trade Agreement between member countries. If realized, this would make the Forum the South Pacific counterpart to the European Community, a prelude to potential political union. It is from such beginnings that a 'Union of Pacific Islands' or some similarly named political entity might emerge during the twenty-first century – one federation embracing all the free peoples of the Pacific.

The century has begun, however, with the regional stability of Pacific Islands being threatened: armed insurrections, governmental corruption, alarming class differences, continued foreign exploitation, disproportionate development and serious trade imbalances characterize the region. Nearly every Pacific nation and territory is still subservient to some foreign power. Increasingly, multinational corporations intrude to work against the local prerogative. If in Pacific Islands' past the exclusion of indigenous Islanders by Europeans and Americans created the 'White Pacific', in Pacific Islands' present the tensions between all peoples of the Pacific and the cosmopolitan powers controlling them are creating the 'Feudal Pacific'. While most Islanders of every heritage are aspiring to federalism, they do this while struggling with increasing debt and social and political instability.

This troubled and blessed New Pacific can only become a truly united Pacific if the cosmopolitan mandate weakens while the regional strengthens. Current international analogues suggest this could well occur within one lifetime. As in the past, how Islanders of every background would then come to terms with their union would depend on their innate wisdom, communal resolve and educated piloting of forces often beyond their control. Then again, pan-Pacific unity might remain forever a conceit. For the present, only one thing is clear: most peoples of the Pacific are at last discovering that greater identity informed from their collective history.

Selected Further Reading

The following is necessarily a selective list, focusing on recent books. Other studies, including individual articles, can be traced through the bibliographies in these books.

GENERAL WORKS

Peter Bellwood, *Man's Conquest of the Pacific* (Auckland: Collins, 1978).

Ian C. Campbell, *A History of the Pacific Islands* (Christchurch: Canterbury University Press, 1989).

Ron Crocombe, *The South Pacific: An Introduction* (Suva: University of the South Pacific, 1983; revised edition 1989).

Donald Denoon, with Stewart Firth, Jocelyn Linnekin, Malama Meleisea and Karen Nero, *The Cambridge History of the Pacific Islanders* (Cambridge: Cambridge University Press, 1997).

Kerry R. Howe, *Nature, Culture and History: The 'Knowing' of Oceania* (Honolulu: University of Hawai'i Press, 2000).

——*Where the Waves Fall: A New South Sea Islands History from First Settlement to Colonial Rule* (London: Allen & Unwin, 1984).

Patrick V. Kirch, *On the Road of the Winds: An Archaeological History of the Pacific Islands Before European Contact* (Los Angeles and Berkeley: University of California Press, 2000).

Patrick V. Kirch and Roger C. Green, *Hawaiki, Ancestral Polynesia: An Essay in Historical Anthropology* (Cambridge: Cambridge University Press, 2001).

Brij V. Lal and Kate Fortune (eds), *The Pacific Islands: An Encyclopedia* (Honolulu: University of Hawai'i Press, 2000).

Richard Nile and Christian Clerk, *Cultural Atlas of Australia, New Zealand and the South Pacific* (Surry Hills, New South Wales: RD Press, 1996).

Douglas L. Oliver, *The Pacific Islands*, third edition (Honolulu: University of Hawai'i Press, 1989; first published 1951; second edition 1961).

Nancy J. Pollock, *These Roots Remain: Food Habits in Islands of the Central and Eastern Pacific since Western Contact* (Lā'ie, Hawai'i: The Institute for Polynesian Studies, 1992).

Marshall Sahlins, *Islands of History* (Chicago: University of Chicago Press, 1985).

Deryck Scarr, *The History of the Pacific Islands: Kingdoms of the Reefs* (Melbourne: Macmillan, 1990).

O. H. K. Spate, *The Pacific Since Magellan*, 3 vols (Canberra: Australian National University, 1988).

David Stanley, *South Pacific Handbook*, seventh edition (Emeryville, CA: Avalon Travel Publishing, 2000).

THE FIRST ISLANDERS

A. V. S. Hill and S. W. Serjeantson (eds), *The Colonization of the Pacific: A Genetic Trail* (Oxford: Clarendon Press, 1989).

Geoffrey Irwin, *The Prehistoric Exploration and Colonisation of the Pacific* (Cambridge: Cambridge University Press, 1992).

Jesse D. Jennings (ed.), *The Prehistory of Polynesia* (Cambridge, MA, and London: Harvard University Press, 1979).

Patrick Kirch, *The Lapita Peoples: Ancestors of the Oceanic World* (Oxford: Blackwell, 1997).

Christophe Sand, *'Le temps d'avant': La préhistoire de la Nouvelle-Calédonie* (Paris: L'Harmattan, 1995).

M. A. Smith et al. (eds), *Sahul in Review: Pleistocene Archaeology in Australia, New Guinea, and Island Melanesia*, ANU Prehistory Occasional Paper 24 (Canberra: Australian National University, 1993).

J. E. Terrell, *Prehistory in the Pacific Islands: A Study of Variation in Language, Custom, and Human Biology* (Cambridge: Cambridge University Press, 1986).

Marshall I. Weisler (ed.), *Prehistoric Long-Distance Interaction in Oceania: An Interdisciplinary Approach*, New Zealand Archæological Association Monograph 21 (Auckland: New Zealand Archæological Association, 1997).

J. P. White and J. F. O'Connell, *A Prehistory of Australia, New Guinea, and Sahul* (Sydney: Academic Press, 1982).

MELANESIANS, MICRONESIANS, POLYNESIANS

D. Bayard, *The Cultural Relationships of the Polynesian Outliers*, University of Otago Studies in Prehistoric Anthropology, no. 9 (Dunedin, New Zealand: Department of Anthropology, University of Otago, 1976).

Peter S. Bellwood, *The Polynesians* (London: Thames & Hudson, 1987).

B. Brake, J. McNeish and D. Simmons, *Art of the Pacific* (Oxford: Oxford University Press, 1979).

J. M. Davidson, *The Prehistory of New Zealand* (Auckland: Longman Paul, 1984).

T. Dye, *Marshall Islands Archaeology*, Pacific Anthropological Records, no. 38 (Honolulu: Bishop Museum Press, 1987).

Steven Roger Fischer (ed.), *Easter Island Studies: Contributions to the History of Rapanui in Memory of William T. Mulloy*, Oxbow Monograph 32 (Oxford: Oxbow Books, 1993).

Irving Goldman, *Ancient Polynesian Society* (Chicago: Chicago University Press, 1970).

Roger C. Green, *New Sites with Lapita Pottery and Their Implications for Understanding the Settlement of the Western Pacific*, Working Papers in Anthropology, Archæology, Linguistics and Maori Studies, no. 56 (Auckland: Department of Anthropology, University of Auckland, 1978).

A. V. S. Hill and S. W. Serjeantson (eds), *The Colonization of the Pacific: A Genetic Trail* (Oxford: Clarendon Press, 1989).

J. Hollyman and A. K. Pawley (eds), *Studies in Pacific Language and Cultures in Honour of Bruce Biggs* (Auckland: Linguistic Society of New Zealand, 1981).

Antony Hooper and Judith Huntsman, *Transformation of Polynesian Culture*, Memoir of the Polynesian Society, no. 45 (Auckland: The Polynesian Society, 1985).

W. W. Howells, *The Pacific Islanders* (London: Weidenfeld and Nicolson, 1973).

Geoffrey Irwin, *The Prehistoric Exploration and Colonisation of the Pacific* (Cambridge: Cambridge University Press, 1992).

E. Ishikawa (ed.), *Cultural Adaptation to Atolls in Micronesia and West Polynesia* (Tokyo: Tokyo Metropolitan University, 1987).

Jesse D. Jennings (ed.), *The Prehistory of Polynesia* (Cambridge, MA, and London: Harvard University Press, 1979).

Patrick V. Kirch, *The Evolution of the Polynesian Chiefdoms* (Cambridge: Cambridge University Press, 1984).

David Lewis, *We, the Navigators* (Wellington: Reed, 1972).

Douglas Oliver, *Ancient Tahitian Society*, 3 vols (Honolulu: The University Press of Hawaii, 1974).

Andrew K. Pawley (ed.), *Man and a Half: Essays in Pacific Anthropology and Ethnobiology in Honour of Ralph Bulmer* (Auckland: The Polynesian Society, 1992).

J. E. Terrell, *Prehistory in the Pacific Islands: A Study of Variation in Language, Custom, and Human Biology* (Cambridge: Cambridge University Press, 1986).

I. Ushijima and K. Sudo (eds), *Cultural Uniformity and Diversity in Micronesia*, Senri Ethnological Studies, no. 21 (Osaka: National Museum of Ethnology, 1987).

Marshall I. Weisler (ed.), *Prehistoric Long-Distance Interaction in Oceania: An Interdisciplinary Approach*, New Zealand Archæological Association Monograph 21 (Auckland: New Zealand Archæological Association, 1997).

THE EUROPEAN TRESPASS

J. C. Beaglehole (ed.), *The Journals of Captain James Cook on His Voyages of Discovery*, 3 vols (Cambridge: Cambridge University Press for the Hakluyt Society, 1955–74).

——*The Exploration of the Pacific*, 3rd edition (London: A. and C. Black, 1966).

Ernest S. Dodge, *Beyond the Capes: Pacific Exploration from Cook to the 'Challenger' (1776–1877)* (London: Victor Gollancz, 1971).

John Garrett, *To Live Among the Stars: Christian Origins in Oceania* (Suva: The World Council of Churches and the Institute of Pacific Studies, 1982).

W. N. Gunson, *Messengers of Grace: Evangelical Missionaries in the South Seas, 1797–1860* (Melbourne: Oxford University Press, 1978).

Francis Hezel, *The First Taint of Civilization: A History of the Caroline and Marshall Islands in Pre-Colonial Days, 1521–1885* (Honolulu: University of Hawaii Press, 1983).

Colin Jack-Hinton, *The Search for the Islands of Solomon, 1567–1838* (Oxford: Clarendon Press, 1969).

Brij V. Lal (ed.), *Pacific Islands History: Journeys and Transformations* (Canberra: The Journal of Pacific History, 1992).

Robert Langdon, *The Lost Caravel* (Sydney: Pacific Publications, 1975).

Harry Maude, *Of Islands and Men: Studies in Pacific History* (Melbourne: Oxford University Press, 1968).

Max Quanchi and Ron Adams (eds), *Culture Contact in the Pacific* (Oakleigh, Victoria: Cambridge University Press, 1993).

Anne Salmond, *Two Worlds: First Meetings between Maori and Europeans, 1642–1772* (Auckland: Viking, 1993).

Dorothy Shineberg, *They Came for Sandalwood: A Study of the Sandalwood Trade in the Southwest Pacific, 1830–1865* (Melbourne: Oxford University Press, 1967).

Bernard Smith, *European Vision and the South Pacific* (New Haven, CT: Yale University Press, 1992).

Spanish Pacific from Magellan to Malaspina (Barcelona: Ministerio de Asuntos Exteriores, 1988).

Ralph Wiltgen, *The Founding of the Roman Catholic Church in Oceania* (Canberra: Australian National University Press, 1979).

THE SECOND COLONIZATION

Alban Bensa and Isabelle Leblic (eds), *En pays Kanak: Ethnologie, linguistique, archéologie, histoire de la Nouvelle-Calédonie* (Paris: Éditions de la Maison des Sciences de l'Homme, 2000).

Peter Corris, *Passage, Port and Plantation: A History of Solomon Islands Labour Migration* (Melbourne: Cambridge University Press, 1973).

David Hanlon, *Remaking Micronesia: Discourses over Development in a Pacific Territory, 1944–1982* (Honolulu: University of Hawai'i Press, 1998).

Kerry R. Howe, Robert Kiste and Brij Lal, *Tides of History* (London: Allen & Unwin, 1994).

Samuel Kamakau, *Ruling Chiefs of Hawaii* (Honolulu: Kamehameha Schools, 1961).

Ralph Kuykendall, *The Hawaiian Kingdom*, 3 vols (Honolulu: University of Hawai'i Press, 1938–67).

Brij V. Lal (ed.), *Pacific Islands History: Journeys and Transformations* (Canberra: The Journal of Pacific History, 1992).

Hugh Laracy, *Marists and Melanesians: A History of Catholic Missions in the Solomon Islands* (Canberra: Australian National University, 1976).

Sione Lātūkefu, *Church and State in Tonga* (Canberra: Australian National University, 1974).

Harry Maude, *Slavers in Paradise: The Peruvian Slave Trade in Polynesia, 1862–1864* (Canberra: Australian National University, 1981).

Malama Meleisea, *The Making of Modern Samoa* (Suva: Institute of Pacific Studies, 1987).

Clive Moore, Jacqueline Leckie and Doug Munro (eds), *Labour in the South Pacific* (Townsville, Queensland: James Cook University, 1990).

W. P. Morrell, *Britain in the Pacific Islands* (Oxford: Oxford University Press, 1960).

Deryck Scarr, *I, The Very Bayonet* (Canberra: Australian National University, 1973).

NEW PACIFIC IDENTITIES

'Atu Emberson-Bain, *Labour and Gold in Fiji* (Cambridge: Cambridge University Press, 1994).

Michael J. Field, *Mau: Samoa's Struggle for Freedom* (Auckland: Pasifika Press, 1991).

Stewart Firth, *New Guinea under the Germans* (Melbourne: Oxford University Press, 1983).

Peter Hempenstall, *Pacific Islanders under German Rule: A Study in the Meaning of Colonial Resistance* (Canberra: Australian National University, 1978).

Francis Hezel and Mark Berg (eds), *Micronesia: Winds of Change* (Saipan, 1979).

Herman Joseph Hiery, *The Neglected War: The German South Pacific and the Influence of World War I* (Honolulu: University of Hawai'i Press, 1995).

Brij V. Lal, *Broken Waves: A History of the Fiji Islands in the Twentieth Century* (Honolulu: University of Hawai'i Press, 1992).

Timothy Macnaught, *The Fijian Colonial Experience: A Study of the Neotraditional Order under British Colonial Rule prior to World War II* (Canberra: Australian National University, 1982).

Norman Meller, *Constitutionalism in Micronesia* (Honolulu: Institute for Polynesian Studies, 1985).

Hank Nelson, *Black, White and Gold: Gold Mining in Papua New Guinea, 1878–1930* (Canberra: Australian National University, 1976).

——*Taim Bilong Masta: The Australian Involvement with Papua New Guinea* (Sydney: George Allen & Unwin, 1982).

W. H. Oliver and B. R. Williams (eds), *The Oxford History of New Zealand* (Oxford: Oxford University Press, 1981).

Mark R. Peattie, *Nan'yo: The Rise and Fall of the Japanese in Micronesia, 1885–1945* (Honolulu: University of Hawai'i Press, 1988).

Jane Samson, *Imperial Benevolence: Making British Authority in the Pacific Islands* (Honolulu: University of Hawai'i Press, 1998).

Deryck Scarr, *Fiji: A Short History* (Sydney: George Allen & Unwin, 1984).

John A. Williams, *Politics of the New Zealand Maori: Protest and Cooperation, 1891–1909* (Auckland: Oxford University Press, 1969).

Maslyn Williams and Barrie Macdonald, *The Phosphateers: A History of the British Phosphate Commissioners and the Christmas Island Phosphate Commission* (Melbourne: Oxford University Press, 1985).

PACIFIC ISLANDERS IN TRANSIT

John Connell, *New Caledonia or Kanaky? The Political History of a French Colony* (Canberra: Australian National University, 1987).

Ron Crocombe and Admed Ali (eds), *Foreign Forces in Pacific Politics* (Suva: Institute of Pacific Studies, 1983).

J. W. Davidson, *Samoa mo Samoa: The Emergence of the Independent State of Western Samoa* (Melbourne: Oxford University Press, 1967).

Gavan Daws, *Shoal of Time: A History of the Hawaiian Islands* (Honolulu: University Press of Hawaii, 1974).

James Griffin, Hank Nelson and Stewart Firth, *Papua New Guinea: A Political History* (Richmond, Victoria: Heinemann Educational, 1979).

David Hanlon, *Remaking Micronesia: Discourses over Development in a Pacific Territory, 1944–1982* (Honolulu: University of Hawai'i Press, 1998).

Stephen Henningham, *France and the South Pacific: A Contemporary History* (Sydney: Allen & Unwin, 1992).

Kerry R. Howe, Robert Kiste and Brij Lal, *Tides of History* (London: Allen & Unwin, 1994).

Brij V. Lal (ed.), *Pacific Islands History: Journeys and Transformations* (Canberra: The Journal of Pacific History, 1992).

Hugh Laracy (ed.), *The Maasina Rule Movement: Solomon Islands, 1944–1952* (Suva: Institute of Pacific Studies, 1983).

Malama Meleisea, *Lagaga: A Short History of Western Samoa* (Suva: Institute of Pacific Studies, 1987).

W. H. Oliver (ed.), *The Oxford History of New Zealand* (Wellington: Oxford University Press, 1981).

Lin Poyer, Suzanne Falgout and Laurence Marshall Carucci, *The Typhoon of War: Micronesian Experiences of the Pacific War* (Honolulu: University of Hawai'i Press, 2001).

Neville Robinson, *Villagers at War: Some Papua New Guinean Experiences of World War II* (Canberra: Australian National University, 1981).

Deryck Scarr, *Fiji: A Short History* (Sydney: George Allen & Unwin, 1984).

Geoffrey White and Lamont Lindstrom (eds), *The Pacific Theater: Island Representations of World War II* (Honolulu: University of Hawai'i Press, 1989).

REINVENTING PACIFIC ISLANDS

David Bradley, *No Place to Hide* (Hanover: University of New England Press, 1983).

John Connell, *New Caledonia or Kanaky? The Political History of a French Colony* (Canberra: Australian National University, 1987).

Ron Crocombe, *The Pacific Islands and the USA* (Suva and Honolulu: Institute of Pacific Studies, Pacific Islands Development Center, 1995).

Bengt Danielsson and Marie-Thérèse Danielsson, *Poisoned Reign: French Nuclear Colonialism in the Pacific* (Harmondsworth: Penguin, 1986).

Stewart Firth, *Nuclear Playground* (Sydney: George Allen & Unwin, 1987).

David Hanlon, *Remaking Micronesia: Discourses over Development in a Pacific Territory, 1944–1982* (Honolulu: University of Hawai'i Press, 1998).

Stephen Henningham, *France and the South Pacific: A Contemporary History* (Sydney: Allen & Unwin, 1992).

Kerry R. Howe, Robert Kiste and Brij Lal, *Tides of History* (London: Allen & Unwin, 1994).

Robert Kiste, *The Bikinians: A Study in Forced Migration* (Menlo Park CA: Cummings, 1974).

Donald F. McHenry, *Micronesia: Trust Betrayed* (New York, 1975).

Ratu Sir Kamisese Mara, *The Pacific Way: A Memoir* (Honolulu: University of Hawai'i Press, 1997).

P. Mazellier, *Tahiti autonome* (Pape'ete, 1990).

Clive Moore with Mary Koopman (eds), *A Papua New Guinea Political Chronicle, 1967–1991* (Bathurst and London: Crawford House Publishing, C. Hurst & Co., 1998).

Robert Nicole, *The Word, the Pen, and the Pistol: Literature and Power in Tahiti* (Albany: State University of New York Press, 2001).

D. Robie, *Blood on Their Banner: Nationalist Struggles in the South Pacific* (Leichhardt, NSW: Pluto Press Australia, 1989).

Gary Smith, *Micronesia: Decolonisation and US Military Interests in the Trust Territory of the Pacific Islands* (Canberra: Peace Research Centre, Australian National University, 1991).

William Tagupa, *Politics in French Polynesia, 1945–1975* (Wellington: New Zealand Institute of International Affairs, 1976).

F. Thual, *Équations polynésiennes* (Paris: Groupe de l'Union Centriste, Senat, 1992).

Jonathan M. Weisgall, *Operation Crossroads: The Atomic Tests at Bikini Atoll* (Annapolis MD: Naval Institute Press, 1994).

Geoffrey White and Lamont Lindstrom (eds), *The Pacific Theater: Island Representations of World War II* (Honolulu: University of Hawai'i Press, 1989).

THE 'NEW PACIFIC'

D. Ahlburg and M. Levin, *The North-East Passage: A Study of Pacific Islander Migration to American Samoa and the United States* (Canberra: Australian National University, 1990).

Judith A. Bennet, *Pacific Forest: A History of Resource Control and Contest in Solomon Islands, c. 1800–1997* (Cambridge: The White Horse Press, 2000).

G. Blanchet, *A Survey of the Economy of French Polynesia, 1960 to 1990* (Canberra: Australian National University, 1991).

Ben Burt and Christian Clerk (eds), *Environment and Development in the Pacific Islands*, Pacific Policy Paper, no. 25 (Canberra and Port Moresby: National Centre for Development Studies, University of Papua New Guinea Press, 1997).

John Connell (ed.), *Migration and Development in the South Pacific* (Canberra: Australian National University, 1990).

Ron Crocombe, *The South Pacific: An Introduction* (Suva: University of the South Pacific, 1983; revised edition 1989).

Ron Crocombe and Ahmed Ali (eds), *Foreign Forces in Pacific Politics* (Suva: Institute of Pacific Studies, 1983).

Ben Finney, *Polynesian Peasants and Proletarians* (Cambridge, MA: Harvard University Press, 1973).

Antony Hooper (ed.), *Culture and Sustainable Development in the Pacific* (Canberra: Asia Pacific Press, 2000).

Antony Hooper *et al.*(eds), *Class and Culture in the South Pacific* (Suva: Institute of Pacific Studies, 1987).

Michael Howard, *Mining, Politics, and Development in the South Pacific* (Boulder, CO, 1994).

Helen Hughes (ed.), *Women in Development in the Pacific* (Canberra: Australian National University, 1985).

Colin Hunt, *Pacific Development Sustained: Policy for Pacific Environments* (Canberra: Australian National University, 1998).

M. Jolly and M. Macintyre (eds), *Family and Gender in the Pacific: Domestic Contradictions and the Colonial Impact* (Cambridge: Cambridge University Press, 1989).

Brij V. Lal and Kate Fortune (eds), *The Pacific Islands: An Encyclopedia* (Honolulu: University of Hawai'i Press, 2000).

David Lamb, *Exploiting the Tropical Rain Forest: An Account of Pulpwood Logging in Papua New Guinea* (Paris: UNESCO, 1990).

Michael Lieber (ed.), *Exiles and Migrants in Oceania* (Honolulu: Institute for Polynesian Studies, 1977).

Jocelyn Linnekin and Lyn Poyer (eds), *Cultural Identity and Ethnicity in the Pacific* (Honolulu: University of Hawai'i Press, 1990).

Grant McCall and John Connell (eds), *A World Perspective on Pacific Islander Migration: Australia, New Zealand and the USA* (Sydney: University of New South Wales Press, 1993).

Bernard Narokobi, *The Melanesian Way* (Boroko and Suva: Institute of Pacific Studies, 1980).

Uentabo Fakaofo Neemia, *Cooperation and Conflict: Costs, Benefits and National Interests in Pacific Regional Cooperation* (Suva: Institute of Pacific Studies, 1986).

John Timothy O'Meara, *Samoan Planters: Tradition and Economic Development in Polynesia* (Fort Worth, TX: Holt, Rinehart and Winston, 1990).

John Overton and Regina Scheyvens (eds), *Strategies for Sustainable Development: Experiences from the Pacific* (Sydney: University of New South Wales Press, 1999).

Elizabeth Rata, *A Political Economy of Neotribal Capitalism* (Lanham, MD: Lexington Books, 2000).

Pamela J. Stewart and Andrew Strathern (eds), *Identity Work: Constructing Pacific Lives* (Pittsburgh: University of Pittsburgh Press, 2000).

R. Gerard Ward, *Widening Worlds, Shrinking Worlds?: The Reshaping of Oceania* (Canberra: Australian National University, 1999).

Index